Emergency Planning Officers' Handbook

Emergency Planning Officers' Handbook

Brian Dillon

Consultant Editors
Ian Dickinson
Frank Whiteford
John Williamson

OXFORD
UNIVERSITY PRESS

OXFORD

UNIVERSITY PRESS

Great Clarendon Street, Oxford OX2 6DP

Oxford University Press is a department of the University of Oxford. It furthers
the University's objective of excellence in research, scholarship, and education
by publishing worldwide in

Oxford New York

Auckland Cape Town Dar es Salaam Hong Kong Karachi
Kuala Lumpur Madrid Melbourne Mexico City Nairobi
New Delhi Shanghai Taipei Toronto

With offices in

Argentina Austria Brazil Chile Czech Republic France Greece
Guatemala Hungary Italy Japan Poland Portugal Singapore
South Korea Switzerland Thailand Turkey Ukraine Vietnam

Oxford is a registered trade mark of Oxford University Press in the
UK and in certain other countries

Published in the United States
by Oxford University Press Inc., New York

First published 2009

British Library Cataloguing in Publication Data

Data available

Library of Congress Cataloging-in-Publication Data

Dillon, Brian.
   Emergency planning officers' handbook/Brian Dillon; consultant editors,
Ian Dickinson, Frank Whiteford, John Williamson.
      p. cm.
   Includes bibliographical references and index.
   ISBN 978-0-19-956136-0 (pbk.: alk. paper) 1. Emergency management—
Handbooks, manuals, etc. I. Dickinson, Ian. II. Whiteford, Frank.
III. Williamson, John. IV. Title.
   HV551.2.D53 2009
   363.34'561—dc22

                                                    2008054688

Typeset by Laserwords Private Limited, Chennai, India
Printed in Italy
on acid-free paper by
Legoprint S.p.A.

ISBN 978-0-19-956136-0

1 3 5 7 9 10 8 6 4 2

Foreword by Ian Dickinson

This is a book for Emergency Planners written by an Emergency Planner. It is unusual in the Emergency Planning community because it seeks, in a very pragmatic way, to impart the essential knowledge and skills required to help those engaged in emergency and contingency planning to do their job better. It is also a valuable resource for those who simply wish to extend their understanding of emergency management procedures generally. It is not intended as an academic work, nor a theoretical analysis of the planners' environment. It is a practitioners' guide—more of a working handbook or professional learning manual than it is a textbook.

The author, Brian Dillon, is an acknowledged expert in his field, formerly as a police emergency planner; he held a number of national UK responsibilities and 'knew his job inside out', as one of his colleagues described recently while bemoaning the fact that he had retired from the police. Yet as a police officer when Brian started out in the role, he found little or no information available to assist him in understanding how to go about being an Emergency Planner. He sought out courses, read articles and talked to colleagues, but nothing seemed to meet his immediate need of being told what Emergency Planners do, how they do it, and why. He took a Masters degree in Risk Crisis and Disaster Management, which added to his theoretical and legal understanding, but it still did not offer to meet the real and immediate need of an emergency planning officer of 'how do I do this job?'

After years of learning on the job, Brian has taken his hard-earned understanding and experience and written this book to fill that need; it is the book he wished he had been able to read to tell him how to do his job when he started. It fills the need in a way which would have been appropriate for him

Foreword by Ian Dickinson

when he was a new Emergency Planner—but is also written with sufficient detail and professional 'clout' to ensure that it will be equally valuable as a personal development programme or as a professional manual for the more experienced planner who is looking to benchmark their own performance against a recognisable standard.

The book takes the reader through structured and progressive lessons using language which is readily understood and in a style that is both straightforward and direct. He emphasizes strongly three factors which are essential to quality and effective emergency preparedness: the first is the Emergency Planning Officer—the skills, abilities, and understanding that are essential to be effective; the second is understanding the Civil Contingencies Act 2004 which is essential for the Emergency Planner and which provides the UK framework and national standards; the third is the resilience of organizations themselves, shaped and prepared by Emergency Planners to maintain continuity and which are able to absorb the impact of emergencies.

Building on these three core themes the reader will be able to emerge from Chapter 10 very well placed to cope with the demands of being an Emergency Planning Officer and be able to assure themselves and their managers that they do, indeed, 'know their job inside out'.

Ian Dickinson
Associate lecturer at the Cabinet
Office Emergency Planning College

Foreword by Frank Whiteford

Emergency planning is a profession that has been created by modern circumstances and the lessons learned from recent events; natural disasters such as flooding, industrial incidents, and terrorist atrocities. We need to respond more and more effectively and preparedness is the key. In order to put together a useful emergency plan you need to know what it's for, what it should contain, who will use it, when, and where. Many books and papers have been written on Emergency Planning and Disaster Management and these have been used to take the science of Emergency Preparedness forward. All of these are vital to our understanding of this work in a society that has an ever higher expectation of the organizations who respond to disasters or incidents.

This book 'does what it says on the tin': it is the Emergency Planners' handbook, providing invaluable guidance and tips for the newcomer to Emergency Planning and recent and relevant information for the more experienced practitioner. It is packed with no nonsense ideas and helpful tips. The Handbook is designed in an accessible, easy to read and understand format, which guides the reader through each step in the process and also gives vital reasons for actions. Each section is clear and concise with a refreshing pragmatism. All Category One or Category Two responder organizations, as defined in the Civil Contingencies Act, will see how the 'blue light' services prepare and practise their emergency plans. Such insight is essential for planners' consistency and will make the synergy of their own plans easier, ensuring they fit together with multi-agency plans.

It can be a confusing and complex subject but the book's layout takes you through the steps in a logical and pragmatic way, allowing you to see the rationale and the concepts of what the Emergency Planning cycle will look like. In Chapter 5, the mysteries of the Gold, Silver, and Bronze roles used

Foreword by Frank Whiteford

by the Emergency Services are explained— without a doubt this still remains a confusing element of Command and Control in the response phase which this book addresses by clearly explaining how things are managed and by whom. Logically, the book ends with the Debrief Process but for me this is the beginning of a new cycle which identifies the lessons needed to provide an even better response.

Brian Dillon is one of the experts in the field and one that has 'done the job' and I can thoroughly recommend this book to all emergency planning professionals.

Frank Whiteford
Associate Director of Health
Service Resilience, NHS Northwest

Foreword by John Williamson

Major emergency incidents occur very often without any warning and even those that do provide some warning (occasional natural disasters for instance) frequently surprise us with their ferocity and destruction. The impact of terrorism has left us feeling vulnerable right across the world. There is very often a feeling of disbelief during the first phase of the incident. The only way to be prepared for these occurrences is to plan for their eventuality. Emergency planning has evolved from experiences of previous disasters and very often from the mistakes and omissions encountered along the way.

Major incidents and disasters bring all of the emergency services together and very often it will be the first time that these people will have worked together. Each organization is used to working with its own people as a team but very often the 'team' can experience difficulties when organizations come together. The problem can often be complicated because people do not understand or appreciate each other's role. They only really get together on the job and this is really not the place to learn.

The only way to achieve successful outcomes is to plan for them. Brian Dillon has provided us with a one stop shop for this planning. The Emergency Planning Handbook provides everyone who might be involved in a major incident or disaster at any level with a complete guide. This guidance comes from someone who has been involved at the sharp end for many years. He uses his experience and vision to bring the emergency services together so that they can plan a cohesive strategy to deal with whatever might face them.

John Williamson
Chairman of the Institute of Fire Safety Managers

Contents—Summary

Contents

Contents

Contents

Contents

How to Use this Book

Although the subject matter in this book is comprehensive and reaches an advanced level, the author has assumed no prior knowledge of the reader. This is for two reasons. Firstly, in order to make the subject accessible and useful to those who have just started to study the subject, and secondly to act as a review or a 'back to basics' for those who have some knowledge.

Likewise, the book does not assume that the reader will be a member of the emergency services, as the emergency planning officer (EPO) may move into the emergency services with little or no prior knowledge of service structure or culture. However, it is hoped that the correct balance has been achieved to meet the needs of all those who are existing or aspiring EPOs, from whatever background. Although the term 'emergency planning' is used within this book, the content is just as relevant to all those associated with, and involved in, civil contingencies, contingency planning and business continuity activities.

The layout of this book has been designed to take the reader through a logical and gradual progression of the essential knowledge and skills required of an EPO. Where possible, diagrams and illustrations have been used to add clarity.

To get the most from this book the reader should have access to the two documents—*Emergency Preparedness and Emergency Response and Recovery*. These documents are the basis upon which civil protection is built in the UK. Continued references are made to these two documents throughout the book, which will require the reader to frequently reference parts of both publications. Including them in the book would have been too bulky and unnecessary as they are easily accessible on line at <http://www.ukresilience.gov.uk/>.

How to Use this Book

Hard copy versions are also available by e-mailing the
Cabinet Office Emergency Planning College on epc.library@
cabinet-office.x.gsi.gov.uk.

Within the book, there are numerous 'Tasks' in shaded
boxes. These are questions, points to consider, research
issues, or tasks, all of which have been introduced and
designed to expand or reinforce key topics.

The book also contains numerous tables, checklists, and
charts, which with some modification can be adapted and
configured to meet the needs of the EPO.

A glossary has also been included to assist in understanding the many acronyms that tend to permeate emergency
service language.

It is hoped that the practitioner-focused style and
approach of this book will act as a constant source of reference for the EPO in their day-to-day activities.

About the Author

In 1997 I was a police Inspector working in a large town in Lancashire. I had little knowledge about 'Emergency Planning', but had attended many major incidents and perhaps without realizing it actually managed to deal with each one in a reasonable fashion, or so I thought. But I attended very few debriefs and when I did it was a very hit and miss affair, with the presumption that if it went well there was no need to debrief it. I really had little knowledge of the role of the other organizations and to be honest was not sure of the role of the police. In any event, I saw the job of Emergency Planning Officer (EPO) advertised in our internal vacancies and thought it would be an interesting change in career. I applied on the basis that I had attended many incidents and therefore qualified on the basis of experience at least. I attended the interview having done a speed read of the Association of Chief Police Officers (ACPO) Emergency Planning Manual. This was just *slightly* easier to find than the Holy Grail, but to be fair it was informative and I clearly remembered enough to impress the panel. Within days I was the lead emergency planning specialist in the force.

I then started to learn about the role of an emergency planning officer. So I searched around for information about exercising, writing plans, debriefing and training on the subject but to no avail. Apart from the ACPO Manual, which at best was superficial at that time, there was nothing else. I would say on reflection that I was not really proficient in the role until two years had passed, but I did get by with the help and support of some older and wiser colleagues.

Since those days, however, the whole landscape of emergency planning and the role of the EPO has changed beyond recognition, not least because of the terrorist attacks in New York in September 2001. Within a few years of those tragic events, I realized two things, firstly that there are now many

About the Author

more EPOs across a whole range of both private and public sector organizations and secondly, there was still very little to assist them understanding the role of an EPO or assisting in developing their skills. Therefore, I sat down to prepare this book to at least provide a grounding and understanding of the key skills and essential knowledge needed for the job. There is a considerable amount of energy and enthusiasm in the emergency planning community and my hope is to make a worthwhile contribution to continue that momentum and enhance our overall emergency preparedness.

Brian Dillon

Author

Brian Dillon MSc SBCI MIFSM is a former Police Inspector and was a Local Resilience Forum Secretary and Strategic Commander Centre Manager for over 10 years. He was a police instructor responsible for both internal and external training in all aspects of risk crisis and disaster management. Brian is a specialist in exercise planning and management responsible for directing and umpiring major live play exercises, in particular civil nuclear emergencies where he represented the police service at Government level. His plans have been used to manage a wide range of emergencies including the Morecombe Bay cockling disaster of 2004.

Consultant Editors

Ian Dickinson B.Ed QPM is former Assistant Chief Constable of Lothian & Borders Police, where he served at the rank of chief officer for more than 20 years. He is an experienced Gold Commander, having led the Scottish response to terrorist incidents and many major events, incidents and civil emergencies in the Lothian and Borders Area. Since 2002 he has had responsibility for Specialist Operations, including the planning of the G8 summit, the Edinburgh Tattoo, Hogmanay, the Golf Open and civil nuclear resilience issues. He is an associate lecturer at the Cabinet Office Emergency Planning College.

John Williamson Dip FM, MSc, FIFSM is Chairman of the Institute of Fire Safety Managers. He is a former Assistant Chief Fire officer and has commanded many major incidents, such as the Piper Alpha platform disaster. John is a Fellow of the Institution of Fire Engineers and provides expert evidence for the Courts. He also lectures on fire risk assessment and fire safety.

Frank Whiteford is the Associate Director of Health Service Resilience in the North West. Frank has worked for the NHS for over 30 years, serving with the Ambulance Service as Deputy Director of Operations in Lancashire. He is responsible for overseeing performance management in Emergency Preparedness across all NHS organizations in the North West and is also the Lead for Pandemic Flu for the Strategic Health Authority. He has been in charge of several major incidents at the Tactical and Strategic level and has taught medical emergency preparedness across the NHS and Blue Light Services in the UK, as well as in Kuwait, Spain and Brazil.

List of Figures

List of Figures

List of Abbreviations

ACPO	Association of Chief Police Officers
ARCC	Aeronautical Rescue Co-ordination Centre
BCM	Business Continuity Manager / Management
BERR	Department for Business Enterprise and Regulatory Reform
CBRN	Chemical, Biological, Radiological and Nuclear
CCA	Civil Contingencies Act 2004
CC	Control Centre
CCRF	Civil Contingencies Reaction Force
CCS	Civil Contingencies Secretariat
CCTV	Closed Circuit Television
CEO	Chief Executive Officer
CNC	Civil Nuclear Constabulary
COMAH	Control of Major Accident Hazard Regulations
COBR	Cabinet Office Briefing Room
CPS	Crown Prosecution Service
CRR	Community Risk Register
Defra	Department of Environment Food and Rural Affairs
DoH	Department of Health
DoT	Department of Transport
DTI	Department of Trade and Industry
ECC	Emergency Control Centre
EP	Emergency Procedures
EPO	Emergency Planning Officer
FCP	Forward Control Point
FLO	Family Liaison Officer
FMB	Forward Media Briefing
FRC	Family Reception Centre
FSA	Food Standards Agency
GO	Government Office (Regional)
GPMS	Government Protective Marking Scheme
GSB	Gold, Silver and Bronze

List of Abbreviations

HAC	Humanitarian Assistance Centre
HSE	Health and Safety Executive
ICP	Incident Control Post
IEM	Integrated Emergency Management
LA	Local Authority
LGD	Lead Government Department
LRF	Local Resilience Forum
MA	Marshalling Area
MACA	Military Aid to the Civil Authority
MACC	Military Aid to the Civil Community
MACP	Military Aid to the Civil Power
MBP	Media Briefing Point
MCC	Media Co-ordination Centre
MDP	Ministry of Defence Police
MI	Major Incident
MOU	Memorandum of Understanding
NAIR	National Arrangements for Incidents Involving Radioactivity
NARO	Nuclear Accident Response Organisation (MOD)
NCC	National Co-ordination Centre (Media)
NHS	National Health Service
NPIA	National Police Improvement Agency
PA	Public Address
PCT	Primary Care Trust
PIO	Police Incident Officer
PNICC	Police National Information and Co-ordinating Centre
QA	Quality Assured
RADSAFE	Radiation Safety (Transport)
RAWG	Risk Assessment Working Group
RC	Rest Centre
RCCC	Regional Civil Contingencies Co-ordinating Committee
REPPIR	Radiation Emergency Preparedness and Public Information Regulations
RNLI	Royal National Lifeboat Institution

RPD	Radiation Protection Division of Health Protection Agency
RRF	Regional Resilience Forum
RRT	Regional Resilience Team
RVP	Rendezvous Point
RWG	Recovery Working Group
SAR	Search and Rescue
SCG	Strategic Co-ordinating Group
SCC	Strategic Co-ordination Centre
SIM	Senior Identification Manager
SIO	Senior Investigating Officer
SRC	Survivor Reception Centre
STAC	Scientific and Technical Advice Cell
TOR	Terms of Reference

List of Useful Websites

<www.ukresilience.gov.uk>
<www.eps.co.uk>
<www.dh.gov.uk/en/managingyourorganisation/
   emergencyplanning/>
<www.hpa.gov.uk/cepr/default.htm>
<www.defra.gov.uk/environ/fcd/floodincidents/contin. htm>
<www.preparingforemergencies.gov.uk>
<www.environment-agency.gov.uk>
<www.co-ordination.gov.uk>
<www.keywaypublishing.com>

Chapter 1

Introduction to Emergency Planning

Overview

In this chapter we will cover the following topics:

- The Emergency Planning Officer
- Personal qualities
- The EPO image
- Personal kit
- Who's who in the emergency planning world?
- Introduction to the Civil Contingencies Act 2004
- The resilient organization

1.1 Introduction

What is emergency planning? It is quite simply an activity which is intended to prevent and reduce harm to society from hazards produced by both man and the environment. The profile of emergency planning has certainly increased and gained prominence in recent years. Since the terrorist attacks in New York in September 2001 there has been a significant increase in planning for major terrorist attacks, and recent flooding events in England in 2007 have also heightened awareness of the devastating effects of such events.

Successful emergency management is dependent on a number of factors, all of which will be examined and explained in more detail within this book. However, it is suggested here from the outset that there are three factors in particular that will drive effective emergency preparedness.

The first is the Emergency Planning Officer or EPO, someone who is responsible for ensuring that statutory regulation and associated guidance is implemented where necessary; that their organization is alive and responsive to developing emergency preparedness, which can be achieved by analysing organizational risk, preparing plans, training staff and exercising those plans. The second influential factor is the Civil Contingencies Act 2004. As we will see in this book, the Act is the framework around which emergency management is based, forming a consistent approach and delivering a unified national standard. Thirdly, high levels of preparedness can be achieved by having and creating resilient organizations that have the capacity to respond to crisis and emergencies in a way that enables them to continue to operate and deliver services.

1.2 **The Emergency Planning Officer**

Emergency planning is now a complex occupation. It now requires considerable knowledge and skills. For many years it was a role bolted on to other responsibilities, if indeed it was recognized or acknowledged at all. The original role allocated to the EPO was in fact to prepare and train the emergency services and the local authority for nuclear war. Funding for such posts came from central Government. Following the diminishing threat of nuclear war it was inevitable that the role of the EPO would transform or perish. During the 1980s a series of disasters shook the emergency planning community in the UK. This led to a review of roles and responsibilities across the emergency planning community and to the publication of the seminal Government Home Office publication called 'Dealing with Disaster'—a document that laid the foundations for emergency response as we understand it today. The evolution of the EPO from the previous 'war duties' officers working for the emergency services and local authorities in the 1970s and 1980s was now developing into a specialist profession as a result. The role essentially moved from one solely dealing with war preparation to one of civil protection generally. Issues relating to risk—both from industrial and environmental hazards as we know them today—were planned for, albeit in a very ad hoc and un-coordinated way. However they led to a growing recognition of the increasingly important role of the EPO. In particular many police forces established dedicated EPOs to manage their emergency planning obligations as co-ordinators within the emergency response phase of an emergency or major incident as outlined in 'Dealing with Disaster'. The role began to develop and evolve across the country, but at different rates with differing priorities, confused financing and different levels of commitment from senior managers and executive officers. Then in 2001 the terrorist attacks in New York occurred and the role of the EPO changed overnight, followed by the creation of the Civil Contingencies Act 2004 a few years later. The EPO became a high profile figure with organizations within the public sector, primarily charged with implementing the Civil Contingencies Act. The profession had come of age.

The word 'profession' is used because that is what emergency planning has become in its own right requiring thorough training and qualification. Although a still relatively 'new' role compared to long standing business professions there is evidence of its growing stature within the public services and the commercial sector. The professional development and qualification element for the EPO is developing at a rapid rate and is now often seen on university prospectuses although it is suggested that there has been a remarkable lack of practical advice and guidance available to those undertaking the emergency planning role. It is intended that this book will address that. In addition, National Occupational Standards, which this book supports, are being developed for the Civil Contingencies role to ensure a consistent standard is achieved within the profession across the country.

Professional bodies such as the Emergency Planning Society (<http://www.eps.co.uk>) and the Business Continuity Institute (<http://www.thebci.org.uk>) are also driving up standards and the profile of the profession. Both offer services and support for the practising emergency planning and business continuity professional. Although many universities offer training and academic qualifications in related emergency planning subjects, the Cabinet Office Emergency Planning College (<http://www.epcollege.gov.uk>) has become the focal point for training development in the UK for emergency planning. Page xxix of this book has a list of useful sites that may assist as reference.

1.3 **Personal Qualities**

What makes a good EPO? The EPO is there to inform, educate, advise and guide. Apart from gaining the knowledge, skills and qualifications, being an effective emergency planning officer means being a good communicator too. Inevitably situations arise where there will be conflicts of interest. This is unavoidable, especially within a multi-agency environment where people have differing perspectives and priorities. Indeed this conflict may arise between the public and private sector where emergency arrangements for industry may demand considerable expenditure. Issues will also occur where persuasion and negotiation are required, for example in securing funding or agreeing where responsibility for actions lie. All of these require an approach which is confident, robust and authoritative but yet being sensitive and understanding to the other position. As an EPO, being able to communicate at all levels in all situations—from protracted negotiation to dynamic crisis management, from training to umpiring—requires high levels of skill. One key factor for an effective communicator is to 'know your stuff'. If the EPO is confident in their own knowledge and skills they will project and instil confidence in others. This is very important when giving presentations and briefings—which every EPO will have to do. Good communication skills also come into play when called upon to debrief a Task or an incident (again, adopting the 'facilitator' approach as opposed to the 'crisis' management approach which we will discuss later).

In preparing plans a critical, analytical approach with attention to detail and a flare for logic and sequencing is vital. This will ensure ideas and thoughts are translated into a form that others will understand easily. Creative thinking and innovation will attack problems and render solutions, sometimes which are different, where negotiating skills may be required to persuade people to change. Being prepared to be receptive to new ideas and accept change is also an important attribute.

The EPO is now without question a vital part of any organization's management team, who will be a valuable advisor across a range of organizational activities. To be able to fulfil that role they must fully appreciate and understand their organization. They should be familiar with the organizational structure, functional areas, processes, policies, systems, business continuity plans, crisis management plans, critical incident criteria, philosophy, strategic aims and objectives, goals and ambitions—in short know the organization, its strengths and weaknesses.

1.4 **The EPO Image**

The EPO should always create an impression of competency and confidence. Developing a good reputation is important. Firstly, the EPO must look the part. It is perhaps an area that seems to be perceived as less important in working environments today where casual wear seems to be more readily acceptable. However, in a business environment impressions and image are important, in particular when dealing with senior managers and members of the public.

In meetings the EPO should always contribute. They should have a personal introduction prepared in advance when attendees 'go around the table'. The EPO should make notes during the discussion as this shows involvement and engagement, which will be noticed by others in the room. Mobile phones should always be switched off unless it is essential to remain in touch, in which case the vibrate mode should be used. It is very off-putting and a sign of indifference to the business at hand to be constantly looking and playing with a mobile phone. Others around the table will notice, as will the chairman.

A good impression and reputation affect business dealing. You will achieve more.

Task 1.1

Using the web site references provided together with personal research, familiarize yourself with the key emergency planning forums that will become your sources of reference. Consider membership where appropriate, if you think it will assist you.

TIP: Look at your stakeholder's web sites and find their references to Emergency Planning. You will gain good insights into their attitude and approach to planning. It will assist you when you meet them.

1.4.1 Personal Kit

As an emergency planning professional, the EPO should be in possession of appropriate health and safety equipment (Personal Protective Equipment—PPE) as determined by the circumstances. At least a high visibility coat specified to highways standard, an industrial hard hat, reinforced rubber boots and a good torch as a minimum. The high visibility coat should ideally have a logo on the back indicating 'Emergency Planning Officer' or similar. This is important so that other people who are involved in an incident or Task can recognize the EPO. Depending on the role, which may include call out, being prepared is essential. Many EPOs attend scenes of major incidents to offer onsite dynamic advice and guidance. Visiting sites, task locations and real incidents can be hazardous and an EPO should not rely on someone else to provide the equipment although there is some obligation on site owners to supply appropriate PPE.

Many EPOs and many senior officers and managers carry hand held computers and laptops which hold emergency plans. But it is essential that these are secure and not left in places where they will or could be stolen or lost. This may seem obvious but it occurs regularly. In London alone in 2006, 6,000 laptop and handheld computers were stolen; taking into account burglary offences, that figure reached 15,000. Many of those computers contained sensitive information.[1]

Carrying a digital camera is also useful to record images that can be used in presentations or documents, to illustrate plans and emphasize a point at debriefs. Communication is also vital so a mobile phone is essential with a spare battery with charger options. Always ensure that mobile phones are keypad locked at all times.

1.5 Who's Who in the Emergency Planning World?

Having looked at the EPO role, we should now place the EPO into a wider context within the public and private sector risk management community. Not only has the profile of the EPO increased but the numbers too and variations in the role. Emergency planning offices and departments across all emergency responder organizations have grown incredibly to meet the ever increasing demands and the requirements of the Civil Contingencies Act. Private sector organizations also recognize the need to be resilient both

---

[1] <http://software.silicon.com/security/0,39024655,39167148,00.htm>. 2008

from a commercial perspective and in the way they support the community following an emergency or obligations to their customers; for example in the transport industry. Many organizations have both emergency planning officers and business continuity managers.

This proliferation of disciplines, and indeed job titles, all related to planning can be confusing. References will be made to emergency, contingency and continuity so it may be useful also at this point to take a brief look at some job titles and descriptions that may be experienced within the wider profession. There are several titles describing the role of EPO-related work, for example, Emergency Planning Officer (or manager), Contingency Planning Officer (or manager) or the Civil Contingencies Officer are all currently in use. They broadly describe the same role but there are subtle differences to be noted. Essentially, the Emergency Planning Officer and Contingency or Civil Contingencies Officer all perform similar roles. To put the business continuity manager into context they will be focused more on the risk evaluation, mitigation and the 'cost' of risk which is business orientated in a commercial sense; whereas the emergency planning officer and contingency planning officer to a large extent are more aligned with preventing injury and loss of life, but each discipline is complementary.

Emergency is described as 'an unexpected and potentially dangerous situation requiring immediate action'.[2] There is a sense of urgency in the description of emergency which will determine how to prepare plans and tends to relate to life saving situations. Contingency on the other hand, describes a future event or circumstance which is possible but cannot be predicted with certainty. This title is broader in context and caters for a whole range of events which may not be considered 'urgent' but nevertheless present critical situations. For clarity and to avoid repetition, Emergency Planning Officer and Emergency Plans will be used in this book, but with a recognition of the need to read across

---

[2] Oxford Concise Dictionary.

'contingency' and 'business continuity' as they are dependent and integral parts of the overall function of emergency preparedness.

1.6 **The Civil Contingencies Act 2004**

One vital piece of knowledge that unites all those within the planning world is the Civil Contingencies Act 2004, which we will now take a brief look at.

The terrorist attacks in New York on 11 September 2001 changed the way in which emergency response is perceived worldwide. The ability to respond effectively to and manage a catastrophic event was brought into question. It also raised the prospect of dealing with new threats involving mass casualties brought about by the use of chemical, biological or radiological devices. Perhaps more disturbing was the realization that existing benign technologies can be turned against society with catastrophic effects. Combined with the global threat posed by climate change and pandemic disease, it is perhaps not surprising that emergency management is on everyone's agenda. Managing the consequences of such events is a real challenge and developing the necessary skills and knowledge is now a key priority for many organizations.

In response to the growing risks presented by manmade and natural threats, the UK Government introduced legislation in the form of the Civil Contingencies Act 2004 (CCA). For the first time this legislation put certain statutory duties on emergency responders and established a national framework to manage the risks through groups known as Local Resilience Forums (LRF) located across England and Wales and usually within police force boundaries. Understanding this emergency planning structure created by the CCA is essential for the EPO and for the development of emergency plans. Through the LRFs the CCA aimed to:

• Provide a single framework for civil protection.

1 Introduction to Emergency Planning

- Improve resilience at Local, Regional and National levels.
- To deal effectively with emergencies.
- Prevent disruption to essential services.

The CCA established new responsibilities and definitions, listed below:

> **Checklist—New responsibilities and definitions established by the CCA**
>
> - Created a statutory duty for the first time. Prior to the CCA, commitment to emergency planning was largely unregulated and very ad hoc.
> - Defined what an 'emergency' was. Up to that point 'emergency' was subjective and therefore open to a very wide interpretation, which led to anomalies in levels of response. However, we will see that the term 'major incident' is still in use for good reason.
> - Required risk assessment activities as a basis for planning. This process gave some degree of rationale and quantification to risk.
> - Created a framework for preparing and responding to emergencies outlined in two volumes of guidance. This set of guidelines ensured a consistent and integrated approach to emergency planning. Up to that point the only reference was the Home Office publication 'Dealing with Disaster', which was a very useful and productive document but lacked detail and authority to enforce standards.
> - Promoted effective warning and informing the public. This followed recognition that communities, indeed informed and educated communities, in terms of emergency response, would be safer communities because informed people clearly make better decisions. It required warning and informing obligations to have ownership.
> - Encouraged business continuity planning and hence business continuity management. Building resilient businesses and organizations created a better chance for them to survive a crisis or emergency. It also allowed for less reliance on the emergency services and other support agencies so leaving them with more resources to concentrate on the 'at risk' and vulnerable communities.

- Redefined 'State of Emergency'. This allowed the Government to make special temporary powers and this could apply to one area or region as opposed to the whole country.
- Incorporated performance measures and sanctions for those who do not fulfil their responsibilities under the CCA. This is a critical element as it 'enforces' the regulations. Many Category 1 responders now have their requirements under the CCA embedded into their performance measures. This allows objective comparisons and evaluation of effectiveness in emergency planning.

Quite a list! As can be seen, these are fundamental changes that had a profound effect and impact on the emergency planning community nationally.

The legislation also created two categories of responder known as Category 1 and Category 2 responders.

KEY POINTS

Category 1 and Category 2 responders

Essentially, **Category 1** responders are those who we think of as the emergency services, health services, local authorities and Environment Agency—the front line.

Category 2 responders are those key support utilities, transport infrastructure, Health and Safety Executive and Strategic Health Authorities.

Task 1.2

- Find your Local Resilience Forum web site and familiarize yourself with the members and their organizations.
- Who are your Category 1 and Category 2 Responders?

TIP: Find out their names or get hold of an Emergency Planning Directory—get to know your stakeholders <http://www.keywaypublishing.com>

---

1 Introduction to Emergency Planning

The CCA enabled two sets of guidance documents to be produced:

1. *Emergency Preparedness*
2. *Emergency Response and Recovery*

Emergency Preparedness together with the accompanying *Emergency Response and Recovery* sets out the generic framework for civil protection.

Every EPO must read and understand both of these documents as they form the basis upon which all emergency planning is driven in the UK. They are also invaluable reference documents and form an integral accompaniment to this book and should be available to be read in conjunction.

Although this book is not solely concerned with the Civil Contingencies Act 2004, it would be fair to say that the CCA resulted in a massive shift in attitude and approach to emergency management. It created a benchmark in standards, a uniformity and accountability within the emergency planning community. The CCA also embraced business continuity as a vital component in the drive for effective emergency planning. Business continuity and emergency response are now more closely linked than ever before.

The CCA drives a principle that organizations who are well prepared for managing a crisis or emergency will not only be more likely to survive from a business perspective but will take some pressure off the emergency services. They can do this by being more self-sufficient and in many ways they can shape how the emergency is managed themselves by early intervention—the 'Golden Hour' will be discussed in a later chapter but endorses the principle that remedial action within the first hour of an incident will have the most impact.

In addition, any organization including the commercial sector for that matter should not take for granted that the emergency services have all the answers to managing an emergency. Indeed, long held assumptions about what the emergency services will or can do need to be dispelled or moderated. Although well trained and practised through daily routine, a crisis or emergency will stretch everyone, blue lights included. The message is a resilient organization is a smart organization.

1.7 **The Resilient Organization**

'Resilience' is a term used extensively within the Civil Contingencies Act 2004. Resilience (according to the Oxford English Dictionary) is defined as the ability to withstand, recover quickly from or spring back into shape having been bent! This definition is extended within the context of the CCA to refer to the 'ability of the community, services, an area or infrastructure to withstand the consequences of an incident'.[3] Resilience is the overall aim that supports effective emergency preparedness. To build in resilience for Category 1 responders the CCA placed a statutory duty on them to maintain plans to ensure that they can continue to deliver their core services in the face of an emergency to which they may have to respond. This concept also embraced the idea of not only looking closely into internal organizational dependencies but reliance on external services that may be contracted. Although the Business Continuity Management (BCM) requirement within the CCA is quite narrow, only applying to 'emergencies' defined within the CCA the process and Task driving that requirement will and does inevitably address a much wider range of threats and crises. In effect the CCA is creating more resilient organizations which are defined under the CCA. The implication for a Category 1 organization not being able to deliver emergency services because they are suffering from an internal crisis or not having foreseen a threat that could compromise public safety should be planned for and avoided at all costs.

---

[3] Civil Contingencies Act 2004. Guidance—Emergency Preparedness, p 222.

The Carlisle floods in Cumbria in January 2005 illustrated this point: police stations, police resources, and the Strategic Command Centre (SCC) were compromised by the flood water. Clearly, issues such as that now need to be factored into relocating those resources and facilities. This is a feature of any planning and project proposal which is to examine and analyze the risk of 'compromise' to that facility—how resilient is it?

But the concept of the resilient organization does not just extend to emergency preparedness only but can make good business sense and increase the chances of commercial survival. We will see in a later chapter how exercising can in fact help build resilience into an organization.

The key factors are therefore, the EPO, the Civil Contingencies Act 2004 and the resilient organization. These three pillars form the foundation for emergency preparedness.

Task 1.3

- Consider why organizational resilience is important to emergency planning.
- How would you rate your organization's resilience?
- What performance measures under the Act, if any, affect your organization?

1.8 **Summary**

- You should understand the role of the EPO and the relationship with others in the planning community.
- The significance of the Civil Contingencies Act 2004 with its main points.
- The Role and function of the LRF
- The key documents that drive the Civil Contingencies Act.

- The relationship between emergency planning and business continuity planning.
- Understanding how resilience is a key driver for emergency preparedness.

1.9 **Conclusion**

The role of the Emergency Planning Officer has become a vital management tool for both the public and private sector over the last ten years to ensure emergency management is developed and maintained. Emergency planning itself has transformed in the last three to four years, brought about by the Civil Contingencies Act 2004. The ability to withstand and recover from a crisis or emergency is a primary objective for many organizations today, from a commercial, reputational and legislative perspective. There is a stark global recognition that we are living in a 'risky' society. Planning to respond to the many threats and hazards now facing society is a priority for everyone.

This book will prepare the foundations to acquire the necessary skills to begin that planning process. In the next chapter we will examine the need to plan and the part exercising has in building resilience into an organization.

Chapter 2

Plans and Exercising

Overview

In this chapter we will cover the following topics:

- Types of plan
- The emergency planning cycle
- Integrated emergency planning
- Measuring risk for planning purposes
- Assessment
- Over planning
- Preparation, Response and Recovery
- Prevention
- Who creates plans?
- LRF planning
- Regional and national planning
- Local Authority planning
- Multi-agency plans in perspective
- Individual organizational plans
- Making planning decisions
- Business Continuity planning
- Do we need to exercise?
- The benefits of exercising plans
- Senior management buy-in
- Corporate manslaughter

2.1 **Introduction**

What is an emergency plan? The Oxford English Diction-ary, for example, states that a plan is 'a detailed proposal to achieve something'. That concept is well understood and

---

accepted; but the nature of a 'plan' and what it means is perhaps less well understood, or indeed taken for granted. Emergency plans are never finished. When a plan is written it enters a cycle, the emergency planning cycle, for the duration of its life (see Figure 2.1). It begins degrading immediately. An emergency plan needs constant maintenance and attention because it is dynamic. It describes activity, gives instruction, directs policy and crucially is only effective when implemented by people trained in its use. A plan that is not used, reviewed, updated and tested will in a short time become redundant and will ultimately fail to deliver what it was designed to achieve.

But having agreed what a plan should be or what a plan should be able to deliver, what type of plans are there?

Trying to envisage the multitude of plan types could be bewildering. Trying to choose the right type can also be confusing. Where to start making those choices often leads to questions such as:

- Why produce plans anyway?
- What or who tells us we have to have plans?
- Who is required to produce plans?
- What has to go into a plan?
- What is the best format?
- Do we have to test plans?

In fact the list of questions could go on and on. This chapter is intended to answer those questions and many more to assist the EPO make that choice. The first consideration is the type of plans that are in general use today.

2.2 **Types of Plan**

In general plans will fall into six main categories:

1. **Generic:** This type of plan can be viewed as the default procedures that can be applied to any incident but which will not contain specific detail. It will spell out

management roles and responsibilities, procedures, policy, definitions and checklists. It is used to deal with incidents and events not specifically planned for. These are often formatted in an aide memoire style on a few pages of laminated card.

2. **Site-specific:** A site-specific plan refers to a known location, eg industrial plant, football stadium, airport, port, industrial unit, office block etc. Therefore more detail is known about potential hazards, resource requirements and geography. These plans contain more specific information and can be a statutory requirement from one or more regulatory bodies.

3. **Incident-specific:** These plans refer to incidents which could occur at any location, usually transport- or movement-related, eg aeroplane, train or coach crash, including the spillage or discharge of dangerous chemicals, plumes or radiation into the environment. Terrorist type activities such as explosions or system failures on large networks would also fall into this category.

4. **Individual or single agency:** These plans are produced within an agency or organization and are intended for internal use. They will describe how the organization will respond to an incident within the organization which includes how it will respond, react or support a multi-agency plan to which it subscribes. These are really the driving force of an organization's response and therefore the building block behind all multi-agency and multi-level plans. This type of plan will be used as the example in the next chapter.

5. **Multi-agency:** Multi-agency plans are a composite of individual plans and planning arrangements by many organizations. They are brought together and amalgamated into one set of arrangements by a lead organization. They tend to be very comprehensive but designed for reference and slow time activation compared to single agency or individual plans, which can be applied rapidly and dynamically. They have a co-ordinating function to ensure the combined response operates in harmony.

6. **Multi-level:** These plans are produced to address more than one level of the civil protection framework. They can be national or regional and then local, but all dealing with a single issue—for example, foot and mouth disease, coastal pollution, pandemic influenza etc. Each layer or level will describe a part of the response but they will fully integrate. This multi-level arrangement works well where there may be slight differences in structure between localities or regions.

Although there appears to be quite a number of plans, each has a specific role to fulfil. Too generic and the specific detail and information is lost. Too specific and there is a danger of duplication and overlap, leading to potential confusion. The key is getting the balance right but it is important to be able to distinguish between types. What they have in common is that they are all living dynamic and changing. They all also form part of the emergency planning cycle.

Task 2.1

List five examples for each of the following:

1. Site-specific plans;
2. incident-specific plans; and
3. multi-agency plans.

Tip: Check out your Local Resilience Forum website.

2.3 **The Emergency Planning Cycle**

Producing plans and exercising those plans lies at the heart of emergency planning. It is a skill that is essential for every EPO. Creating plans and exercising forms part of a cycle of emergency planning (Figure 2.1) activity that ensures that plans are up-to-date, viable and efficient.

This activity also supports the principle of building a resilient organization, with properly trained staff working with

Figure 2.1 Emergency Planning Cycle

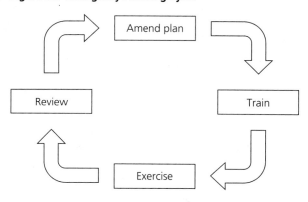

effective emergency plans. In this chapter we will examine the issues that drive the planning and exercise processes. What directs the production of plans and having produced the plans how we can ensure they will work?

2.4 **Integrated Emergency Planning**

The CCA supports and endorses the principle of Integrated Emergency Management (IEM) which is based upon six activities:

1. Anticipation—Identifying threats and hazards.
2. Assessment—Quantifying and analysing those threats and hazards into risk.
3. Prevention—Putting in place measures to reduce the risk or stop the event happening.
4. Preparation—Making a plan, this includes training and exercising staff.
5. Response—How to deal with the event when it happens.

6. Recovery management—How to return to near normality.

We will now look at each activity in turn.

Figure 2.2 Integrated Emergency Management

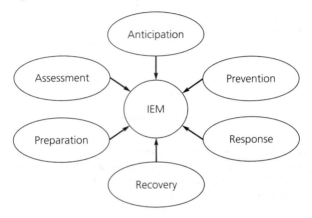

2.4.1 **Anticipation**

The whole planning process is underpinned by the IEM activities. Each activity has to be considered in turn to ensure that all aspects of the planning process are fully addressed. The key planning areas centre initially on Anticipation and Assessment—establishing a need to plan and risk assessing the potential hazards. What to plan for? Anticipation means trying to identify what new hazards and threats could arise, sometimes referred to as 'horizon scanning'. This may result from many factors such as environmental, industrial, legislative, and economic or disease. Having identified potential hazards their impact has to be assessed to inform the level of planning needed to mitigate or eliminate the risk.

2.4.2 **Measuring Risk for Planning Purposes**

Assessment—how can risk be measured? There is no 'ideal' plan to suit all events for all organizations, nor is there a totally reliable risk model to inform the decision to produce plans. Risk is a slippery concept which can to a degree be measured but the risks most of us face are quite obvious and the decision to make plans is clear. Nevertheless, a risk assessment process is needed to ensure all aspects of risk have been addressed. Dealing with a 'process' will ensure a level of consistency and objectivity in making those risk assessments and ultimately whether to plan for them or not.

Before beginning the process of attempting to measure risk with a view to producing a plan, it is important to establish a 'position' on plans. The implications of having a plan as opposed to not having one is a risk judgement in itself before the risk assessment itself. Not having a plan eliminates the consequences of it going wrong and having to write, maintain and exercise it. Producing a plan has consequences, and not just the time spent in creating and maintaining it. A plan will be the tangible proof of an organization's commitment to prepare for and mitigate a threat or hazard that has been deemed to be a significant risk. The plan could be examined and analyzed by a third party such as a court, inquest or inquiry to establish any shortcomings and deficiencies. A plan will have an effect on someone and the mere existence of the plan can at some level create a 'duty of care' towards those affected by the plan, in particular employees. In addition, if people have been informed that there is a plan and they will be affected by it, the plan can't simply be discontinued or modified without involving those affected. Therefore, it is quite a responsibility and the plan must be robust, tested and fit for purpose.

Not having or even considering a plan in the face of a potential hazard is a very high risk strategy in itself and one which could have very serious consequences if the incident in question occurs. This position is a short sighted and dangerous view, albeit one that exists.

2 Plans and Exercising

So how can risk be quantified? An event that is potentially catastrophic but extremely unlikely may be worth writing a plan for, because of the serious consequences it could have. A moderate event which happens relatively frequently may also lead to creating a plan: although the consequences may be less serious, the event would still have regular adverse impact on the community, albeit low level. How is moderate or frequently defined? Risk is subjective. Trying to measure risk accurately is a complex activity, which can be and is often unreliable. But to focus one's thoughts, the use of the traditional risk assessment matrix such as the one in Figure 2.3 may help to categorize the risk. There are numerous forms and formats for this chart but

Figure 2.3 Risk Assessment Matrix

Likelihood →

Impact	RISK	IMPROBABLE	POSSIBLE	PROBABLE	HIGHLY PROBABLE
	MINIMAL	Low	Medium	Medium	Medium
	MODERATE	Low	Medium	High	High
	SEVERE	Medium	Medium	High	High
	CATASTROPHIC	High	High	High	High

essentially they do the same job. It must be remembered that the trigger point, or level at which one decides to create a plan, can be determined in a number of ways. Within the context of a national framework created by the Civil Contingencies Act 2004 there has to be a degree of consistency across the country. For example, it would be unacceptable for one Local Resilience Forum (LRF) to agree to have a certain plan and a neighbouring LRF not to. Therefore risk level can be directed by legislation, advice from Government Departments or professional advice such as insurance companies or company policy. Where this direction is not so explicit the ultimate decision rests with the individual or appointed committee or group, either public or private sector. But whatever criteria or risk level is agreed, the risk matrix is a very simple way of creating a process in quantifying risk and the process also demonstrates that the risk has been addressed and can provide a rationale for writing or more importantly, not writing a plan.

This risk assessment process can be further quantified by assigning values to the 'likelihood' and 'impact'. For example, likelihood could be given values ranging from once every 100 years for improbable, to once a year for highly probable. The difficulty here is getting the data to validate those values. This of course can be done historically, by modelling or by prediction. If this can be achieved it adds a factor of reliability into the assessment.

Again, impact can be 'valued' by assigning the potential impact on numbers of people in the form of predicted casualties, fatalities or displaced persons. This can be adapted for damage to property or infrastructure. It is a complex process but it too, as in likelihood, renders a more accurate assessment, which in turn can be used to make plans more effective. In short, if reliable numerical data can be obtained and applied with a degree of confidence it should be used.

Referring to the matrix, assume that all 'high' risk hazards will be planned for—that is the chosen criteria. If the hazard is judged to be 'possible' and 'catastrophic' a HIGH rating would result. This would require a plan. If however, the judgement or analysis for another hazard came out as 'highly probable' but 'minimal' impact that would result in a MEDIUM risk and therefore no plan is required.

This matrix method can also be used to quantify more specific risks, such as those used for activities within a plan. Is the task or action required in the plan too risky? Again, apply a threshold beyond which the activity will not be allowed to take place, with ever reducing levels of risk being addressed or mitigated by the use of risk 'treatments' such as providing protective equipment for example or modifying the task to make it less risky or simply not doing it.

Task 2.2

What is the six step risk assessment process? Refer to the CCA Guidance notes.

2.4.3 **Over Planning**

One of the important advantages of using a risk assessment methodology is to prevent 'overplanning'. Setting a risk threshold too low or not using an assessment at all can result in producing plans unnecessarily with all the attendant problems that may incur. An informal or casual approach to planning can lead to a situation where every conceivable potential adverse event seems to result in a plan. This is an exponential activity in which a final conclusion is never reached, because many incidents can be the combination of a series of unforeseen unconnected events that are completely random. It is impossible to plan for everything. This approach could be classed as paralysis by analysis! What is reasonably foreseeable is the key and the applied test.

2.4.4 **Preparation, Response, and Recovery**

Having managed the risks presented, the next stage is to consider preparing for and responding to the event if it happens. These activities will focus on creating the plans and everything that supports that process, such as training and exercising. Preparation, Response and Recovery within the IEM are the three activities that produce the main area of planning activity and indeed form the basis for the two Civil Contingencies Act guidance documents. This book is primarily focused on these activities. Recovery management is a post incident activity and usually managed by established groups (like the Recovery Working Group [RWG]—we shall discuss later) set up for the purpose of restoring and rebuilding the community in the aftermath of an incident when the emergency phase of the incident is over. It will also be demonstrated later that the RWG has a role to play in the emergency phase of an incident to ensure that issues under consideration and decisions made are taken in the light of their potential impact on longer term recovery.

2.4.5 **Prevention**

The remaining activity within IEM is 'Prevention'. Prevention is mainly addressed through legislation generally on safety and putting in place the physical barriers and procedures to reduce the likelihood of the event happening in the first place. For example, this is seen in the very high safety standards within the aviation and nuclear industries. This area is often the focus for Health and Safety legislation monitored by the Health and Safety Executive (HSE) and other legislation that governs safety on industrial sites and transport. In terms of the CCA, prevention does have a place in response in that activating a plan can avert an emergency occurring and so prevent it happening.

2 Plans and Exercising

Having established the planning framework we now need to consider who the lead planners are and where their planning obligations stem from.

2.5 Who Creates Plans?

It will be useful at this stage to consider the main planning groups that may be encountered and identify how they integrate plans. The CCA encourages information sharing and collaboration in many areas of emergency management but particularly in plan preparation. Plans written in isolation have limited use. Having an understanding of the different planning levels and types will assist the EPO to develop an appreciation how plans produced by different organizations can, and should build into a coherent meaningful response.

2.5.1 Local Resilience Forum planning

Within a Local Resilience Forum the risk assessment process is usually carried out by a 'Risk Assessment Working Group' or RAWG, a sub-group of the LRF. Based upon the risk assessment outcome, plan preparation is recommended or not, with the ultimate objective to reduce, control and mitigate the effects of an emergency created by that risk. The issue for the LRF is to agree what criteria should apply to trigger the creation of a plan. Some planning is obligatory following direction from Government or legislation but other hazards, often localized are not subject to that direction and rely wholly on a risk assessment process to inform that decision. That decision has to be based upon a level of risk that is acceptable or unacceptable to the LRF and that will direct them to declare that a plan must be created. Therefore, each LRF should have set criteria that trigger the production of a plan together with a process to identify who the lead organization(s) will be to produce that plan. The risk assessment process must have a 'product' or 'outcome' otherwise the risk assessment can become meaningless and diluted.

In terms of identifying a lead organization it is difficult to see how LRFs can achieve this effectively as they have no authority to direct any agency to carry out work. If it cannot be agreed it is incumbent upon each organization with a stake in the response to create their own plans (individual or single agency) this option will be discussed under multi-agency plans later. The tendency is to mitigate the risk identified by the LRF by listing and producing existing emergency arrangements prepared by individual Category 1 and 2 responders and using them in a generalized way. Although not common practice at the moment, the establishment of a multi-agency planning team is a more focused and efficient means of fulfilling completely integrated emergency management and a consideration for all LRFs. In this way lead Category 1 responders can work more closely together, co-located to apply their individual expertise in creating multi-agency plans on behalf of the LRF.

Notwithstanding who contributes to the planning process all local hazards and risk assessments are contained in a public document called a 'Community Risk Register' or CRR, produced by each LRF. In it can be seen how each identified hazard is assessed and treated and what plans are in place. These important documents can be examined by approaching the local LRF and/or by viewing the document on their local web sites. The CCA makes this process a statutory duty for Category 1 responders, which is usually discharged through the LRFs. The CCA also stipulates what must appear in each plan and how plans are treated; these stipulations can be read in the CCA guidance documents.

Task 2.3
- Find your LRF CRR.
- Where can it be found apart from the web site?
- Examine the risk treatments—what kind of plans are in place?

2.5.2 **Regional/National Planning**

The CCA guidance refers to the role of a regional tier of civil protection to improve local co-ordination and introduced a non statutory framework to achieve that aim. In effect, it introduced additional layers of resilience management to ensure better communication and co-ordination at both Regional and National level. This established the Regional Resilience Forums (RRF) and Regional Resilience Teams (RRT) working under a Director from Regional Government Offices. The RRF attendant sub-committees supported by the RRT create plans to address both regional and national issues.

The RRFs have no statutory duty but do prepare plans with a view to enhancing that regional co-ordination role by preparing plans and linking into all LRFs. The plans they prepare are usually of national significance and in response to advice and direction from Government departments. They also publish a plan that co-ordinates a regional response to a civil emergency and they do acquire statutory powers if a 'state of emergency' is invoked. It is not intended to cover that level of detail within this book but a complete explanation is contained in the CCA guidance documents.

2.5.3 **Local authority planning**

Depending upon the local authority (LA) structure, District, Unitary, County Council or Metropolitan, the planning function and who within the authority carries that out

---

may differ. But local authorities do have certain emergency planning responsibilities. They usually relate to planning under the Control of Major Accident Hazards (COMAH) Regulations 1999 including the Pipeline Safety Regulations 1996 and the Radiation Emergency Preparedness and Public Information Regulations 2001 (REPPIR). These pieces of legislation were set aside from the CCA on the premise that the regulations fulfilled the principles underpinning the CCA already. Therefore the LA have a requirement to prepare multi-agency plans for fixed chemical sites as required by COMAH and fixed nuclear sites as required by REPPIR. Many LAs also prepare other multi-agency plans and link in closely with the LRF to ensure a fully integrated and co-ordinated approach. These plans would include those to assist managing the Voluntary Services and their role in caring for the community, for example plans for rest centres, call handling facilities, faith community plans, emergency mortuaries etc.

2.6 Multi-Agency Plans in Perspective

As we have seen the LRF, RRT and Local Authority subscribe and support multi-agency plans. There is a duty on Category 1 responders to consider the production of multi-agency plans where each organization has a role to play in dealing with a particular emergency. The CCA also stipulates that each organization should agree who will take the lead. However, that may not always be possible or achievable but the CCA directs:

> Where they [LRF] are unable to agree that a multi-agency plan is needed, or which organization should take the lead responsibility, each has a duty to maintain its own plan'.
>
> CCA Guidance—Emergency Preparedness 2005, p 61, para 5.92

But having agreed to create a multi-agency plan, consider: what is it and how useful is it? A multi-agency plan is just that—it co-ordinates the combined response. Multi-agency plans will 'outline' the roles and responsibilities of each participating organization and describe an agreed set of arrangements. But if an organization contributes to that plan they will need to set up their own internal arrangements in support of that plan, an individual or single agency plan. In fact many organizations do hold their own plans which direct and reflect their own emergency arrangements. These are not multi-agency plans per se but could be viewed as internal management tools for that organization alone. The police for example will probably have numerous internal plans because they have to co-ordinate the overall emergency response to so many incidents and have additional responsibilities to support many multi-agency plans. The lead organization is often the local authority for multi-agency plans or a group formed from the LRF.

Task 2.4

- What are the three types of regional plan? Refer to the CCA Guidance.
- What is the membership make up of a RRF?
- Outline the relationship between the LRF and the RRF?
- What role has the RRF in mutual aid?

2.6.1 Individual organizational plans and plan format

If not driven by explicitly to create plans, why go to the trouble to do so? In making that decision, consider the risk assessment approach to identify in the broadest sense what are the implications for the organization if they do not plan for identified hazards. Can an organization anticipate what incident or event could compromise the organization? Could it be to avoid one or more of the following?

- Possible injury to employees or the public
- Damage to the environment
- Legal action
- Financial loss
- Adverse publicity
- Loss of reputation

If the answer to any one of these is yes, there may be need to look more closely at what it is that could cause these events to happen and the impact they may have. One option as already alluded to is to not have a plan at all and 'risk' it, but having a plan in place may eliminate or reduce that adverse effect on the organization, making it more resilient. For the police for example, if they fail to properly co-ordinate a multi-agency response to a specific incident or to plan for an event because they were ill prepared or having not made proper arrangements, it could lead to loss of life and damage to property. For any industrial or transport activity, lack of plans could result in danger to employees, the public and a probable breach of legislation. Every organization must consider risk and how to manage it, in particular where an organization has obligations to contribute to a multi-agency plan.

Whatever motivates or requires plans to be prepared, be it producing plans under legislation or producing plans simply as good business practice or contributing to a multi-agency plan, requires a decision, as to what type of plan is needed. What type of plan meets the requirement? Individual plans can range in content from merely call out lists to highly complex notifications, activations and actions. It is a matter of experience, judgement and consultation among stakeholders in making that decision as to the scale and complexity of the plan required to deal with the risk. The plan is designed to address the risk—the risk is not configured to fit the plan. Plan formats will vary from organization to organization but the plan format described in the next chapter in this book is flexible enough to cater for arrangements that are simple as well as complex. The key point to remember with individual plans is that they are prepared to meet the need for an organization, to slot into existing organizational practice and policy, they are unique to that organization. They will be and should be configured to support and be compatible with other plans produced by other stakeholders but the emphasis is that they are there to support that individual organization. Within the major planning framework individual plans are vital for organizational and business resilience.

2.7 **Making Planning Decisions**

Whatever process is put in place to consider risk and produce plans, a planning group will need to be assembled to address the issues. For example, the LRF considers the production plans by using the RAWG to inform their planning process. In the same way organizations too who require plans will need to identify a core planning team to assess risk and create the plans, in effect their own RAWG. This can be centred on a specific department, as large organizations may have a dedicated unit whereas a smaller company or organization may only have a business continuity manager or emergency planning officer who can co-ordinate the activity. It may be that a consultant is hired to address and co-ordinate the process.

The benefits of having a core planning team are illustrated and endorsed by Business Continuity Management requirements.

2.8 **Addressing Business Continuity**

Business Continuity Management (BCM) plans set out a whole menu of contingencies to address issues that can threaten a business or organizational operation. By contrast, emergency plans address the issues that could be considered as a threat to human health and well being. Computer failure or loss of heating can create a business crisis but is not threatening to life and limb. But a critical part of a BCM plan is the emergency planning aspect. In other words the emergency plan will sit alongside the BCM plan and should be crossed referenced.

The emergency plan element is therefore absolutely critical as it affects lives. Failure to address the risks presented in the risk assessment or not to have in place an effective plan could have serious implications for any organization including potential prosecution.

This book will deal principally with emergency plans.

However, the EPO needs to have an appreciation of BCM and where possible work closely with the Business Continuity Manager. Although the focus of this book is on emergency planning, business continuity is so closely linked now to emergency planning by the CCA that it needs consideration. In terms of business continuity planning, it's a good example of an internal plan that builds and supports resilience. It is a sobering thought that '80% of businesses affected by a major incident fail with 18 months'.[1] It is probably no surprise therefore that the CCA requires that all Category 1 responders have effective internal BCM plans in place and that the local authority are charged with providing advice and assistance to businesses and voluntary organizations on BCM issues in general.

This requirement is designed to ensure that the key responders can respond effectively even if they are affected by the emergency themselves. It means they can continue to deliver their daily function and still respond to an emergency. But in addition there is a view that a strong resilient business will be more able to look after itself and not rely on the emergency services or other statutory agencies to help them. This can only occur if that organization has effective and robust plans themselves. As already alluded to, this not only makes sense to take the pressure off the emergency services but also it makes good business sense and will give

---

[1] Lancashire Resilience Forum website: <www.lanmic.org.uk> 2008.

a business the best possible chance of survival following an emergency.

In terms of business continuity generally which includes emergency responders who have to plan for BCM within their own organizations under the CCA, they need to identify what could threaten their company or organization. That could be anything from fire, flood (remember Carlisle) or storm damage to IT failure to widespread staff sickness. Considerable concern exists relating to the prospect of pandemic influenza. Could an organization cope with significantly reduced staffing? As previously mentioned it is not intended to deal in detail with BCM here but the following process will illustrate the basic procedures to addressing BCM. This is known as the 'Business Continuity Lifecycle' and can be summarized in five steps as follows:

Step 1: Analyze your business
Step 2: Hazard Identification List
Step 3: Risk assessment
Step 4: Develop response and recovery plans
Step 5: Testing and exercising plans

The similarity can be seen to plan development and to the IEM described within the CCA.

The process is quite straightforward. The Business Continuity Manager supported by the EPO should gather the key people in the organization, for example managers or department heads and together create a list of the things that could adversely affect business activity and if these events did occur, what impact would it have? Rate these risks in order of severity as previously described, which would have the most impact on the organization's ability to continue production or offer services and which would have the least?

Consider the use of contractors—are they as resilient as they should be? They should be able to demonstrate that they have BCM plans too and can support the organization in the event of a crisis. These requirements should be incorporated into any contract.

Using the 5 steps outlined above will guide the production of the BCM plan.

Day-to-day risk, or what could be described as 'routine' risk, can be addressed in normal daily operations and will not need a specific plan; indeed most organizations will probably have an in-house health and safety policy document covering daily activity such as office, workshop, or operational activity, within which full assessments have already been completed. In cases of this type of 'routine' disruption once this risk is realized, a generic procedure may be used to bring together key managers to deal with the problem. This may be all that is required without having to prepare structured procedures and processes within a BCM plan—be aware of 'over planning'.

In general, the hazard/threat and impact analysis will inform the basis of the plan. Remember too that business continuity advice can now be obtained from the local authority. The key message here is to be prepared, have sound BCM plans in place to ensure the organization is resilient and flexible.

The diagram illustrated in Figure 2.4 shows an overview of a planning network. It shows how individual plans produced by a variety of organizations and private companies support the individual plans produced by both Category 1 and 2 responders under their statutory obligations. It also illustrates the relationship with BCM as an integral part of planning for resilience. It also shows the influence of the Regional Resilience Forum in informing the production of multi-agency plans and the separate requirements of the local authority to create specialist multi-agency plans. It can be seen that planning and building resilience is not just an issue for the emergency services or a designated group of emergency responders but it affects the wider community. Working together, all the planning processes will join up and produce a seamless and robust response to any crisis or emergency.

Figure 2.4 Planning Network

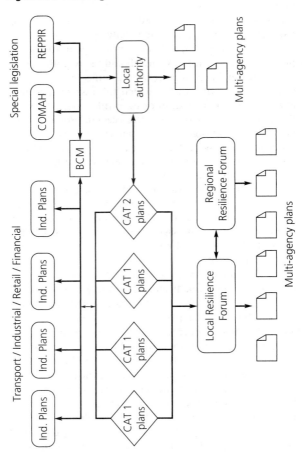

Task 2.5
- List five reasons why an organization should consider a risk management approach to planning.
- Explain the relationship between emergency planning and business continuity planning.

Having decided on the need to plan, whether it is driven by the CCA, legislation or a need to produce individual plans to direct organizational emergency activities, the next consideration is exercising. Is there really a need to exercise?

2.9 **Do We Need to Exercise?**

Having a plan is not enough. The CCA under section 2(1)(c) or (d) requires certain categories of organization to carry out exercises to ensure that the plans are effective <u>and</u> train those people who would be charged with carrying out that plan. What this means in real terms is that there is a recognition of the importance of exercising and for some organizations it is now a statutory obligation. However, the message for everyone involved in preparing emergency plans is that exercising must form part of the emergency planning cycle, see Figure 2.1. It is suggested that those who fail to exercise their plans could become vulnerable to severe criticism or even litigation.

Having comprehensive and robust plans is not sufficient for organizational resilience. Not using or exercising a plan can have dire consequences and can mean the difference between organizational survival and failure. A study showed that 38% of companies surveyed had actually invoked their plans[2] and 43% of companies experiencing disaster never recovered. With as many as 30% of those not reviewing their emergency plans it is hardly surprising that

---

[2] Source: *London Chamber of Commerce* May 2003 and *Compass* January 2004.

---

companies and organizations fail to respond effectively to a crisis or emergency. Being infected with complacency with regard to emergency preparedness is a fatal flaw in any company or organization, a major symptom of this malaise is a failure to exercise.

If producing plans for a crisis or emergency is a requirement for an organization or is accepted that it is just common sense and good management, can it really be assumed that those plans will work? How will those who play a key role in the plan react or perform? Are there sufficient resources? How will other organizations, such as contractors, impact upon the plan? How can an organization know they will survive the inevitable scrutiny? The only way to find the answers to these and numerous other questions is to test or exercise the plans.

Task 2.6

Consider what the CCA guidance directs relating to exercising and training—summarize.

2.9.1 Benefits for the organization—why exercise?

Perhaps the question should be why not exercise? Having a plan creates a 'comfort blanket' and in fact in some cases a false sense of security. Having seen that there may be a reluctance to exercise plans, why do some organizations seem to avoid it or only exercise as a last resort? There is in many cases a fear that exercising will expose weakness or the plan when tested will fail, coupled with that is the potential 'finger pointing' and blame. In addition, many organizations believe that exercising is expensive and takes away from valuable staff time. All very understandable fears and concerns, but exercising plans can have major benefits for organizations in their day-to-day activities.

Testing plans brings people together to share in problem solving, facing unusual threats together and coping in a crisis. Working with all levels of management promotes team building, fosters understanding and builds confidence. Exercising can bring together disparate departments, branches and other stakeholders, both internal and external who would never meet during 'normal' business. Opportunities for networking develop and key partnerships can be forged or consolidated. Following many major incidents a comment often heard amongst responders relates to how useful it was 'knowing' the people involved, seeing a friendly face and how easy it made communication, especially in that chaotic phase when a rapport already existed. This can only be created and nurtured during exercises.

As long as exercising is seen as an enjoyable activity which does not create confrontation, frustration, embarrassment, belittle or confuse it will be become a valuable management asset.

Perhaps one of the key benefits of exercising is the part it plays in 'active' learning generally. This can extend to understanding the organization better and not just in terms of emergency response. 'Active learning is an umbrella term that refers to models of instruction that focus the responsibility of learning on learners'. Bonwell and Eison (1991) suggested learners work in groups, discuss materials while role-playing, debate, engage in case study, take part in cooperative learning, or produce short written exercises.[3] This is the essence of exercising. Getting involved, giving advice, assisting others are all effective learning methods. Simply telling staff to read plans and memorize procedures is 'passive' learning and not very effective for embedding behaviour and knowledge. Active learning involves engaging staff through exercising on what they know or should know. It consolidates knowledge and highlights training needs.

---

[3] C Bonwell and J Eison (1991) *Active Learning: Creative Excitement in the Classroom*. AEHA ERIC Higher Education report no.1 Washington DC.

2 Plans and Exercising

Exercising can seem to many a complex, expensive or a risky activity. Neither is it arduous or time consuming. This book will provide the information and knowledge to explain the processes and administration that will help prepare exercises that are organizationally effective, fun and cost-effective. But there has to be the will and practical support too.

2.9.2 Senior management 'buy-in'

It is important that the benefits of exercising are recognized and supported by senior management. Without high level support and backing it is difficult, if not impossible to achieve real progress in organizational resilience. Having a sound exercise programme supported by an organizational 'policy' on exercising will create an organization that is strong and resilient against crisis and emergencies. Create an exercise policy—an exercise policy will demonstrate a commitment to continued improvement and development within an organization in terms of building that resilience. A senior management team will support that view. Having a policy will provide the 'ammunition' or the organizational weight to drive exercising in an organization. It can also mean minimizing financial loss to a business, litigation or paying out compensation. It can also prevent loss of reputation and goodwill earned over many years. This is particularly important where public confidence and support is so important to overall effectiveness, as in a public service organization such as the local authority.

Perhaps even more relevant for senior managers is that exercising can actually help in mitigating or reducing the effects of criminal liability resulting from the crisis or emergency, in particular where lives are lost through accusations of involuntary manslaughter by negligence. The existence of plans and effective exercising can be used to demonstrate the extent to which an organization has sought to prepare and reduce the risk of harm. This is mentioned within the book to simply draw attention to the issue and direct the reader to further research. It is a complex subject area but one the EPO must be aware of.

From April 2008, under the Corporate Manslaughter and Corporate Homicide Act 2007, company directors can be legally responsible for the safety of their employees and for the consequences of accidents that involve the wider public. An organization will be guilty if the way its activities are managed or organized causes a death and its activities are shown to be a gross breach of the organization's duty of care to the person who died. The penalties for non-compliance include fines or even imprisonment.

How will an organization know if it's activities are fit for purpose and adequate without exercising? It is suggested that having regular exercises as part of an active emergency planning cycle can demonstrate to others that an organization has commitment to continuous improvement of risk management procedures and therefore an organization that is responsible and caring.

Another feature of fatal incidents is that relatives of those involved and their legal teams will pursue corporate 'heads' relentlessly and will dissect plans, processes and procedures (which should include an auditable exercise programme). This is done in an effort to identify negligence and blame or simply to make sense of what happened, to find out every possible detail. It is worth mentioning here the 'school of thought' alluded to earlier that if a plan does not exist one cannot be criticized for it—it is suggested that not having a plan would probably have more serious consequences. The motivation of victims' relatives to obtain information is so intense because it is driven by the loss of a loved one or friend. One has only to consider the Marchioness Disaster on the Thames on 20 August in 1989 in which 51 people died or the Hillsborough Football stadium disaster on 15 April 1989 in which 96 people died to see how relatives' action groups can mobilize and initiate change many years following the events. In an era where corporate manslaughter is a real issue for officers of companies or organizations, getting it wrong could have serious consequences. Organization must be prepared for intense scrutiny.

This is a particular problem for the smaller company because it is far easier to attribute a causal link to the incident that resulted in death or injury to a 'controlling' officer of the company. The bigger and more diverse a company's structure, the more difficult it can be to attribute grossly negligent acts or omissions committed in the course of the company's operations to a controlling officer and, therefore, to the company itself. However, even if it is not possible to show that a company has been grossly negligent because there is no controlling mind, offences under other legislation may have been committed.

Task 2.7

- What are the possible implications of not testing contingency plans? List six
- What are the benefits of exercising for an organization? List eight
- List three reasons why senior management should buy-in to exercising.

2.10 **Summary**

You should understand the following:

1. the principles of planning;
2. who creates plans and the processes that inform the decision to agree to produce a plan;
3. risk assessments for planning purposes;
4. the different types of plan;
5. the need for BCM in an emergency planning context; and
6. the rationale for exercising and the consequences of not doing so.

2.11 **Conclusion**

The CCA requires that plans be subject to update and revision by establishing a plan maintenance matrix to check that maintenance work is being done and revised in the light of a revised risk assessment or other factors such as organizational restructuring or failings identified by exercises or an incident. Crucially, the CCA requires that exercising and training be carried out. Plans must include within them provisions for carrying out exercises to validate plans and make them effective

This must include adequate training of staff or other persons to ensure they are properly prepared.

The bottom line is an organization can't afford not to exercise and train their staff.

Chapter 3

Creating Your Plans

Overview

In this chapter you will cover:

- Integrated Planning—Internal
- Electronic or hard copy?
- What should be in the plan?
- Plan Format
- Building the plan
- Plan Contents
- Plan Foreword
- Plan Introduction
- Copyright/Human Rights
- Information security
- Freedom of information
- Plan Title—Distribution—Amendments—Exercises
- Plan Background
- Plan Objectives
- Plan Management—Incident Management—Command and Control
- Working with the police—Vulnerable—Warning the public—Evacuation
- Plan Support—BCM—Media—Welfare—Messages—Administration
- Health and Safety
- Tasking—Appendices
- Completing and marketing the plan

3.1 **Introduction**

Having considered the type of plans in use and who is involved in producing those plans, the next task is actually to look in greater detail at how a plan is put together.

Following the guidance outlined in this chapter will provide readers with all the information needed to prepare comprehensive and effective plans. Expertise in plan writing comes with experience as knowledge is developed and the EPO is required to tackle a range of different plans addressing a whole range of risks. However, there are basic principles which form the core of a good plan and this includes a format that lends itself to being user friendly and therefore more efficient to use. This chapter contains sufficient detail to demonstrate how a plan is made up. It will also assist in reviewing and deciding if specialist support is needed with existing plans. The information within this chapter will also assist those who regularly prepare plans by highlighting issues that may not have been considered before. The proposed plan format outlined in this chapter exceeds the recommendations of the CAA guidance.

3.2 **Integrated 'Internal' Planning**

As we have seen, the Civil Contingencies Act refers to Integrated Emergency Management (IEM) as Anticipation, Assessment, Prevention, Preparation, Response and Recovery Management and is covered in great detail in the guidance documents that accompany the CCA. It must be emphasized that this IEM approach will ensure that there is compatibility, a synergy and interoperability across processes and procedures between organizations. Collaboration, liaison, consultation are key elements in developing plans. But 'internal' integration is critical to creating an effective plan, in particular single agency or individual plans. What is meant by internal integration?

Having decided to produce a plan to offset an assessed risk, it is also important that the new internal emergency procedures are aligned or integrated into day-to-day activity. If that happens it means there will be a seamless move from normal activity into emergency response mode. This will be examined in more detail in Chapter 5 on co-ordinating the emergency response, but in essence, the emergency response should be built upon normal procedures enabling an escalation of those procedures proportionally, either gradually or immediately, to manage the incident presented—right up to disaster. For example, do not designate key roles in the plan to individuals who are never or rarely on site or available.

Do use facilities and equipment that are already available without the need to be sourced from outside at short notice. Do not rely on contractors and suppliers unless they are contracted to provide the additional resources in a fixed time frame and can cope. This is a general resilience issue. Make sure if contractors are engaged they can prove their resilience.

The emergency response should where possible use the personnel and resources available on a day-to-day basis, thus ensuring there are key staff on duty at the time of the incident. This is an important issue for the plan. There will of course be requirements to have use of special equipment, facilities or to require a change of roles but these should fall into place incrementally and in a triggered sequence, which starts from the daily routine. Therefore integrate emergency procedures into daily activity. It will save time and be more efficient.

Figure 3.1 illustrates that gradual movement.

Figure 3.1 Seamless Transition

> **Task 3.1**
>
> Consider why it is import to integrate emergency proce-
> dures into day-to-day activity.

3.3 **Electronic or Hard Copy Plan?**

This is an important issue when considering the production
and use of plans. Surely everything should be electronic in
this day and age! Making the best and most efficient use of
technology is a must, especially where accessing information and data is concerned—which is the case with plans.
Electronic plans are useful in that many people can view
them simultaneously from distant locations and they can
be quickly and easily updated. They can also be integrated
into IT communication or command systems. Hard copy
plans must be considered redundant and obsolete.

On the other hand, the very nature of an emergency
situation may prevent access to the relevant IT systems,
for example in a power failure or a system crash. Accessing electronic versions of plans may also be problematic
if the level of authority is restrictive, bearing in mind that
maintaining security of electronic material can be difficult
within a large organization. Computer viruses, hacking and
deliberate electronic terrorism and sabotage are real issues
that can affect not only law enforcement and government
organizations but large corporate companies too. Portable
computers moving in the public domain are susceptible
to theft and are targeted by computer thieves (see Chapter
1 p 7). Another issue with electronic plans relates to their
ownership and accountability—in particular where they
are 'absorbed' into other electronic systems and begin to
have dependent links into other databases which are managed and created by other people. Can a computer plan be
audited when it becomes so amorphous? There is a danger

that the electronic plan loses structure and direction. A hard copy plan acts as a vital reference for plans which are transferred or developed for electronic use.

KEY POINT

In any case, in terms of electronic plans a hard copy must be viewed at least as a vital backup and should exist if only for that reason. Being completely helpless because the computer breaks down is no excuse and is bad planning!

It must also be remembered that those who are charged with implementing the plans will in fact be relatively few in number. From the author's experience, having a hard copy version is a preferred option for many managers. There is something reassuring in having a hard copy plan to hand and to be able to use the plan to keep notes in it, using it as a working document for later reference.

However, hard copy plans do have drawbacks. They will be in various locations, will always need constant updating and checking to ensure the right version is being used and the amendments have been added. A robust auditable system is essential against numbered copies with regular physical checks to make sure the plans are where they should be. This checking process should be logged and kept on file. If plans are not being updated this must be brought to the attention of the plan holder immediately.

However, there is no reason why both electronic and hard copy plans cannot co-exist and complement each other. The hard copy has ownership, accountability, authority, portability, reliability and has a 'usability' and companionship as an effective working tool. Electronic plans are versatile, quick to use, updated easily and can be integrated into other systems opening a vast array of support data at will. Utilizing both systems has a place in modern emergency management and for the EPO being able to produce a hard copy plan is an essential skill. Without that skill it is impossible to create another form of plan.

With hard copy plans there should only be one 'master' plan copy which is kept by the 'owner' who should also keep a working file containing all relevant papers that support the plan. This forms an audit trail and will contain information relating to distribution, amendments, training sessions and exercising. In addition where updates and amendments come to light which fall between regular updates these can be kept on file until the review or update takes place. This is assuming of course that they can wait for that process! This is a judgement for the plan owner to make. We will look at the title/ownership page shortly.

3.4 **What Should be in the Plan?**

Six types of plan have been listed and it is intended now to describe the preparation of just one type—the single agency or individual plan. This plan has been chosen as it is the one which will feature most often in an emergency situation although the format to be described, with some modification, can be applied across all types of plan. This plan will concentrate on providing sufficient information to enable an effective response to the incident in the crucial initial stages, 'the golden hour' and provide enough detail to provide the reader with a basic understanding of the threat and the necessary response. The 'Golden Hour' principle refers to the period within which most lives will be saved and injuries reduced. It is a medical term in fact but is used to describe generally the period immediately following an emergency when escalation can be reduced significantly. As the incident consolidates and settles down and the response becomes more structured there will be more time to consider options and longer term strategies. The characteristic of the single agency or individual plan is that it is not overwhelmed with information, which in the early stages is not required, and would only inhibit its use and confuse the reader.

But whatever plan is produced, the plan must satisfy a number of criteria:

1. The plan must have ownership or title.
2. The plan layout must be clear and easy to use.
3. The plan must be concise.
4. Roles and responsibilities must be clearly defined.
5. The plan must be revised and tested regularly.
6. Those who have a role within the plan must be trained and regularly briefed.

It may sound pedantic but in terms of hardcopy plans, ease of use is so important. That will include consideration of such issues as:

1. Plan cover—is it easy to see in a bookcase?
2. Folder type—how easy to turn pages and keep it open. Separate pages in a ring binder will lend itself to easier updating too.
3. Font type and line spacing (double spaced and at least font 12)—is it clear and easy to read?
4. Using colour pages—it adds emphasis to functions and tasks.
5. Use of photographs, flow charts, floor plans and diagrams for clarity and understanding.
6. Using numbered paragraphs and sub paragraphs is essential as it will assist in communicating information about the plan between people who may be using the telephone or e-mail.

The plan must be instantly recognisable. When developing a 'corporate format' or style, whichever format is chosen is very important. The format should remain consistent in terms of look and content. It makes training and exercising the plan more effective because only one plan type is being used. No matter what size or geographic location or various parts of the organization the emergency plans are used in, it will always look the same wherever the user is. Everyone within the organization should know what an emergency plan looks like and be able to use them and over time it will embed into the corporate memory.

Task 3.2

Thinking of the organization you work for, or just considering a plan cover generally, how would you design a plan
cover so that it would be recognisable?

What information would go on the front?

3.5 Plan Format

Below is an emergency plan format, which with adapta-
tion, can be applied to most organizational needs. It can be
used for very simple single organizational plans or complex
procedures covering major plans involving many organizations. This system is expressed as follows:

Checklist—'BOMSRCH' system

1. Background (Information)
2. Objective (Intention)
3. Management (Method)
4. Support (Administration)
5. Risk Assessment
6. Communication
7. Health and Safety

This system is known as the 'BOMSRCH' system, pronounced 'Bombsearch'. The titles in brackets are included
for those who may be familiar with the 'IIMARCH' system,
pronounced 'aye aye march' which is extensively used by
many public service organizations including the police.
These headings form the core of the plan but the plan will
consist of other components and in effect every plan is
'built' or 'constructed' in a uniform and consistent way.

3.6 **Building the Plan**

The hard copy plan should be 'assembled' or formatted in the following order or formatted electronically as follows.

Checklist—Building the plan

1. Inner front cover—duplicate of the front cover.
2. Contents Page
3. Foreword/Preface (Optional)
4. Introduction—page numbers start here
5. Title—ownership and signatures
6. Distribution—the plan holders
7. Amendments—changes and insertions
8. Exercises—dates and types of exercise inc. the exercise manager/director details
9. Background—1st Section. Each Section will be divided by card
10. Objective—2nd Section
11. Management—3rd Section
12. Support—4th Section
13. Risk Assessment—5th Section
14. Communication—6th Section
15. Health and Safety—7th Section
16. Tasks—8th Section

Note: For each separate task a new Section is used. For example:
    (i)   Duty Manager—9th Section
    (ii) Media Officer—10th Section
    (iii) Chief Executive Officer—11th Section
    (iv) Etc.

17. Appendices—Final Section

Note: For each appendix a letter is used; A, B, C. For example:
A. Essential Telephone/Fax Directory.
B. Maps/Diagrams/Illustrations.
C. Equipment Inventory.
D. Any other relevant information.

Having described the plan format, each individual section will now be examined in more detail as to what should be included.

> **Task 3.3**
> Why is a corporate plan format important for an organization?

3.6.1 Contents

In an emergency situation the first page looked at will be the contents page! It is important to ensure that the contents list is very detailed and comprehensive. The reader should not have to trawl through the document looking or searching for a relevant point—clarity is essential. This is achieved by clear simple headings. In particular in the '**TASKS**' section, (under 'TASK'), the role of each facility or individual must be listed, eg Duty Manager, Communications Operator, etc. Everything else, although important, can be read at a slower pace once the Tasks are initiated.

Each 'Section' in the plan should be divided by a numbered card divider, which relates to the contents page to make finding the relevant section easier. Ease of use is the key—remember!

3.6.2 Foreword/Preface (Optional)

It is useful if the Foreword or Preface is written by a senior manager. It not only adds weight to the document but is a good means of attracting senior management buy in, in particular when it comes to publishing and circulating the plan. This section can emphasize the corporate approach to plans, training and exercising and generally a motivational and supportive approach to instil the 'resilient organization' message.

3.6.3 Introduction

This page will briefly state the aim and objective(s) of the plan, identifying its scope and any limitations. Reference to other generic source material will be made where appropriate and references to 'assumed' information will be specified. The Introduction should also include reference to any statutory obligation, whether direct or indirect, to write the plan, together with the risk assessed rationale in writing the plan in the first instance.

Copyright

Copyright for some is perceived to be a problem, in particular where commercial interests tend to plagiarize for profit. The difficulty is that so much information is freely in circulation and has been adopted and adapted, that it can be difficult to pin down its source. But if information is used genuinely to promote and develop civil protection it would seem counterproductive to inhibit or hinder that effort. It is a matter of judgement. It is worth noting that the two CCA guidance documents can be produced free of charge in the spirit for which they were intended—to promote civil protection.

However, a copyright warning can be attached although in law it is not required. If being used it is suggested that a copyright warning be placed in the Introduction, for example:

Example—Copyright Warning

The Policy and information contained in this document has been compiled and presented for emergency planning purposes and sole use of 'MegaBolts' and its staff. This is a corporate Policy document for which 'MegaBolts' retains the copyright. Except in accordance with the provisions of the Copyright Designs and Patents Act 1988, written permission signed by the Chief Executive Officer is required to replicate the document in any material form.
© MegaBolts 2008

This section should also contain a reference to **Human Rights audit** and **Diversity and Discrimination audit.** Remember—if a plan is written we assume responsibility for it and its effect on others. A suggested form of words for the Human Rights Act could be:

Example—Reference to the Human Rights Act

Human Rights Audit 'Consideration has been given to the compatibility of this plan and its related procedures, with the Human Rights Act 1988, particularly with reference to the legal basis of its precepts: the legitimacy of its aims: the justification and proportionality of the actions intended by it is the least intrusive and damaging option necessary to achieve the aims: and that it defines the need to document the relevant decision-making process and outcomes of action.'

Information security

It must also state in the wording of the Introduction whether it is suitable for public disclosure or the document contains sensitive information and it must not be disclosed. If appropriate it should be clarified as to whether the document requires a protective marking, as follows: not protectively marked; restricted; confidential; secret or top secret under the Government Protective Marking scheme. The plan author should check this within their own organization. If it applies, there will be a policy on the subject with explanations as to what each marking level entails which will include information on storage, security, handling, transmission and disclosure. If sensitive material does appear in the document it is easier to collect or collate that information into one section which can be extracted for disclosure without compromising the whole document. In this case it would be better in an appendix or appendices which are appropriately marked. The most obvious section would be personal contact details, locations of dangerous substances, times of deliveries etc. Anything which could give information that would be useful for criminal or terrorist use or commercially sensitive. In most cases emergency plans will fall into sensitive categories.

Everyone has the right to request information held by public sector organizations under the Freedom of Information Act 2000, which came into force in January 2005. The

Freedom of Information Act applies to all 'public authorities' including:

- Government departments and local assemblies;
- local authorities and councils;
- health trusts and hospitals;
- schools, colleges and universities (public institutions);
- publicly funded museums;
- the emergency services; and
- many other non-departmental public bodies, committees and advisory bodies.

Some privately owned companies that have an obligation to plan for emergencies under legislation may be reluctant to submit their plans to public authorities in case the information contained within them is disclosed. Local Resilience Forums have been approached to disclose information relating to plans but the CCA guidance advocates publishing plans in any case. The issue is the sensitivity of the information and each request would have to be assessed on a case by case basis.

3.6.4 **Title—Ownership and signatures**

This page will contain the plan title and the signatures of those involved in its production. It is important to complete this page. Firstly, it will give ownership and responsibility. It must be remembered that a signatory to the plan will be deemed to have a 'controlling' effect on its application and usage. This is a sobering thought when a line manager is challenged about having knowledge of the plan if called to account. Getting a signature ensures that senior management have sight of the plan and they are aware of it. This will be useful to generate support and 'buy-in' when it is time to exercise the plan. The ownership page should be signed by the following:

- Plan author—prepared by
- Line Manager
- Departmental Head

3 Creating Your Plans

It is worth noting that under the Corporate Manslaughter and Corporate Homicide Act 2007, Crown bodies such as the police, army and other emergency services are absolved from liability of 'duty of care' except for their responsibilities towards their staff. This is an issue raised for information only and awareness of EPOs. Further details can be obtained by researching <http://www.justice.gov.uk/publications/corporatemanslaughter2007.htm>.

The layout of the page could look like Figure 3.2.

Figure 3.2 Title Page

CONFIDENTIAL-TITLE AND SIGNATURES

Title: ....   **Ref No**..............

This plan is owned by: Department / Organization

Only the 'Owner'of the plan can authorise any alterations.

The 'Owner' will ensure that:

- The master document is retained together with relevant supporting documents.
- The level of circulation of the plan is determined and details are recorded of copy holders.
- It is updated and reviewed.
- It is tested and exercised.
- Health and safety issues are regularly risk assessed.
- Changes and amendments are circulated to plan holders promptly.
- Electronic versions are updated.

Further information and advice on any of the above elements can be obtained from:

Plan prepared by: ....Date: ....

Contact Tel...

Line Manager: ....Date: ....
Inspected

Department Head...Date: ....
Approved

> **Task 3.4**
>
> Research the principles of the Corporate Manslaughter and Corporate Homicide Act 2007—how could it affect the role of an EPO?

3.6.5 Distribution

This page will contain a list identifying the locations and destinations of the plans.

3.6.6 Amendments

Amendments will be recorded as follows:

Update

This requires simple administrative changes only; an update is as the name suggests. This includes a regular, at least annual, check on telephone numbers, areas of responsibility, changes in post holders etc.

3.6.7 Reviewed

A complete review taking in all aspects of the plan. This will involve asking the question, do we need this plan? Involve all those who have a role to play, revisit all parts of the plan. This should take place at least every two years or when the plan is used for real.

3.6.8 Exercises

It should contain details of when the plan was last exercised and by what method, ie 'live' or 'table top', which we will discuss later. It should also contain the name of the exercise manager or director. This will allow future exercise planners to liaise with previous exercise managers and exchange ideas. In the master copy held by the owner it would be good practice to include a list of personnel taking part in the exercises. This should be affixed into this section. In the event of a real incident, these people would be used if available.

Many organizations also include exercise details relating to their employees on their personal files or an information database. This provides an ideal reference in the event of a real incident to quickly identify staff that may have the necessary skills and experience to assist.

3.6.9 **Background—Section 1**

This section, being the first, will contain general details of the scenario(s) giving rise to the formulation of the plan and the risk assessment process used. These details will include information giving rise to the risk, for example flooding or a chemical fire. It could involve information about a company, industrial processes, storage of hazardous substances, the threats involved, hazards to be expected, site location and when the company or organization will implement the emergency procedures.

What will trigger the plan? How is 'emergency' or 'crisis' defined for their company or organization? There is a definition in the CCA of emergency but there will need to be a more specific description as to what constitutes an emergency or crisis for them. All organizations will define differently what an emergency is for them. That in itself will not create a problem as it identifies specific issues that are relevant for that organization alone. It must however comply and fall within the definition of 'emergency' within the CCA guidance if it is to have any meaning to responding organizations, such as the emergency services.

It is also important to agree what will trigger an alert and who will do it. A common problem is who will 'press the button'. There is often a tangible reluctance for some organizations to alert the emergency services or their own organization for fear of being criticized, incurring some liability or cost. The implications for activating an alert can be serious but it would be far more serious not to and as a consequence injury, death or serious damage to property results.

Emergency definitions often have assigned alert levels to direct a particular response or a traffic light code. In this section define the 'alert' levels or colour code. For example:

- Emergency Level 1—Activate Level 1 procedures—Stand-by (prepare).
- Emergency Level 2—Activate Level 2 procedures—Mobilize (move to action).
- Emergency Level 3—Full Emergency.

or

- Alert Amber.
- Alert Red.

These levels will be defined and detailed in the Task sections and within the Management section (later) outlining exactly what will happen if and when each level or colour code is reached.

This section should also *briefly* list any respective roles and responsibilities involving outside agencies. This is why it is crucial to involve these organizations in the planning process. The implementation of any special procedure and/or policy should be briefly explained, bearing in mind that a full and detailed explanation of the subject matter may be contained in other documents. In other words, attention may be directed towards an issue for further reading or reference. For example, the organization may have a generic health and safety policy document covering day-to-day activity, reference may be made to this. This section may refer to other emergency plans that complement and support this one and may be used in conjunction with it. Without this approach, the contents of each and every emergency plan would be overwhelming and defeat the object of the plan. If it is not needed in the plan, leave it out.

3.6.10 **Objective—Section 2**

This section will contain statements of intent in relation to the plan. Remember that one cannot endorse or encourage personnel to recklessly put their personal safety at risk or fly in the face of policy. Very careful consideration of the words used must be given as 'legal responsibility and accountability' could rest on the statements of intent made at any subsequent inquiries. This statement also demonstrates the desire and commitment to staff and those who may provide services to the response or there may be a moral responsibility too.

Common Objectives may include:

- Save life and prevent injury;
- Protect staff, contractors, and persons on company property;
- Protect company property and assets;
- Assist the emergency services; and
- Co-ordinate recovery;

The list of objectives is a matter for the organization, but it is important as it creates strategic focus, prioritizes and provides goals to give the response structure.

Task 3.5

Consider any CCA stipulations regarding plan maintenance and updating of plans.

3.6.11 **Management—Section 3**

This is a chronological narrative giving a management overview of the whole response process and the most comprehensive section.

If being activated the reader must be directed to the relevant 'Tasks' so as not to delay the implementation of the plan by reading this management section first. A simple warning on the top of the page will ensure this happens:

For example: IF ACTIVATING THIS PLAN REFER TO YOUR TASKS—NOW.

Anyone with a role within the plan will know this as they will have undergone training and familiarization of the plan.

This section will commence at the point at which the declaration of the incident is made and acted upon. Up to this point, we have been concerned with the circumstances and threats that may be faced, not our response to them. At this stage the activation levels will have been reached which were outlined in Section 1 – Background. It is the start of the immediate response. It will declare in more detail, in the first instance, what is required at an 'operational' level—the hands on level—to deal with the incident then move up to the appropriate managerial level. It should take the reader through the arrangements, logically, step by step, building gradually in a seamless way. It is a summary of the planned objectives and tasks that will occur as the incident unfolds. Remember—specific and very detailed tasks and responsibilities of personnel involved in the response, although mentioned in brief in this section will be highlighted in the separate 'Tasks Sections'. Therefore, within this section the reader will often be referred to 'TASKS'. The 'TASKS' will be contained in separate sections and appear at the back of the plan.

In preparing this section, imagine how the detail would be outlined to someone with no prior knowledge. Imagine completing this management section as though it was a briefing—explaining to a group who are about to carry out the plan.

There are many issues that will appear in the management section. Precisely what appears depends upon the nature of the response but there are some key issues to consider which will now be specifically discussed, principally because they are so important within the management section. The following explanations have been written generically. There are references to non emergency service considerations and issues. This approach has been chosen as it gives a better insight to those within the blue light services on the issues under consideration by non blue light organizations which in turn may assist them in developing arrangements that are a better 'fit' for themselves and those of partner agencies.

The specific issues dealt with here are:

1. incident management
2. working with the police
3. making planning provision for the vulnerable
4. warning the public
5. evacuation.

Incident management/command and control

Within this part of the management section, outline *exactly* the management structure that will be adopted and at what stages. What will inform the move to another management level? How and when will it be activated? Whichever organization the plan is for, when preparing plans there will be a need to establish clear management or command and control using terminology that is part of the organizational language. Be explicit as to how the plan will work for the organization and how it will integrate into the organizational structure and how it will be integrated into outside agencies if the need arises. For example, this will lend itself to a seamless integration with blue light organizations. Imagine it as a jig saw piece that fits into a bigger picture. This is the heart of a good plan: Who does what, where, when and why!

'Commanders' or managers will be those people who have managerial responsibility and authority for a particular aspect of the response. As long as their role is well defined and designated, a title is all that is required. But their job description should include a descriptor which clearly recognizes their function as either strategic, tactical or operational (see below) so if the need arises their role can be aligned with that of the emergency services. Ensure that they are identified by post and they have a TASK sheet within the plan that is *explicit* as to what action they need to take. At any given time those who have a role to play or are 'in charge' for the organization must be easily identifiable. Using identification tabards or jackets is a useful way of ensuring everyone knows who is doing what.

There will be more detailed information which will assist in understanding that distinction in Chapter 5 with more about co-ordination. Clearly these roles are more clearly defined and familiar within the emergency services but the overall objective is to create a synergy and compatibility across all response organizations so avoiding confusion when they are required to support and contribute to a multi-agency response.

Although discussed in more detail later it is useful at this point to mention briefly the use of the Strategic (Gold), Tactical (Silver) and Operational (Bronze) (GSB) system of Command and Control. Detailed knowledge is not required at this stage but it is relevant to this section. GSB is familiar to many but often non blue light organizations try to emulate the system. But choosing GSB can be confusing not only to non blue light organization but to the blue light organizations themselves. Which Gold is being referred to? There is a real danger of multiple Golds, Silvers and Bronzes proliferating and creating a barrier to good co-ordination. It should be avoided because it will clash and over complicate the overall management structure if and when the emergency services become involved. In most cases it will also be unnecessary.

The scale and level of management structure chosen will largely depend on the management structure 'needed' and by not trying to shoe horn into any other system.

With 'command' arrangements agreed and described within the management section, consideration will now have to be given as to how the response will be controlled and administered, notwithstanding that the managers and/or commanders have been identified. Facilities or a facility to control the response need to be identified in order to support the managers or commanders, even if the incident occurs 'off-site' such as a transport incident. For non blue light organizations who do not have such arrangements as part of their organizational structure the facility can be called the Emergency Control Centre (ECC), for example, but it must not be confused with being part of the GSB framework put in place by the emergency services. For non blue light organizations the location can be anything from a full-blown communications centre to the staff canteen with extra phone lines and a few dry wipe boards, whatever meets the needs of the management arrangements within their plan. However, all plans must be configured to expect to accommodate several other agencies should the incident escalate and expect to have a police liaison officer attend the facility if the situation requires it. These arrangements must be discussed with the emergency services to ensure they are compliant and complement the emergency services response.

Activation of any ECC or control centre (CC), (including the police control centres for example) will form a 'TASK' and that must appear as an action for a person designated within the plan. On declaration of an incident, a decision will be made at an appropriate level of response to open the ECC or CC. Until that facility is functioning, there will be a need to ensure that plans allow for initial incident management from a switchboard operator/supervisor/manager—this is where internal integration comes in and a use of day-to-day facilities to form the initial and first stage of the bigger response. This is important because once the dedicated ECC or CC is managing the incident, this allows business to proceed with as little disruption as possible to the organization and is a demonstration of good business continuity management.

> **Task 3.6**
>
> Think of your own organization or one you have worked in.
>
> What kind of emergency facilities are there in your organization? Could they cater for multi-agency use?

Working with the police

This topic is discussed in greater detail in Chapter 5 but within the management section cognisance needs to be taken of the potential and absolute requirement to be able to work closely with the emergency services and the police in particular. The plan must support the police. It must be understood that the police usually co-ordinate the entire emergency response for all agencies. Companies, non emergency services and other organizations must be prepared to support police co-ordination if requested. That means the police will create the facilities and locations to enable that co-ordination to take place. Police commanders are only in charge of their own staff and they have no authority over any other organization. But it is possible that they may request support at one of the police control centres to offer advice, information and assist in decision making. It is absolutely vital that they are supported and those requested to attend police control centres are at the right managerial level, as we have discussed, by assigning the correct managerial function in the planning stage. Those requested to attend these centres should do so as a matter of absolute priority as it is within these control centres that decisions will be made that affect all organizations, including companies. Not being there means not having a say or input. Obtaining training in 'liaison officer' duties is a good investment for any organization or company that may be called into a police control centre. But one very important issue may become very relevant or a concern for a company in this police environment—are they a suspect? This is an issue that can often be raised prior to arranging debriefs as the full investigation into the incident may not be complete but can manifest itself at the emergency phase too. This will be discussed in more detail in Chapter 5.

Being called into a police station/control centre at any level—Gold, Silver or Bronze—should mean that those attending must be trained or at least have a good knowledge of the systems and processes that they will come across. Failing to appreciate this will put them at a disadvantage. They will or could be overwhelmed or mildly intimidated by the hustle and bustle of this environment. This knowledge and experience can be obtained by taking part in as many exercises as possible and ensuring that full collaboration and planning occurs in the plan preparation stage.

The vulnerable

In preparing plans particular consideration must be given to those who may not be self-reliant. The term 'vulnerable' may extend to those with disability or those who are confined or restricted in some way, for example in nursing homes or nursery schools. The scope is very wide. It can also extend to those within an organization where provision may have to be made to assist or put in place special warnings for them. These are all issues and considerations outlined as a commitment at the beginning of the plan which include diversity and disability. For planning purposes, a little thought and consideration combined with consultation between stakeholders should assist in identifying those vulnerable persons or sections of the community that will need special measures to be put in place to help them. Issues of communication are key to effective planning for the vulnerable and this issue of communication generally is important for communities and organizations as a whole. This leads onto developing effective and viable warning systems and procedures, which are termed 'warning the public'.

Warning and informing the public

A significant issue contained within the Civil Contingencies Act guidance (Emergency Preparedness Chapter 7) is the requirement to have in place public warning and public information arrangements within plans. This approach actually translates across into the workplace too. It really makes sense because people that are well informed will hopefully react in a more measured, calm and positive fashion to an emergency situation: 'Individuals have an incredibly difficult time making sound decisions under conditions of uncertainty, this difficulty limits the efficacy of warnings in promoting accurate risk perceptions and fostering rational decisions'.[1] They will be more likely to follow the advice of the emergency services or managers if they are properly aware and informed and it will reduce the likelihood of panic. It is about education and achieving a risk communication strategy that alerts but not alarms—a fine balance. That will involve shaping risk perception so that the risk is viewed in a realistic way and not over exaggerated. Another key issue for communicating warnings is trust in the message. People will take more notice of a message if they trust the messenger. 'If we do not trust the source then we will not trust the message' (Royal Society, 1992).[2] 'Research on warning response has shown that the source from which an individual receives the first message influences the way in which the warning is evaluated.'[3] Who will the public trust?

Regarding the veracity of warning messages, research presented to the Lancashire Resilience Forum (formerly the Lancashire Major Incident Co-ordinating Group) by the author in July 2003 indicated that the police and the fire

---

[1] Viscusi and Zeckhauser (1996) 'The Risk Management Dilemma' in H Kunreuther and P Slovic (eds) *Challenges in Risk Assessment and Risk Management* (London: Sage) at p 144–55.

[2] Pidgeon et al (1992) in The Royal Society *Risk Analysis, Perception and Management* (London: Royal Society) at p 122.

[3] MK Lindell and RW Parry (1992) *Behavioural Foundations of Community Emergency Planning* (Washington: Hemisphere Publishing) p 183.

service were held in the highest position of trust amongst the immediate resident population living around the nuclear power stations at Heysham, Lancashire. The survey was conducted to establish the most efficient means of framing risk communication messages following a nuclear emergency at the site. Although this is not published research it informed the production and public warning information strategy.

This illustrates an important issue for the EPO. In terms of developing risk communication strategies and on issues of warning and informing the public, small scale targeted surveys can yield valuable information to make plans more effective at a local level. Locally, population profile, attitude and knowledge can vary a great deal. Surveys are a useful way of gauging and measuring public understanding and potential behavioural response which in turn will greatly assist in emergency management. EPOs should not be afraid to engage and listen to the public.

How is risk communication achieved? This is achieved in broadly two ways. Firstly by raising awareness in the public mind of emergency response issues prior to any incident. Secondly, by communication warnings and alerts and then followed by continued information on the situation.

Raising awareness has been approached at three levels. Firstly, by requiring the publication of risk and plan information through requirements in the CCA, this is available to the public to view and increase their level of knowledge. Secondly at national level, for example the Government 'Preparing for Emergencies' leaflet together with web sites such as <http://www.ukresilience.info> and <http://www.preparingforemergencies.gov.uk>. Thirdly, often supported by advice and information locally co-ordinated and financed through LRFs who circulate more emergency information. This may include postal drops, events, newsletters, media outputs, web-based information and so forth to raise awareness with the public generally. There are also those at risk communities, whether it is from a nuclear or a chemical site where certain pieces of legislation such as the

Control of Major Accident Hazard Regulations (COMAH) and Radiation Emergency Preparedness and Public Information Regulations (REPPIR) require a specific public warning and information strategy to be in place as a condition of the company's operating licence. In flood risk areas too, the Environment Agency lead on public warnings. Within an organization prior warning and awareness regarding emergency response will be achieved through exercising, training and briefing.

Warning during an emergency and follow on information is a more critical factor as it is this action that really could save lives and prevent injury and damage to property. It should be made clear and agreed beforehand who is responsible for the warning. How will it be done and by whom? Assuming that certain agencies, such as the police, will always do that kind of thing would be a mistake. If in doubt check this out. The police are bound by health and safety laws like every other employer and some warning tasks may simply be too dangerous for the police to do— remember the risk assessment. In addition, the police and other emergency services do not have infinite resources and simply may not have the capability.

What methods are used to alert and warn of an imminent or ongoing emergency will be a matter that best suits the situation and environment so that it is as effective as possible. A bespoke solution taking into account factors such as time of day, area to be warned, target population or group (including the vulnerable) and type of hazard should be considered. Always choose the most effective means of warning. Consider technological means first. Why? Because it frees up valuable resources and reduces the risks to those that may have to enter hazardous environments such as toxic smoke, flood water or radiation. Every warning task will have to be risk assessed and appear in the plan.

Further and more detailed information about the legal requirements can be found at <http://www.ukresilience. co.uk> and within the guidance contained in your pack. See also 'Dealing with the Media' below.

Evacuation—general

Finally, within this section we consider evacuation. Evacuation is a vital issue when dealing with public safety. The decision to evacuate is a difficult one to make as the activity in itself can be dangerous, bearing in mind what was said about vulnerable people. With a fixed site and site-specific plans including flooding, evacuation can be pre-planned to a degree. It is possible to designate areas and locations which are pre-identified to form evacuation assembly points and rendezvous points where the emergency services can assemble and transport is provided (this is normally arranged by the local authority) to remove people from an area. These points will be supported with safe routes (with alternatives) around and through the site or incident. Many fixed site plans will have sectored areas which make identifying affected areas easier to plot and designate. This is achieved by means of scaled concentric circles on plastic overlays used on a map or a specially printed map. Using post code areas or fixed boundaries such as main roads, railways or rivers is a way in which the public can relate to and understand an affected area more easily. Always bear in mind that an evacuation means removing people from an unsafe location to a safe one, usually caused by something harmful in the air, so taking into account wind shift is vital and allow for alternative routes if the wind changes. This includes considering the positioning of key resources and facilities near a site that could also be affected. Consider using for example red and blue routes as alternatives. Remember—wind direction is always given in terms of where it is coming from, eg a northerly wind is coming from that direction (Figure 3.3).

The use of route maps and photographs, both aerial and ground level are essential for this task to illustrate the plan.

Spontaneous and unknown threats or hazards present a more complex and dynamic approach to evacuation, in which the safest options have to be assessed within an environment which will be unknown, such as topography

Figure 3.3 Wind Direction

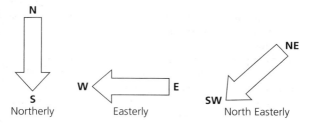

and population profile. This requires considerable effort in an often fast moving situation. This is best co-ordinated by the police using mapping systems based in their control/communication centres. In a slower moving situation a more measured approach can be taken within a multi-agency control centre.

Communicating evacuation advice to the public can take many forms from using the media to utilizing any pre-distributed information such as that provided under the COMAH and REPPIR requirements. These include calendars and leaflets with emergency information printed on them. There is no doubt that the police will assist using all resources available in a spontaneous incident to warn the public on foot and by vehicle if necessary following a dynamic risk assessment. However, wherever possible use of any available warning technology should be considered first, for example, mobile phone technology and the wider facilities available to inform the public generally like public address systems or public message boards. But using public address (PA) systems, such as those on police helicopters or vehicles can have the opposite effect to that which is required. If the message is go in and stay in, do not tell people by PA. They will simply open windows, doors and go outside to hear the message!

One important factor to which the emergency services have little control is spontaneous evacuation. This should never be underestimated or assume that the public will be totally compliant and co-operative. Reaction can be moderated to some extent by prior education and shaping the 'risk' message to avoid possible panic. This is very important around fixed hazardous sites. For example, for planning purposes assuming that those in the immediate vicinity of a site may evacuate because they reside within a specially designated 'danger' area is a realistic assumption. Extend that to perhaps twice or three times the distance from the site because people will take 'precautionary' evacuation steps, perhaps even for only a few hours. That effect will potentially grid lock perimeter roads trapping those nearer the site who may actually need to or are directed to evacuate. The safer planning option in these circumstances is to plan far beyond the immediate site vicinity (usually 1km for planning purposes). It important that spontaneous evacuation be planned for, in particular in terms of traffic management arrangements. This may involve significant traffic diversions and involving local agencies such as the police, local authority and the Highways Agency in particular if planning for wider scale spontaneous evacuation.

Evacuation—town centre

Town centre evacuation presents unique challenges for the EPO. Town centre environments are very dynamic places. They are changing all the time with diverse communities of residents, commuters, visitors and workers to mention but a few. Town layout and geography, infrastructure and building type can vary as much as the population profile. Add to that the fluctuating population, time of day and weather conditions creates an environment which is unpredictable.

Clearly town centres remain a target for the terrorist. It is quite obvious that the town centre environment presents large concentrations of people in relatively confined areas making them attractive targets. Planning for evacuation is now an important multi-agency activity involving the police, local authorities and shopping centre managers, to mention but three. 'Traditional' explosive devices are now only one of a menu of weapons that could be used which include the chemical, biological, radiological and nuclear devices (CBRN). Responding to such events are now well planned, resourced and exercised.

Some town centre evacuation models will pre-designate evacuation assembly or muster points based upon identified zones combined with key evacuation routes with alternatives should some routes become unavailable. This is supported by a warning communication strategy to inform the public of what to do. In fact, this information is often freely available with road signs indicating the assembly points and evacuation routes. This model has the advantage that facilities can be pre positioned and arranged such as transport, medical support if needed, rendezvous points for emergency responders and everyone knows what will happen and what to expect.

However, a dynamic capability will have to remain. In reality the location of the incident or threat, chemical attack or a bomb warning will be unknown. The wind drift if airborne substances are involved will be unknown. The dynamic of the public reaction and behaviour will be unknown and many people will be unfamiliar with the town layout.

Pre-planning is essential to identify all the features mentioned above, but keeping some of that information secure for the use of the emergency services through effective co-ordi-

---

Task 3.7

Consider the guidance contained within Emergency Preparedness concerning 'communicating with the public' and consider the advice relating to warning the public.

---

nation by the police is essential. The key to having effective pre-planned and dynamic response capability is setting up effective means of communicating with the public in town centre environments. Using a combination of strategically placed message screens, public address systems supported by trained and exercised emergency response personnel will ensure that the public are properly and quickly informed with the best advice and reassurance to indicate the most appropriate course of action for them to take. The benefits of CCTV in this situation cannot be overstated, not only from a detection and investigative point of view but assisting in co-ordinating an effective response and evacuation.

3.6.12 **Support—Section 4**

Aside from the central incident management response which takes precedence, the plan should contain additional information, which although not crucial is nevertheless important as these considerations will ensure the emergency response will run smoothly and is fully supported. Consider support as the processes that will underpin the initial response or 'oil the wheels'. These could include for example:

- **Business Continuity Issues**—how the organization will continue to operate by offsetting the effects of the emergency. For example, if a particular member of staff has duties to perform in managing the incident what alternative arrangements have been put in place to cover for them or if a room is being used what alternative rooms can be used? Only brief outlines are needed within the plan. Longer working hours may need to be considered with extended hours of duty, alternative working arrangements will need consideration. What alternative arrangements will be put in place?
- **The Media**—a key area which will assist the overall management of the emergency. This will be considered in some detail in this chapter.
- **Welfare Issues**—looking after staff in terms of both physical and mental wellbeing. Welfare, morale and stress are inter-related. People are at most risk of stress when confronting unfamiliar situations where uncertainty prevails. Stress can undermine confidence and performance

too. Initial and regular briefing is therefore very important to remove uncertainty, by keeping people informed
and setting clear tasks. Watching for symptoms of stress
is important, as early intervention is vital to prevent
longer term problems. Monitor hours of work carefully.
Emergency response is not like working in an office. Burn
out can occur quickly. Supervisors and managers must
watch for stress. How can the organization's personnel
or human resources department assist? If the organization has a medical or nursing section how can they help?
Consider the support of external agencies if necessary, by
seeking advice in the planning stage from local authority social services departments or the local primary care
trust. Psychological debriefing is an area of some contro-
versy as individuals have many different ways of coping.
But managing stress and post incident trauma must be
considered and arrangements should be put in place to
accommodate this in due course, to offer counselling and
support, where requested.

- **Logging/Messages**—what methods will be used in control centres? Reinforce the message to save and protect
  all information regarding the emergency including all
  messages, hard copy and down load computer information onto disc. This will be required later for debriefs and
  inquiries. Ensure that this task is allocated to a person or
  team.
- **Administration**—the necessary follow on staffing
  arrangements, briefing arrangements and continuing
  that ongoing support. Preparing duty rosters and monitoring hours. Planning briefings and refreshments.
- **Logistics and Equipment**—looking at arrangements
  to increase support, from whom and where if required.
  Looking at resource levels, trying to forecast what will
  be needed. Linking into the control centre(s) to ascertain what is needed. Positioning logistic support in the
  right locations at the right times. Co-ordinating distribution and allocation of resources on advice from control
  centres.

3 Creating Your Plans

Each plan may require additional support structures that will have to be considered on a case by case basis. However, the constant to all plans is managing the media which we will now look at.

Dealing with the media

The general public, and therefore the media, in all its forms have an understandable curiosity in all unusual events resulting in loss of life, injuries and large scale damage. The power of the 24 hour media cannot be underestimated. The media must be used as an ally, a communication link, a means to inform, to warn, to educate and to minimize risk. When an event occurs it is essential that an early press release is produced and should be a priority followed with regular updates, even if there is nothing to add.

The vast majority of the press and media are responsible reporters. Being sympathetic to their needs and expectations will allow a mutually beneficial relationship to emerge. There may be a separate media plan within an organization, which is good practice, but the Local Resilience Forum will have special arrangements in place to manage the media. Viewing a copy would be of great benefit when considering producing a plan.

It is important that there is a designated media spokesperson or persons within an organization to address the media. Depending upon the size of the organization this can range from a full department to perhaps one or two people. It is money well spent to have some form of media training for the spokesperson. Again the Local Resilience Forum can assist in finding suitable courses or someone who can assist in that area. The BBC has special responsibilities to promote public safety information and again may assist with information locally.

Being prepared, trained and confident to manage the media is an absolute must for any organization. But close liaison with the police is essential to co-ordinate the information going out to the public. It is a primary responsibility of the police service to co-ordinate a media response during an emergency. The co-ordination of the media response is covered in Chapter 5, but for the purposes of this chapter, within this section of the plan, it is useful to include some essential basic information to assist those who may be called upon to address the media and this section can provide a valuable aide memoir.

In some circumstances an interview may be inevitable. This may be as a result of the rapid onset of the emergency or the need to quickly get essential messages out to the public, in particular warning messages. It may not always be possible to secure the attendance of the 'media professional' from within the organization in time. But choosing the right person amongst those who are available may be the only option but can be the single most important decision in holding a successful media briefing. Is the person about to go in front of the media really the right person?—If not choose another person, be realistic and honest. It may be possible to get assistance from another organization or emergency service. Some people are very good and natural, their body language, facial expression, intonation, facial animation all contribute positively to the message. Being uncomfortable, ill at ease and nervous can all detract from the message and as we have seen, trust in the messenger is vital to the public accepting and believing what they are being told.

Preparing for the interview is a key part to ensuring success and getting the message across. Here are some other issues to consider for inclusion in the plan under this section:

- Before any interview make sure the objective of the interview is understood. Is information being asked for—an appeal? Is it for creating a warning, giving information and advice or defending a position? This will inform the way answers are prepared and give an opportunity to obtain further information or facts before the start.
- Establish the format of the interview, where the interviewer will take the interview or lead the interviewee. The reporter should be asked what their first question

will be...the first answer can then be prepared and help build that initial confidence.

- It is live! If it is recorded it can be stopped and started again.
- The interviewee should write down the key messages having analyzed the interview objective—they must get those points across.
- Think of a way to emphasize the messages—a phrase perhaps that will grip the viewer or listener.
- Try to anticipate the 'awkward' question. What would the interviewee least like to be asked—then prepare for it.
- If in front of a camera, dress correctly and avoid sun glasses.

Having prepared, what should now be considered whilst stood in front of the camera or microphone?

- Telling the truth at all times may seem obvious but there is a tendency to be over helpful which could colour the answers. If the interviewee does not know, they should say so and go and find the answer. They should never speculate.
- Remaining calm, composed, and taking sufficient time is important.
- They should never say NO COMMENT.
- They should try to be themselves and natural. Smiling when it is appropriate. They should not be over sincere— it will appear false. Trying to be conversational and not talk in a series of statements is more natural.
- Avoiding jargon and acronyms or words where the meanings are unsure should assist understanding. Keep it simple.
- Do not be distracted onto side issues. They should deflect the question and return to the message—a politician's skill—this is not easy.

If a prepared media statement is required, it should be prepared by taking time to write down the message objectives first and build the statement around that.

Example—Media

If it is a message to warn people about a toxic smoke plume, the key points will be:

Go in—Stay in—Tune in

- Cover those who are residents, people in the open and car drivers
- Consider parents with children unaccounted for or pets outdoors
- What action they should take when indoors—close heating vents and close windows
- Those who may be affected by the smoke—medical action to take
- Reduce anxiety
- Stay tuned in
- Do not overload the emergency services with 999 calls
- 'All Clear' arrangements
- Any local issues such as traffic congestion.

Using these key points prepare a warning message. Listing points in this way will ensure that all the key issues are covered and result in an effective message. Keeping the wording to about 100 words is a useful guide to have the entire message used by the media. If it is longer it will probably be edited.

Task 3.8

Using the key points above prepare a press statement to give over the radio.

3.6.13 **Health and Safety—Risk Assessment— Section 5**

A plan is produced having identified the overall hazard or hazards through a risk assessment process, as already described. There will now be a need to carry out a risk assessment to establish the level of risk associated with managing the hazard or hazards from a response point of view. In other words, the tasks required within the plan may require risk assessment to establish how the tasks will be accomplished safely (Figure 3.4).

In Figure 3.4 the overall process begins with the hazard. The hazard is risk assessed and if appropriate, a plan is produced. Within the plan 'TASKS' are identified to enable the plan to work. Those tasks are risk assessed and if necessary modified to make them as safe as possible. From that analysis the TASK sheet can be produced. Specialist advice may be required and guidance to do this for example, if the hazards are outside general experience such as chemicals or radiation or infection. Those risks can be rated or assessed as already mentioned and then the EPO has to decide what action, if any, is needed to take to eliminate or reduce that risk to an acceptable level.

That may involve not carrying out the action associated with that hazard, special training for the individual or providing personal protective equipment or PPE. Then and only then can the task appear in the TASK sheet (Figure 3.5). It is important that the risk assessment process is documented and appears in the plan. There are many risk assessment forms on the market that can be used.

3.6.14 **Information Sharing—Section 6**

Information sharing here is defined in the broadest sense. It could be termed information management. It is about how information will pass, be shared, recorded and the securing of information. No matter how good a plan may be, if people can't talk to one another, it is useless. Include here:

- Reference to telephone numbers/directories—both internal and external.
- Radio call signs.
- Communication contingencies/backups.

Figure 3.4 Hazard Risk Assessment

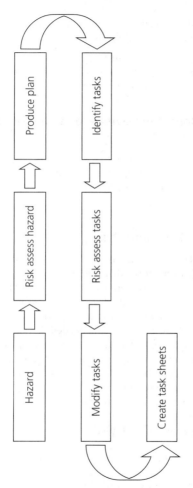

3 Creating Your Plans

- Reference to and encouragement to use information sharing and messaging systems in control centres.
- Anticipated meetings such as Tactical Co-ordinating Group and Strategic Co-ordinating Group.

At this stage it is sufficient to appreciate how to populate this section. We will consider in more detail the issues of information sharing in Chapter 5.

3.6.15 Managing Health and Safety (General)—Section 7

Health and safety issues embrace those areas of general policy and are distinct from hazard identification associated with the plan—see below. This section reminds personnel of existing H&S policy.

3.6.16 Task (Action) Sheets 8—Section 8

The Task Sections will be the first reference point if activating the plan for those with a role—referred from Section 3—Management. Tasks are listed here for activating facilities and/or direct individuals to carry out functions. Tasks should not be buried in the text where they will be hard to find especially when urgency is needed. Each separate task sheet(s) ie for each individual or facility (Emergency Control Centre, etc.) should have a separate Section.

If the plan contains distinct and separate emergency scenarios, such as for different buildings or hazards, for example, fire, bomb threat, chemical leak etc. each one will have a task sheet.

The beginning of a typical Task Sheet may look like Figure 3.5.

Task should be short, concise, clear and in numbered paragraphs. The user of the plan should use the task pages like a checklist, marking off each task as it is completed or adding notes on the progress of the task. These task pages could be used as contemporaneous notes at a future inquiry

Figure 3.5 Task Sheet

PLAN: Title of plan included here.

**TASK SHEET: COMMUNICATIONS OPERATOR/
SWITCHBOARD MAIN BUILDING**

1. Upon notification of declared emergency notify:

a) Duty Operations Manager
   Tel. 23453   Completed Yes / No

b) Media Office/Duty media officer
   Tel. 67856   Completed Yes / No

c) Human Resources Dept.
   Tel. 65895   Completed Yes / No

2. Arrange for Emergency Control Centre to be opened.

   Tel. Operations 65789   Completed Yes / No

3. Notify Headquarters

   Tel. 67890   Completed Yes / No

4. Etc

---

or debrief. Similar task lists could appear in electronic versions of the plan and where possible including an audit trail or a failsafe means of recording completed tasks.

3.6.17 **Appendices**

The final section of the plan. These pages are separated from the main body of the plan as they are likely to be changed more frequently, and therefore make amendments easier to include during the 'update' process.

As a whole, Appendices appear as one Section and each appendix is given a letter. They will include such things as maps, telephone details, special arrangements, evacuation assembly points and maps, etc. The list can be extensive but an appendix is essentially a supplementary piece of information which would otherwise clog up the body of the text and make the plan difficult to use.

3.7 **Completing and Marketing the Plan**

The plan must now be quality assured. It must be circulated to all those who contributed to it and feedback obtained. A final sign-off meeting can be held and minuted. A clear audit process must be recorded and retained in a file because this feedback may become very relevant in the event of the plan being activated as part of the debrief process or inquiry. Should any issues arise as to the content, this feedback can be produced to demonstrate support or otherwise.

Once the plan is complete it must be introduced to those who may have to implement it. There is no point having a plan if nobody is aware of it. This is the point at which a seminar exercise will introduce the plan and indeed form the final QA before it is published. We will take a closer look at this type of exercise later.

> **KEY POINT**
> Those who have a role within the plan must be *trained*.

A marketing strategy is also required to publicize the plan. Depending upon the stakeholder profile during the sign-off meeting, arrange for opportunities to engage with all those who may need to be aware of the plan. For example, use in-house newsletters, notice boards, magazines or e-mail messages.

Single agency plans need not be openly published as required with plans produced by the LRF. Single agency plans need only be disclosed, or parts of them which are not subject to 'sensitivities', under the Freedom of Information Act and only if the organization is a public body.

The creation of plans is a specialized process. The guidance given here is intended to give enough information to produce a plan (in this case a single agency plan) and to give an insight and enough knowledge to critically review existing arrangements or to identify a need to produce a plan.

3.8 Summary

You will now be aware of:

1. Integrating emergency procedures into day-to-day activity.
2. Comparing the advantages and disadvantages of electronic or hard copy plans.
3. Putting the plan together.
4. What are the essential parts of a plan.
5. Key plan components
6. Supporting the police
7. Evacuation
8. Dealing with the media
9. Completing and marketing the plan

3.9 Conclusion

This chapter has introduced the basic principles of preparing an emergency plan. There is a lot of information to take in and in many ways this is the core of the book. Real confidence and expertise will develop the more plans are produced. Having understood the basics of plan preparation we will now proceed to look at the role of the emergency services and how they respond to incidents.

This will provide an essential insight into the methods and expectations of the emergency services and how, by having that understanding, effective integrated plans and response procedures can be produced.

Chapter 4

Understanding the Emergency Response

Overview

In this chapter we will cover:

- The 'Golden Hour'
- Emergency and Recovery Phase
- Emergency response terminology
- The emergency response
- What is a major incident?
- Who declares a major incident?
- The Police
- Incident scene management
- Cordons
- CBRN
- Facilities and people that support the response
- The Fire and Rescue Service
- The Ambulance Service
- The Local Authority
- Maritime and Coastguard Agency
- Support Organizations

4.1 Introduction

With the exception of a wholly internal organizational crisis, the likelihood is that at some point another external organization will become involved and affect how an emergency or crisis is managed or responded to. The most obvious agencies that become involved are the emergency services such as the police, fire and ambulance services. For many organizations, including those that work closely with the emergency services, the way in which they operate can be difficult to understand at times. Even the emergency services themselves can find it confusing.

Questions often relating to the emergency services include:

- What are their expectations?
- What powers do they have?
- Who is in charge ?
- How do they organize themselves?
- What part can be played to assist them?
- What support can they afford to an organization in difficulty?

Understanding these crucial issues can have a direct effect upon how plans are prepared and how those plans are exercised. This chapter will begin with an explanation about the emergency services' roles, their responsibilities, and their incident management procedures. For those already involved with the blue light services it will provide a much broader insight into the collective role the blue lights play and how they interact with each other and other agencies.

Within this chapter there is a heavy emphasis on the role of the police. This is because it is the police who are so involved with the co-ordination and management of the incident. This role is key to planning the response. It is also the police who will try to create and facilitate a situation in which the expertise of the other emergency responders can be fully focused and proceed unhindered. The most vital period to get that right is in the initial stages of the response—the 'Golden Hour'.

4.2 **'Golden Hour'**

The 'Golden Hour' as we have seen, is the critical time within which most lives will be saved. That initial response, or the 'Golden Hour' to any land-based spontaneous (sudden impact) emergency is typically led by the emergency services who respond immediately and their response activity will diminish over a relatively short time, usually starting with the ambulance service followed by the fire service and the police. Organizations like the local authority and the business community usually take more time to mobilize but remain involved for longer, in some cases years into the recovery phase.

4.3 **Emergency and Recovery Phases**

Incident response is divided into two distinct phases. The 'Emergency' phase and the 'Recovery' phase are almost self-explanatory. The emergency phase is usually co-ordinated by the police and is the period within which there is or exists a threat to public safety, personal safety or damage to property. The recovery phase, or return to normality, is the period following which there is consolidation, investigation, remediation and recovery. The phrase 'return to normality' is somewhat of a misnomer in that following a major emergency, in particular where lives have been lost, there is no return to 'normality'. That will change forever.

It is usual that the recovery phase will be led or co-ordinated by the local authority in whose area the incident took place. This handover from police to local authority is a formal process undertaken within the SCG or Strategic Co-ordinating Group that we will discuss later.

Figure 4.1 represents the response and recovery phase in a graphical form.

4.4 **Emergency Response Terminology**

Initially attempting to categorize the scale and nature of any incident will be difficult and at best is often a subjective judgement based on partial and incomplete information. But there are certain definitions that attempt to clarify the nature of an incident for management purposes. Before

Figure 4.1 Emergency Response/Recovery Phase

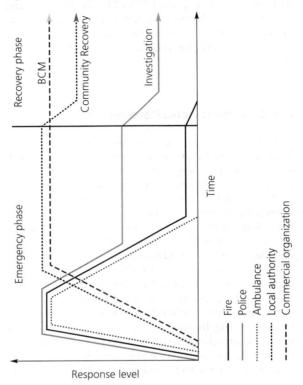

describing the emergency response in detail and categorizing what type of incident is being dealt with it would be useful to introduce the terms used to identify incidents and how using a common emergency response language can assist communication. See the terms below for more information.

KEY POINT

Terms used to identify incidents

- *Emergency*: the term was introduced by the CCA 2004. This describes a very broad range of incidents which in themselves have a significant impact upon the nation, region or locally.
- *Major incident*: is a term that the emergency services have used for many years, which is well understood in terms of the nature of the response required to manage it.

These terms are closely related and their relationship must be understood to apply them correctly. More complete explanations and their application follow in this chapter.

- *Critical incident*: for completeness this term is included here. This term the police use to describe any incident where police action may have an impact on the confidence of a victim, their relatives or the wider community. This term is often used in situations of racial tension. However, this is a term that requires caution in its use. It can arise from time to time and is used by some organizations to describe a level of incident or circumstances that may fall short of a major incident. It is a term that causes confusion and must be used and applied in the context intended by the organization using it.

Scene management layout (see Figure 4.5) and terminology is agreed between all the emergency services to ensure that there is a clear methodology and approach to every incident. It also assists the police to manage effective co-ordination at and around the scene if all those responding subscribe to the same emergency management principles. The police set out their emergency procedures (EP) policy in a document produced by the National Policing Improvement Agency (NPIA) on behalf of the Association of Chief Police Officers (ACPO). This document sets out guidance across the whole emergency management process and provides a consistent approach for all police forces in England, Wales and Northern Ireland.

The configuration of scene management structure has changed in recent years to deal with new threats including chemical, biological, radiological and nuclear type incidents (see Figure 4.5). To that extent the ACPO EP guidance was revised in 2008 in the light of the new threats and to accommodate the Civil Contingencies Act 2004.

Having established the basis for understanding these terms we will now consider their practical application in both planning and the emergency response itself.

4.5 The Emergency Response

The first few minutes of an incident will inevitably be chaotic as the situation unfolds, but the emergency services will quickly begin to meet to discuss immediate priorities and implement the appropriate management or command structure as required to manage the incident.

One of the first considerations will be if it is a 'major incident' (MI).

4.5.1 What is a major incident?

This term 'major incident' still dominates the emergency planning world. This is because it describes to an organization a situation that requires a special response from them. Why is this important? Declaring a major incident will:

- initiate plans
- mobilize and alert support organizations and other emergency services
- release resources
- focus attention
- drive the operational response
- combine multi-agency response
- define a command structure

But a major incident for one service may not be for another. For example, a plane crash with no survivors will not create a major incident for the ambulance service but will for others involved in the response. This is where the principle of 'Combined Response' is adopted. The combined response principle ensures that the overall response is co-ordinated. The 'unaffected' service(s) will liaise closely to determine their response—full response, standby or stand down in support of that agency. This will avoid 'catch-up' for a service that would not be routinely informed. It is for an individual service to determine if they are needed at a scene and it is *not* for another service to stand them down or decide they are not needed.

Task 4.1

Can you think of five emergencies which would not require all three of the three emergency services?

Recognising a 'major incident' may not be so easy to determine in the early stages of an incident. It is very important to understand the circumstances and criteria that will trigger a 'major incident' for an individual organization. It may be a number of factors unique to a particular organization, but whatever criteria or circumstances define a major incident for them, the whole process must now take into account the influence and direction of the Civil Contingencies Act 2004, which defines what an 'Emergency' is. A major incident must sit within that definition.

Definition—Emergency

'An event or situation which threatens serious damage to human welfare in a place in the UK, the environment of a place in the UK, or war or terrorism that threatens serious damage to the security of the UK.'

CCA 2004 *Emergency Preparedness Guidance 2005*, p 5.

Please note: an emergency outside the UK with effects within the UK can be classified as an 'Emergency'.

---

4 Understanding the Emergency Response

It should be noticed that the word 'major incident' does not appear in the definition of 'Emergency'. However, it has been accepted that 'major incident' will continue to be used as a term because it is so embedded and understood by all emergency responders and its application is flexible. It is important though to appreciate where major incident fits within the CCA and all the organizations that go to support the legislation. See Figure 4.2.

Looking at Figure 4.2, all organizations should subscribe and embrace the CAA definition but within that definition each organization must construct a definition of major

Figure 4.2 What is a Major Incident?

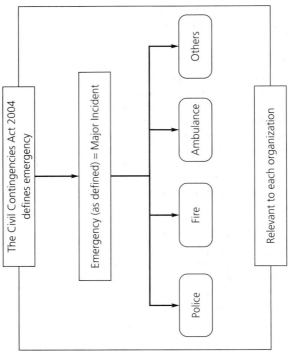

incident that applies to them alone and put in place stated and documented conditions and criteria that will trigger that declaration. However, be aware of using the term 'critical incident' as it has a specific meaning for the police which may confuse.

How would an organization define its major incident? The first consideration in defining a major incident is to understand that major incidents are about consequences and not cause. It is the impact and effects of an incident and how it affects an organization that will determine at what point to move to declare a major incident. Issues to consider for determining a major incident may be:

- The response required to manage it falls outside your daily capability
- It requires additional resources or special arrangements to deal with it
- It is large scale and having serious and widespread impact
- It puts your ordinary service delivery at risk

Task 4.2

Think about an organization you work for or have worked for. What do you think would constitute a major incident for them?

Once an organization has determined what for them constitutes a major incident they should then define what criteria will trigger that response. This may be a staged response moving up in levels eventually reaching 'major incident'. Each level will determine a course of action that will appear in the plan, which we will consider later.

A key point here is not to confuse 'major' with 'unusual'—in many cases the unusual can be dealt with quite easily. For example, a helicopter crash in open rural countryside is an unusual event but in terms of management it is quite straightforward in terms of resources.

4.5.2 Who will declare a major incident?

The CCA is quite clear about how this process occurs for 'emergency' and requires the plan to include the following information:

1. Which post holder will declare the emergency.
2. How they will be advised of the incident and who is consulted.
3. Who they will inform.

It is suggested that this is a good basis also for allocating responsibility and clarity as to who has the duty or responsibility to declare a major incident within an organization. The early recognition and declaration of a major incident is crucial to the effective management of the incident. Although the CCA directs an individual to be identified it is often quite ambiguous who that person is in reality. Traditionally emergency service organizations have left that decision to the first responders. It could be argued that in the more obvious incident such as a plane crash or train crash it is quite easy, but some major incidents are 'slow burn' and it is not quite so simple or obvious. First responders are often too involved in scene management and rescue to be in a position to assess the overall impact of the incident, the availability of resources or indeed if all the conditions and criteria apply to call it a major incident. There is no doubt that the first responder would inform the decision to call a major incident but a more reliable and robust method would concentrate that decision on a management level. For example, a duty manager within the organization or duty officer perhaps in a control room environment. Often these decisions can be assessed or quality assured more thoroughly through control rooms—people who have the detailed overview of the circumstances and probably the experience to make those subjective decisions at the earliest opportunity. In the author's experience it is often the delay in declaring a major incident that inhibits that early response and the Golden Hour effectiveness and advantage. It is suggested that by default the decision to declare major incident should be integrated into a managerial function.

4.6 The Police—Category 1 Responder

The Police ranks are included here for general information to assist those involved in emergency responses in recognizing the ranks of those they are dealing with.

The primary function of the police in emergency management is to co-ordinate the response. Without effective co-ordination the response will be inadequate and probably fail entirely.

Checklist—the primary functions of the police service in emergency management

- To protect life and property.
- Co-ordination of the emergency services and other support organizations.
- To investigate, gather and present evidence of criminal activity and enforce the criminal law.
- To identify those involved in major incidents or disasters.
- To collate and disseminate casualty information and inform relatives.
- To investigate death on behalf of the coroner.
- To co-ordinate evacuation.
- To identify, along with the Ambulance Service, a suitable location to accommodate those involved or surviving an incident to receive support and enable documentation to take place, known as a Survivor Reception Centre (SRC).

The police priorities will be to ensure the emergency services and other emergency responders can perform their tasks effectively. They can do so by:

- Facilitating inter-agency communications and consultation at the scene—initially at the Incident Control Post (ICP) or Forward Control Point (FCP)

4 Understanding the Emergency Response

Figure 4.3 Police Ranks

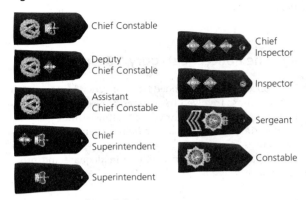

Chief Constable

Deputy Chief Constable

Assistant Chief Constable

Chief Superintendent

Superintendent

Chief Inspector

Inspector

Sergeant

Constable

(Image courtesy of Kent Police)

- Facilitating access and egress in and around the scene
- Setting up traffic management and diversions
- Setting up appropriate cordons—both inner and outer
- Managing RVPs and Marshalling Areas
- Dealing with the media

Protecting and assisting the public by:

- Providing support and assistance with care for the welfare of survivors
- Establishing the identity of persons involved in incidents
- Co-ordinating any evacuation
- Assisting with warnings, advice and information
- Protecting property

Establishing or assisting in the establishment of the facts of the incident by:

- Protecting and preserving the scene and any deceased persons
- Identifying witnesses/suspects
- Investigating or assisting in the investigation

It should be noted and appreciated that the police will secure a scene to obtain evidence or assist others to get evidence such as the Fire and Rescue Service, forensic services and the Health and Safety Executive. It is their duty. Being prepared for this type of disruption is an essential part of business continuity planning and one the emergency services must consider when assessing the impact cordons may have on communities and businesses. It could mean that getting access to the scene may be restricted or excluded for hours or even days. This is an important factor for businesses. How will their business survive? This is a good reason to ensure that where possible, businesses should engage with the police at an early stage of planning for emergency and crisis.

The priority of all the emergency services at a scene is to save life and prevent injury as far as possible. The first response will be an operational response by the emergency services. The operational response is activity seen on the ground, what would actually be seen and is described as the routine response, ie the vehicles and personnel attending the scene.

Upon arrival at the scene of an emergency the police will use the following list to assess the scene; this is known as SAD—CHALETS:

- **S**urvey, **A**ssess and **D**isseminate. Think...
- **C**asualties—number, severity, contaminated?
- **H**azards—fire, chemical, explosion risk, gas?
- **A**ccess—identify safe routes?
- **L**ocation—be precise?
- **E**mergency services—in attendance or required?
- **T**ype of incident—RTC, explosion, CBRN?
- **S**afety—do not put yourself at risk!

4.7 **Incident Scene Management**

To illustrate the co-ordination function of the police we will look at the process as it begins from a 'typical' spontaneous (sudden impact) incident.

At a scene the police will arrange a **Rendezvous Point** (RVP) in liaison with the Fire Service (if they are present) in a safe area and nearby a **Forward Control Point** (FCP). The FCP is the initial 'Control' where Commanders (Incident Officers) from other blue light services will meet and decide on priorities to manage the incident. The police will then establish an **Incident Control Post** or ICP nearby but outside the inner cordon.

4.7.1 **Incident Control Point**

An ICP is intended to be the first management building block to accommodate the police and other agencies to achieve multi-agency co-ordination at or near the scene, a place where they can meet and discuss options and priorities. This facility would need to be large enough, with sufficient administrative support and facilities to be effective. In reality this type of facility is usually not available. However, most emergency services have their own 'command' vehicles which are limited in facilities and space for full multi-agency use, but one such vehicle could be used in the initial stages of the incident to fulfil that ICP function.

4.7.2 **Forward Control Point**

The FCP is set in a location as close as safety permits and the RVP is where responders will meet before being directed to the ICP. The RVP and ICP will be supported by a **Marshalling Area** (MA) which will hold resources until and when needed at the incident site. These locations are managed by the police as part of their co-ordination role (see Figure 4.4 Access Control).

4.7.3 **Cordons and access control**

At this point it is worth mentioning the use of cordons. How to get through police cordons? Cordons are put in place for very good reasons. They are usually maintained by the

Figure 4.4 Access Control

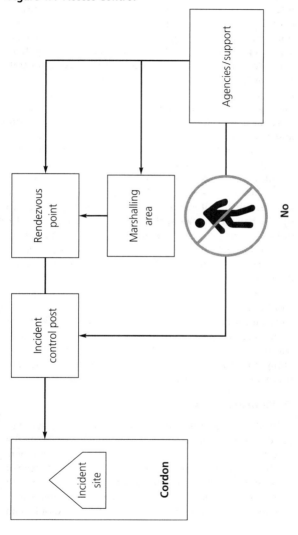

police and the fire and rescue service and are very resource intensive to maintain their integrity. Usually there are two cordons, an inner and outer cordon. In addition, the term hot zone, warm zone and cold zone may be used to manage a scene involving contamination, but essentially these zones are cordoned areas. Each cordon has 'access control' to ensure only authorized people can gain access. Security is maintained by the police and the inner cordon safety management is usually left to the fire and rescue service. Cordons are for safety reasons primarily, in which the fire and rescue service have overall primacy within the inner cordon unless it is a terrorist-related incident in which case the police will take primacy.

Unless the incident is a result of a terrorist action, the police cannot force people to leave cordon areas but clearly it is sensible to follow police advice as it will be backed up by other agency advice such as the fire and rescue service or health professionals. The police obtain their powers to impose and enforce cordons following terrorist incident from Section 33–36 of the Terrorism Act 2000. The police do not impose cordons lightly.

At the ICP, the police, fire, or ambulance services may require the assistance of other agencies, for example, the local authority, utility companies, Environment Agency or even a company representative, to name but a few. They will be asked to attend the Rendezvous Point and will be brought forward to the ICP by the police. Then if required they will be taken to the Forward Control Point.

Traffic management

Beyond the cordon area there will be traffic management in place. This will restrict access to a general area. Clearly the objective is to keep people away for safety reasons but there will be occasions when staff need to attend a site, a scene or a police control centre to offer assistance. Getting through police lines can be an interesting experience! This is why it is important to brief those who may be called out to an incident as to the correct approach to adopt when trying to access cordons or police traffic management. If there is a genuine reason to request access through a police line the person requesting access should make it clear to the officer the reason why they need to get through. Production of photo identification is essential. The person requesting access may also politely ask that a message be forwarded to the police control centre advising them of the request to get access. Although this approach may seem excessive, non-blue light emergency responders may have real difficulty persuading an officer that their role is essential and only by verification via control can this be confirmed.

Requesting a police escort to get through traffic is generally unrealistic unless it is arranged in advance at the time of call out or the attendance is vital to save life.

During the initial scene management process police, officers will be appointed with specific jobs to do, like implementing cordons, managing RVPs, marshalling areas and cordon access control in order to protect the area. They will be engaged in traffic management to assist in controlling traffic in and out of the area too. This is a very resource intensive time, the level of resource needed can easily be underestimated. As we will see later, during exercises it is often an important issue to ensure those taking part in the exercise are given 'realistic' levels of staff and equipment to reinforce the level of resources needed to manage even a relatively small scene.

In and around the incident site the activity will be frenetic and it is important that key managers and commanders are readily identifiable with high visibility jackets. It is vital that they are easily identifiable to other response agencies and take an active, decisive and robust role at a scene to co-ordinate the activity. The police will wear 'Incident Officer'

Task 4.3

Research the legal powers that give the police authority to enforce cordons.

---

jackets to indicate their role. More detail about the role of the police Incident Officer will be dealt with in Chapter 5.

An example of a comprehensive scene management structure is shown in Figure 4.5. No two scenes will be the same and the exact positioning of various facilities will vary but the diagram gives an overall impression of the general layout.

Figure 4.5 Scene Management

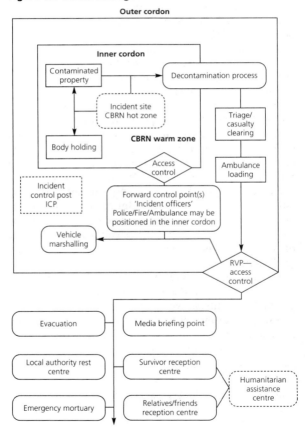

4.7.4 **Chemical, Biological, Radiological, and Nuclear (CBRN)**

These terms are now commonplace in emergency planning and have very different impacts if used. It is not intended to give a definitive explanation of their effects on humans or the environment here, but they have some characteristics that the EPO should be aware of from a planning perspective. More detailed information can be obtained at <http://www.ukresilience.gov.uk/emergencies/cbrn.aspx>.

Essentially, the objective in a CBRN response is to deal with contamination effects resulting from chemical, suspected biological or radiological substances. It is worth considering the effects these substances have in the initial stages of exposure. Chemical substances will have an immediate effect as people inhale the toxic substance or it is deposited on the skin. The emergency services use the 1-2-3 system of approach in these circumstances. Biological and radiological exposure will be far less dramatic with the harmful effects emerging within a matter of hours or indeed days. A nuclear explosive device will create catastrophic devastation instantly. This is opposed to a radiological device which is intended to spread radioactive material around by means of conventional explosive. Both the fire and rescue service and ambulance service have limited radiation detection devices to alert staff if that is the case.

Steps 1–2–3

This system was developed to assist emergency responders approach a scene safely by making them alert to potential chemical attack situations.

- Step 1—if one casualty down—normal procedure.
- Step 2—if two casualties down—approach with caution.
- Step 3—if three or more casualties down, without obvious cause—do not approach. Possible chemical attack.

4.7.5 **Decontamination**

Decontamination of those affected by a range of CRBN substances is now a well practised and core activity for the emergency services and support agencies. Portable structures containing showers and other cleaning materials are used to treat casualties exposed to contaminants. Very sophisticated systems are now in place with warm water, private undressing/dressing areas and emergency clothing, all provided for the comfort and wellbeing of the casualty. Hundreds of walking and stretcher casualties can be decontaminated per hour when the systems are fully operative. However, the difficulty of containing and restraining those affected to await de-contamination is a major factor for the emergency services. This is an understandable reaction from those affected, who will be frightened and probably in a state of panic. They may try to attend hospitals, but in doing so they will contaminate and probably shut down hospital emergency rooms and affect other people they come into contact with. In the initial stages of a chemical attack stripping off outer clothing immediately is vital to remove the majority of the contaminant followed by a very basic decontamination, such as a hose and sponge down, in order to save life.

A point to note is that this decontamination procedure now extends also to the accidental or negligent spillage or discharge of these substances and not just terrorism. The focus of the response concentrates on the effective and speedy decontamination of those exposed—in particular, the new role of the ambulance service as the primary decontamination agency (supported by the fire and rescue service to deal with mass decontamination). All blue light services are now trained and equipped to deal with such incidents and have been provided with specialist equipment to do so. The key concern in these situations is keeping the public calm and reassuring them to remain where they are at the location to undergo decontamination and so prevent the spread of the toxic substance.

4.8 **Facilities and People that Support the Response**

4.8.1 **Forward Media Briefing (FMB) Point**

The Forward Media Briefing (FMB) point represents the focal point of media activity around the incident site. The demands of 24 hour news media require a robust and facilitated approach to meeting those demands. Although remote Media Briefing Centres (MBCs) still form an important facility in managing large numbers of media personnel, the emphasis has certainly shifted. Some LRFs are pre-identifying potential Forward Media Briefing (FMB) locations strategically placed across their areas to enable a rapid media set-up that can offer all the facilities and logistic support that is needed. Places to consider are hotels, conference venues, clubs, police stations, local authority facilities, sports, and leisure centres. Each one is then surveyed and a basic set-up plan is prepared in terms of layout, reception, security, IT facilities, accommodation, parking, access etc.

Allowing access to safe locations to enable filming and live broadcasts from the incident site is now an expectation that needs to be met. This can be achieved by pooling and managing the media through briefing at the Forward Media Briefing point and taking them forward to a safe location. Issues of 'good taste' (in terms of what is filmed) are a matter for negotiation and agreement between the media and primarily the police. There is no doubt that there is mutual benefit to be gained by both the media and the police having a joint consensus in media reporting arrangements from an incident site. The police will have media arrangements in place to manage the media demand which will involve consultation with other agencies resulting in a co-ordinated approach to managing the media. The LRF will also have joint media response arrangements in place. Media co-ordination will be managed through a Media Co-ordination Centre (MCC) usually chaired by the police who will then report and sit within the SCG (discussed later). The MCC is made up of media liaison officers from all participating organizations , who can, through the MCC contribute and where necessary resolve any issues of conflict in terms of media output. It is important that any one agency does not unilaterally address the media without reference to the MCC and SCG. If that occurs there is a real danger that confused and mixed messages will be released that may compromise the overall response.

4.8.2 Rest Centres (RC)

The provision of Rest Centres is a matter for the local authority supported by the police and voluntary services. The centre will provide food, drinks, non emergency medical support, and children's facilities. In many cases provision for pets will have to be considered as being separated from pets will cause some people to be very anxious. Again as with the Forward Media Briefing points, many LRFs have pre-identified suitable locations and facilities to act as Rest Centres. They tend to be local authority facilities such as leisure centres or community buildings. The concept of a rest centre is to accommodate those who are temporarily displaced from their homes. Although an essential facility in those circumstances, many people faced with evacuation will try to find accommodation with family and friends or indeed in a hotel. The prospect of sleeping in a rest centre environment can be distressing for many people who will feel insecure and vulnerable. It is therefore important that the police provide that level of reassurance and security where possible by being present and visible.

Those attending a Rest Centre will be documented by the local authority and voluntary services to ensure that they are accounted for and details can be passed to enquiring relatives and friends. Many local authority documentation forms are also compatible for police casualty bureau purposes in the event that the situation requires a casualty bureau to be opened and the data can be transferred to the casualty bureau without having to re-interview those already documented.

4.8.3 **Survivor Reception Centre (SRC)**

Survivor Reception Centres are temporary facilities which are set up near an incident site to accommodate those who have been involved in the incident and could be classified as 'casualties'. They are distinct from Rest Centres and serve a different purpose. Following an incident involving many people, the ambulance service will sort or triage those involved and those requiring hospital treatment will be taken to designated hospitals. There may be significant numbers of people who are not physically injured but will need general comfort, support, assistance and advice. The location of the SRC is made spontaneously by the ambulance service and the police. Any suitable local building will be used. Casualties will need to be documented there by the police for 'casualty bureau' purposes (see later) and

---

Task 4.4

Can you think of a situation where you could have a Rest Centre operating and a Survivor Reception Centre operating at the same time?

---

investigative reasons. A point to note here is that those at the SRC are asked to attend there are voluntarily. There is no power to require a person to stay or attend at a SRC unless other circumstances apply in which the police will take the necessary action.

4.8.4 **Friends and Relatives Centre (FRC)**

The Friends and Relatives Centre (FRC) is complementary to the SRC. It is a location chosen to enable those concerned about their family and friends who have been involved in an incident to go to and seek information. It is a natural reaction for people to do this which the authorities must be able to manage. In many cases it will involve large numbers of people. As with the Rest Centres and Forward Media Briefing Points pre-identification can be a valuable exercise in speeding the set-up process. The best locations tend to be hotels as they have accommodation, catering, large rooms for briefings and interviewing families. Also bear in mind that following a major incident the local hotels will be block booked by the media very quickly. The FRC is a location where Family Liaison officers will attend and begin the support process for the families involved (see FLO). The key point for a FRC is 'information'. The provision of 24 hour TV broadcasts and regular briefings by the police or local authority are essential to keep everyone informed. Even if a briefing states that there is nothing to add this will reassure and ensure that everyone feels involved.

Police teams, often supported by Social Services Crisis Teams will take details from the relatives and friends to inform and assist in the identification process for those involved (see 4.9 below).

A point to note is that holding reunions of families and those involved within the FRC can be distressing for those who have not been reunited. Also note that those engaged in mortuary duties should not share the same accommodation as the families and friends—this can be distressing for them.

4.8.5 **Humanitarian Assistance Centre (HAC)**

Although having some similarity with the FRC, this facility is intended to provide longer term support offering practical advice and guidance to those involved in the incident, whether it be individuals, families or communities. Indeed, support should extend to rescuers and response workers too. It is a truly multi-agency activity tapping into the health services, local authority, faith communities and the private sector, such as insurance companies. Detailed guidance can be found in the UK Resilience website <http://www.ukresilience.co.uk>.

4.8.6 **Emergency/Temporary Mortuary**

An incident involving many fatalities (or many body parts) may require the setting up of an 'Emergency Mortuary' as hospitals may become overwhelmed by the number of deceased persons. This is a responsibility of the local authority. The decision will be a joint one as to the need for an emergency mortuary made between the coroner and the police. The need is also determined by the number of probable body parts as opposed to persons missing. This is because each body part for administration and processing purposes is treated as a person for identification purposes. Extensive emergency mortuary planning has already been undertaken in advance of a potential influenza pandemic and following concern over mass fatalities resulting from a CBRN type attack. The options for an emergency mortuary can vary from pre-designated sites to temporary structures erected on secure sites. Each LRF will hold plans outlining their approach and policy.

4.8.7 **The Senior Investigating Officer (SIO)**

The SIO is responsible for the overall investigation of an incident where there is potentially any criminal liability associated with the circumstances. Where fatalities occur in circumstances other than wholly natural situations, where the coroner is not involved the police will act on behalf of the coroner to inquire into the circumstances of the death. As a result of that investigation prosecutions may follow. As we have seen, the police will also support and investigate with other agencies such as the HSE and Department of Transport. The SIO commands a large team of officers covering many investigative disciplines such as gathering forensic evidence and it is for that reason that the SIO must be involved in major incident management from the very start. The guidance and advice offered by the SIO is invaluable to secure and preserve evidence wherever possible once every possible effort has been made to save life. The SIO will arrange for the scene to be forensically searched, examined, witnesses to be seen, suspects to be detained or arrested and interviewed. All these activities have implications for the multi-agency team managing the incident. It is therefore important that the SIO or deputy is part of the Strategic Co-ordinating Group to assist in decision making (see Chapter 5).

4.8.8 **The Senior Identification Manager (SIM)**

The SIM is a relatively recent role. It emerged following the Marchioness river boat disaster on the Thames in London and the subsequent Lord Justice Clark report into issues relating to identification of the deceased. The SIM is a very senior police position alongside that of SIO. The SIM will work with the SIO and Gold Commander in developingstrategies and tactics to complete the identification of all those involved in an incident, both fatalities and those injured.

In collaboration with the coroner and supervising pathologist, the SIM will ensure that the deceased are correctly and properly dealt with in terms of efficient identification which is appropriate and respectful with the families involved throughout the process. The SIM will oversee all activity at the mortuary, the casualty bureau (if deaths are involved) and the role of the Family Liaison Officers. Again the SIM or deputy should have access to and be part of the SCG.

4.8.9 **Family Liaison Officers (FLOs)**

FLOs are police officers often supported by Social Services crisis support teams. FLOs are allocated to a family who have suffered bereavement in circumstances in which the police are investigating or where a family member is

---

Task 4.5

Police Family Liaison officers are supported by Social Services Crisis Support Teams and care for the needs of those affected by major incidents involving injury and death.

Using the CCA guidance and information available from your LRF web-site and other material, research their role and responsibilities.

---

missing. They are essentially evidence gathering, which includes making identification enquiries (for example DNA and physical descriptions). They are also there to support and offer advice and guidance to families throughout the identification and investigative processes. It can be a very emotional and difficult job taking many months.

4.9 Casualty Bureau

The casualty bureau is a police facility set up to manage the identification of those involved in an incident. This can include those who have died, have been injured or are missing and unaccounted for. Casualty bureau facilities are often shared between police forces and linked in terms of call handing to ensure sufficient call takers are available to manage the demand for those seeking information about relatives and friends involved in incidents. Technology has enabled direct electronic input from remote sites such as hospitals and emergency mortuaries and from FRC with information provided by relatives and friends.

The casualty bureau concept is straightforward. It is there to match information from someone who is missing or dead against information from those reporting them missing and therefore to make a positive identification. See Figure 4.6.

Figure 4.6 Casualty Bureau

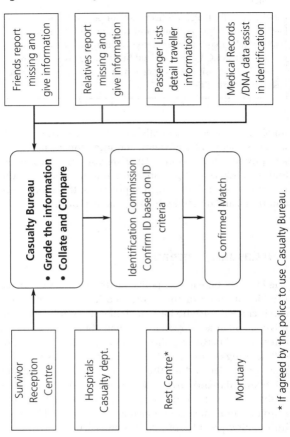

Friends report missing and give information

Relatives report missing and give information

Passenger Lists detail traveller information

Medical Records /DNA data assist in identification

Casualty Bureau
- **Grade the information**
- **Collate and Compare**

Identification Commission Confirm ID based on ID criteria

Confirmed Match

Survivor Reception Centre

Hospitals Casualty dept.

Rest Centre*

Mortuary

* If agreed by the police to use Casualty Bureau.

When an incident takes place resulting in loss of life or injury it is understandable that close friends and family will be anxious for information concerning their friend or relative. Depending on the circumstances and numbers involved, the police will decide if a casualty bureau is required. If an incident is a 'closed' incident, for example a small aircraft where all the passengers are known with certainty, a casualty bureau may be dispensed with. If they decide to open a casualty bureau, an 0800 (usually) or free phone number is released through the media. The police will activate the pre-planned arrangements and call takers will be positioned to handle the incoming calls. These could in fact be in different locations across the country within police forces subscribing to a national or regional scheme. In this way the number of call takers can be scaled up or down to meet the demand. All incoming information will then be channelled to the designated casualty bureau. Although the police will issue a number for the casualty bureau or information centre, in many cases with large transport undertakings such as airlines and rail operators' protocols exist to share and collaborate with information sharing.

> **Task 4.6**
> Establish what emergency/temporary mortuary arrangements apply in your LRF area.

4.9.1 How does the system work?

When a relative reports someone missing and they assume that they have been involved in the incident, the police will grade that information. The grading will be decided by the SIM and colleagues such as the casualty bureau manager. The grading can be for example 1–5, 1 being that the person reported missing is very likely to have been involved and 5 unlikely. For example, if it is a train crash, the relative may have actually put the person on the train in question so they are certain that they were on it. On the other hand a relative may report that they are aware that their relative is touring in that area and always uses trains. That may be graded as a 5. Depending on the level of certainty any grade between 1 and 5 will be used. Casualty bureaux will also have a proactive team who actively re-contact relatives and friends to establish if the person they reported missing has turned up. This is often overlooked by the reporting person as they are so relieved they forget to tell the police!

4.9.2 Making the identification

Data is compared and collated with information coming in from various locations such as hospitals, SRCs and later in the process, mortuaries. To make formal positive identifications an 'Identification Commission' is established to assess the identification information and make a decision. They will use a combination of Primary, Secondary, and Assistance means of identification.

For example:

Primary	Secondary	Assistance
DNA	Personal jewellery/effects	Visual ID
Fingerprints	Medical records/X-ray	Photographs
Odontology	Blood group	Personal description
Distinctive deformity	Distinctive clothing, tattoos	Body location
Distinctive medical	Marks and scars	Clothing
	Physical disease	

A combination may be any two primary or a minimum of three secondary. Only assistance means can support primary and secondary. It should be noted that visual identification in itself cannot be a positive identification. 'Viewing' the body or indeed part of the body is a matter for the rela-tives to decide as it may greatly assist them coming to terms with their loss.

Task 4.7

Can you think of reasons why visual ID is not a primary form of ID?

Once identification is confirmed by the Identification Commission that will be communicated to the relatives. This is done by a personal visit which will involve the police.

Having looked in depth at the police response we will now examine the role of the other emergency services and key support agencies.

4.10 **Fire & Rescue Service—Category 1 Responder**

Figure 4.7 Fire and Rescue Service Ranks

Firefighter

Group Manager

Crew Manager

Area Manager

Watch Manager

Brigade Manager

Station Manager

4 Understanding the Emergency Response

For general information, the Fire and Rescue ranks are included above to aid those involved in their recognition of various ranks at scenes and Control Centres.

The Fire and Rescue Service has undergone major change in recent years, in particular in relation to their role in responding to large scale catastrophic events in the wake of the terrorist attacks in New York in 2001, under the New Dimensions programme. They now have substantial equipment strategically placed across the UK to respond to major incidents including de-contamination units and high capacity pumps.

The Fire and Rescue Services have scene management arrangements that are configured on creating sectors with a sector commander in charge of each one. See Figure 4.8.

Checklist—the primary areas of Fire and Rescue Service responsibility at a major incident

- Life-saving through search and rescue.
- Fire-fighting and fire prevention.
- Rendering humanitarian services.
- Providing and/or obtaining specialist advice and assistance where hazardous materials are involved.
- Salvage and damage control.
- The provision of specialist equipment, eg pumps, rescue equipment and lighting.
- Safety management within the inner cordon (hot and warm zone).
- Provide equipment and manpower to support the mass decontamination of the public in support of the NHS.
- Provide manpower and equipment to perform urban search and rescue.
- Initiate environmental protection measures.

Task 4.8

The Fire Service operate a system of sector management. Will this conflict with police co-ordination?

Figure 4.8 Sector Command

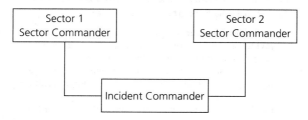

The fire and rescue service will approach a scene and 'sectorize' it into manageable areas but the system is still compatible with overall co-ordination, as the Incident Commander will liaise with the other emergency services on site. Other developments have included changes in working practices and the way equipment is managed and deployed.

4.11 **Ambulance Service—Category 1 Responder**

The ambulance service, like many other public sector organizations, has undergone rapid change in recent years again being touched by the effects of terrorist attacks in New York in 2001. Following those events and a review of the UK capability of dealing with mass casualties, the ambulance services became the primary body responsible for casualty decontamination working closely with the Fire and Rescue Service who assist them by decontaminating large numbers of people.

Task 4.9

Who has primacy for decontamination? What is the distinction if any?

> **Checklist—primary areas of responsibility for the Ambulance Service at a major incident**
>
> - To save life in conjunction with the other emergency services.
> - Provide treatment, stabilization and care of those injured at the scene including decontamination of casualties.
> - Initiate casualty decontamination procedures at the scene including mass decontamination arrangements in conjunction with the Fire and Rescue Service.
> - Provide sufficient medical and other staff, equipment and resources.
> - Establish effective triage systems to determine the priority evacuation needs of those injured.
> - Act as a gateway to all NHS services and co-ordinate NHS activity at the scene.
> - Provide communication facilities for NHS resources at the scene, including communication links with hospitals and other control centres.
> - Nominate and alert appropriate hospitals to receive casualties from the incident.
> - Arrange for the provision of a Medical Incident Officer and Mobile Medical/Surgical teams and provide transport to the scene where necessary.
> - Provide appropriate means of transporting those injured to hospital or other treatment centre.
> - Maintain an emergency service throughout the county and return to a state of normality as soon as possible.

4.12 Maritime and Coastguard Agency (MCA)—Category 1 Responder

The primary role of the Maritime and Coastguard Agency is to co-ordinate the emergency response offshore. This can cause some confusion as to where the police and MCA co-ordination starts and finishes. In practice, the MCA will always cover areas covered by water and dry areas by the police. In the area from high water to low water it will be a combined effort.

The MCA control and co-ordinate the response to major maritime emergencies until such time as the emergency is closed or has become a mainly land-based operation. They manage these offshore incident from strategically placed Control Centres around the coast. They mobilize, task, and co-ordinate declared and additional SAR facilities, which include:

- RNLI and other lifeboats
- Military Search And Rescue (SAR) helicopters and fixed wing aircraft through the military Aeronautical Rescue Co-ordination Centre (ARCC)
- Maritime and Coastguard Agency resources including boats, vehicles, beach, mud and cliff rescue teams
- vessels and support units in the vicinity
- Port Authority and associated resources, eg tugs, pilot vessels, etc.

The MCA will also alert other relevant emergency services local authorities and organizations. Part of this alert process is to facilitate and arrange the embarkation of survivors and casualties to nominated landing points and to agree with the police the location for landing any deceased.

The MCA will provide an early warning system for oil, chemical and other forms of sea and coastal pollution, including the alerting of the Regional Operation Manager— Counter Pollution and Salvage (ROM-CPS) of the MCA, and local authorities. As part of their environmental protection role they will assist with counter-pollution and clean up by providing co-ordinating facilities and communications.

4.13 **Local Authority—Category 1 Responder**

The local authority provide a vast amount of resources and support in major incident management. It must be remembered however that they are not a blue light emergency service and must be given a very early call out to allow them to mobilize themselves and the voluntary agencies that support them.

Checklist—the primary areas of responsibility for local authorities

- To support the emergency services and those engaged in the response to the incident.
- The provision of a wide range of support services.
- To activate the voluntary agencies bearing in mind the time taken to respond, and co-ordinate their response.
- To provide suitable accommodation at Rest Centres for those evacuated or otherwise displaced from their homes including the documentation of those displaced.
- To provide support at a location used to care for and provide support to those involved in or surviving an incident, known as a Survivor Reception Centre.
- To provide facilities and location(s) for relatives and friends of those involved in an incident to enable information, support and reuniting, known as a Friends and Relatives Centre.
- Will provide, in consultation with the police, emergency mortuary arrangements (Emergency/Resilience Mortuary).
- Will facilitate the remediation and reoccupation of sites or affected areas.
- To lead the recovery and return to normality, whilst at the same time maintaining services at the appropriate level.
- To activate faith groups bearing in mind the time taken to respond, and co-ordinate their response.

The local authorities have certain responsibilities relating to flood management, in particular relating to flash flood and water runoff and drainage inundation. This work is sometimes contracted out to United Utilities.

Task 4.10

Establish the emergency planning structure for your local authority—is it County, Metropolitan or District based?

4.14 **Other Key Agencies**

4.14.1 **The Health Protection Agency (HPA)—Category 1 Responder**

The HPA is a non-departmental body providing public health advice to the Government, the NHS, and the statutory agencies and directly to the public. They are a key agency in managing the impact of major incidents.

They also provide:

- A central source of scientific and medical information. This includes information relating to the deliberate or accidental release of chemicals, poisons, CBRN or radiation. The Radiation Protection Division (RPD) specialize in offering advice and information relating to radiological incidents and deliver training to other emergency response agencies.
- Specialist advice on the planning and operational responses to public health and other emergencies. This includes assisting in formulating messages relating to health protection measures in order to reduce public anxiety.

4.14.2 **The Food Standards Agency (FSA)**

The FSA is an independent Government Department offering a range of services relating to food safety generally including advice and guidance relating to food affected by contaminants. They also monitor radiological safety as it relates to discharges into the environment and its affect on the food chain.

4.14.3 Animal Health and Welfare (formerly State Veterinary Service), Department for Environment, Food and Rural Affairs (Defra)

Many major incidents, in particular where contaminants are involved, will have a serious impact on animals, from domestic, to farm animals to wild animals. Animal Welfare has a number of offices across the country that will provide advice and guidance relating to animal welfare issues.

4.14.4 Department of Health (DOH)—Category 1 Responder

In the event of a national or international incident which is deemed to be complex and of a serious nature the DoH will take control of NHS resources. This will be managed from their Emergency Preparedness Division Co-ordinating Centre. This will provide the necessary co-ordination for the NHS as a whole and offer support to Ministers.

4.14.5 Primary Care Trusts (PCTS)—Category 1 Responder

PCTs provide a range of health professionals such as doctors (GPs), dentists, opticians, and pharmacy services. The PCT will work with local authorities and other agencies that provide health and social care locally to ensure that the needs of the community are met. PCTs within the LRF area often nominate a lead PCT to co-ordinate and sit on the LRF to ensure an effective PCT response following a major incident.

4.14.6 **Acute Trusts—Category 1 Responder**

Hospitals are managed by acute trusts. They have:

- Arrangements in place via A&E in dealing with emergencies as receiving hospitals for casualties.
- They will have tried and tested Major Incident procedures in place and can link into police casualty bureau systems and technology to assist in identifying casualties.
- Clinical response capability to an emergency.
- Mobile response capability to incident scenes.

4.14.7 **Strategic Health Authorities (SHA) in England—Category 2 Responder**

Strategic health authorities are responsible for:

- developing plans for improving health services in their local area,
- making sure local health services are of a high quality and are performing well,
- increasing the capacity of local health services—so they can provide more services, and
- making sure national priorities are integrated into local health service plans.

Strategic health authorities manage the NHS locally and are a key link between the Department of Health and the NHS.

4.14.8 **Local Health Boards (LHBS) in Wales— Category 1 Responder**

The LHB is responsible for local co-ordination of NHS emergency planning and response. They are the lead health co-ordinator over a wider area covered by each LRF and report and liaise with the Welsh Assembly Government's Health and Social care department to support a pan-Wales response.

4.14.9 **Public Health**

The Chief Medical Officer is represented across the country by the Regional Directors of Public Health. In the event of an emergency they will work closely with the HPA. They provide public health advice, support and leadership to help the SHAs and the NHS to manage the emergency. They will also provide co-ordination with regional tiers such as the RCCC in preparing and responding to outbreaks of infectious diseases and other public health emergencies.

In Wales, public health advice is provided by the National Public Health Service for Wales.

4.14.10 **Port Health Authorities—Category 1 Responder**

The focus in collaboration with other agencies is the control of infectious diseases, protecting the environment, import controls on foods and general hygiene on vessels.

4.14.11 **The Environment Agency (EA)— Category 1 Responder**

The Environment Agency's role is to protect and improve the environment in England and Wales by:

- prevention or minimization of the effects of an incident upon the environment
- investigating such incidents and prosecute where appropriate
- pursuing remediation, clean-up or restoration of the environment.

Their primary role relates to flooding where they are responsible for issuing warnings, operating flood defences and educating the 'at risk' communities to manage flood events. They will also seek to prevent and control pollution events and monitor pollutants into the environment.

They will provide advice and monitor and regulate the disposal of wastes such as diseased animals.

4.14.12 **Health and Safety Executive—Category 2 Responder**

In 2003 the police (ACPO), the Health and Safety Executive, and the Crown Prosecution Service agreed a joint protocol for liaison when investigating work-related deaths. The role played by the HSE cannot be over-emphasized as they have extensive powers when conducting investigations in particular now with the Corporate Manslaughter and Corporate Homicide Act 2007 in force. The HSE inspectors should be seen as an integral part of the investigation team. HSE also regulate nuclear installations, mines, factories, farms, hospitals, schools, offshore gas and oil installations and other workplaces to ensure a safe working environment for both the workforce and public.

4.14.13 **Department of Transport**

The DoT carries out accident investigations relating to transport incidents. The main branches are:

- **Air Accident Investigation Branch (AAIB)** is part of the DoT and investigates all civil aircraft accidents and incidents. Its primary aim is to establish the cause and circumstances of accidents to preserve life and make improvements for the future. It is not to apportion blame or liability.
- **Marine Accident Investigation Branch (MAIB)** is a separate branch within the DoT. It is not part of the Maritime and Coastguard Agency (MCA). There is a memorandum of understanding however between the HSE, MCA and the MAIB to ensure full co-operation and collaboration during investigations.
- **Rail Accident Investigation Branch (RAIB)** is an independent body within the DoT. It reports directly to the

Secretary of State. It was established by the Railways and Transport Safety Act 2003 following the Ladbroke Grove rail accident in 1999 and recommendations contained within the Lord Cullen report into that incident. Again the RAIB has extensive powers of investigation and will work closely with the police (British Transport Police) relating to incidents on railways involving the death of a person, serious injury to five or more people or extensive damage to rolling stock, the infrastructure or environment.

4.14.14 **Ministry of Defence/Military**

The military have taken a much higher profile in becoming engaged with assisting and planning for civil emergency matters. Every LRF will have a military representative within their group. Military assistance has been available to the civil authorities for many years but has recently been formalized into the Civil Contingencies Reaction Forces (CCRF) based around Territorial Army volunteers. The CCRF was set up to assist the civil authorities in times of local or national emergency. Clearly however, military operational commitments both home and abroad have a significant effect on how the military can respond to civil requests.

Arrangements have existed under the terms of what is known as Military Aid to the Civil Authorities (MACA) which is divided into MACP—Military Aid to the Civil Power, which is concerned with national security and MACC—Military Aid to the Civil Community. It must be stressed that there are strict criteria for accessing military aid and can have very significant financial implications. If the situation is not directly life threatening, advice must be sought from the local Military Liaison Officer to clarify the cost implications. These decisions are usually taken through the SCG or Strategic Co-ordinating Group.

4.14.15 **Private Sector**

> **Task 4.11**
>
> Can you think of the kind of support the voluntary sector can provide following a civil emergency? List at least 10 activities.

The CCA 2004 identified and recognized the contribution certain organizations and companies bring to emergency management and designated them as Category 2 responders. These include:

- electricity distributors and transmitters
- gas distributors
- water and sewerage
- telephone providers
- railways operators
- airport operators greater than 50k passengers
- ports
- Highways Agency

4.14.16 **Voluntary Sector**

The voluntary sector, including groups such as the Red Cross, can provide a great deal of support through the local authority in terms of offering support to the community generally, those involved in major incidents, casualties and friends and relatives.

Although not specifically covered in this book detailed information relating to their role within a major incident can be found on their respective web sites and by referring to the Local Resilience Forum. As a matter of good practice every emergency planning officer should regularly update themselves on current developments within all emergency response organizations.

4.14.17 **Faith Communities**

Connected to voluntary work is the support offered by many faith groups from denominations and religions. This support is normally co-ordinated through the local authority. Their advice and guidance can be invaluable in terms of understanding cultural or language issues. In particular, many faith leaders and community leaders can assist in communication with sections of the community that would otherwise be less effective.

4.15 **Summary**

In this chapter you have examined how the emergency response is structured and the activities of the emergency services and support agencies. In particular we have looked in great detail at the police response and how they combine their management arrangements into overall co-ordination. This is very important to understand as it is the primary driver within emergency response in the UK. Scene management has also been explored giving you an insight into the arrangements you may have to support or plan for.

4.16 **Conclusion**

Understanding the role of the emergency services and all the agencies that make up the multi-agency approach is vital to the EPO. Working together in a co-ordinated way will greatly enhance the effectiveness of the response and therefore reduce the impact upon the community. The number of response agencies as we have seen is large and without co-ordination the overall effort will fail. The next chapter examines in detail how effective co-ordination is achieved. The focus will be on the police and how they create the environment and facilitate co-ordination from the start of an incident.

Chapter 5

Co-ordinating the Emergency Response

Overview

In this chapter we will cover:

- The role of the police in co-ordination
- The police—who are they?
- Gold, Silver, Bronze
- Police Incident Officer—PIO
- Activating management levels
- Strategic Co-ordination Centre
- Multiple Silvers?
- Two essential SCC Sub-Groups
- Regional and National Co-ordination
- Lead Government Departments
- Managing within the SCC/SCG
- Recording information
- Running meetings
- Resourcing police controls
- Criminal liability
- Putting it all together

5.1 The Role of the Police in Co-ordination

As we now operate in a multi-agency environment the key to being an effective EPO is to fully understand the relationship, interaction and responsibilities of each organization and perhaps most importantly where they and their organization fit into the whole picture. The range of response agencies is quite extensive as we have seen. Each emergency response organization will have detailed 'tried and tested' internal procedures for dealing with crises, major incidents and civil emergencies developed over many years and it is not intended to go into detail here about individual organizational procedures.

This chapter is about describing how effective co-ordination is achieved from the initial response right up to Government level. For the purposes of familiarization only, a summary of the main emergency response organizations has been given so far in the previous chapter, however the role of the police is examined even further now. As already alluded to, this focus on the police is because it is the police who are charged with the responsibility for the overall co-ordination of the emergency response. Being able to understand that co-ordination role is vital for any EPO in terms of preparing plans, exercising and training.

The role of the police cannot be overstated when it relates to major incident management. The police service is responsible for the overall co-ordination of the emergency response phase to an incident where there is an immediate or a potential threat to public safety. In this context this relates to physical harm where the threat is likely to result in death and injury brought about by violent means either man made or by nature. There will be occasions when public wellbeing is threatened such as that from diseases in which case other agencies will take on the co-ordination role. But the police will always play a crucial role in such circumstances.

5.1.1 **The Police**

At this point it should be made clear what is meant by the 'police'. This book concentrates on emergency procedures in England and Wales and therefore the focus is on police co-ordination as outlined in the ACPO Emergency Planning Guidance as already described. In Scotland the processes and administration are different. There is no significance to the term 'police' or 'constabulary'. Historically city and borough forces used the term 'police' and county police used the term 'constabulary'. Some county forces have now adopted the term 'police' perhaps as it is perceived as more modern. The other main police forces in England and Wales are:

5.1.2 The Civil Nuclear Constabulary (CNC)

Until 2005 the CNC was called the UK Atomic Energy Authority Constabulary which focused on guarding civil nuclear sites and nuclear material in transit. It receives its strategic direction from the Department for Business, Enterprise and Regulatory Reform (BERR). There are approximately 750 police officers and staff working from 17 sites in the UK. They are routinely armed. Post the terrorist attacks in New York in 2001 and coupled with the subsequent increased terrorist threat posed against civil nuclear sites the CNC was expanded considerably and have enhanced security levels at all nuclear sites, that previously were not staffed full time by CNC. They typically have jurisdictions up to several miles around nuclear sites.

The CNC also have responsibilities in relation to the transport of dangerous nuclear materials. The CNC co-ordinate the National Arrangements for Incidents Involving Radioactivity (NAIR) in case of a release and can alert the nearest 'expert' nuclear site to attend and manage the incident. The NAIR scheme is there primarily to assist the police and it can be used for any radiological-related incident for which there are no other set arrangements in place. Another scheme co-ordinated by the CNC is the RADSAFE scheme and it again provides 24/7 advice and response to accidents involving civil nuclear material in transit but excludes military nuclear material which is managed by the MOD (see below).

5.1.3 **Ministry of Defence Police (MDP)**

The prime role of the MOD police is armed security at approximately 100 MOD sites throughout the UK. Every officer is trained in the use of firearms. The MOD has special arrangements and responsibilities for managing MOD nuclear incidents or accidents and has the Nuclear Accident Response Organization (NARO) in place to respond if needed. NARO works closely with all civil agencies.

5.1.4 **British Transport Police (BTP)**

The BTP, a category 1 responder, is made up of approximately 2,700 officers supported by Special Constables (250 approx.), Police Community Support Officers (210 approx.) and Police Staff (1,200 approx.) They cover the whole rail network including the London Underground, Docklands Light Railway, Glasgow Subway, Midlands Metro, Croydon TramLink and Eurostar. They work very closely with train operators and Network Rail and with each local police force.

In terms of co-ordination, protocols and memoranda of understanding exist between these forces and the main 'Home Office' forces to ensure that roles and responsibilities are clear when dealing with major incidents.

5.1.5 **Co-ordination and Command**

The role of the police as co-ordinators does not mean they are 'in-charge' of other services or agencies. They act more like a conductor of an orchestra ensuring that the score (or plan) is followed and the right instruments (resources) are used. They co-ordinate in a truly multi-agency environment or setting, involving the other blue light services and other response agencies including the voluntary agencies and private industry as necessary. Increasingly the private sector is becoming an important contributor to major incident response in particular where their specialist knowledge can assist critical decision making. This may take the form of technical or organizational information. And of course being at the centre of decision making can have a profound effect on the ability of any company to survive the incident commercially.

What all police forces have in common is the use of the Gold, Silver, and Bronze (GSB) command structure which we will now look at in some detail. Understanding GSB is essential to all those engaged in emergency planning, no matter what organization they come from.

5.2 **Gold, Silver, and Bronze (GSB)**

To enable co-ordination to occur, the police have developed a command and control system that is fully integrated into day-to-day police practice and is capable of incremental development to manage major incidents. The police use Gold, Silver, and Bronze (GSB) to co-ordinate their emergency response arrangements. This is accepted nationally. GSB describes a flexible management structure which separates management activity. It creates Operational activity known as Bronze, Tactical activity known as Silver, and Strategic activity known as Gold. This can be further described as 'What to do'—Strategic, 'How to do it'—Tactical and 'Doing it'—Operational. For the purposes of this chapter the terms Gold, Silver, and Bronze will be used but recognizing that Strategic, Tactical, and Operational are also as valid.

Most people associated with emergency response will at least have heard of this system and indeed many will profess to understand it fully. The difficulty is that over time it has been interpreted and shaped into many forms and formats. It was always envisaged as a flexible system of incident management that recognized the need to separate the Gold, Silver and Bronze elements in order to make the decision making process clear and unambiguous. It is dependent on function and role, not rank. The reality is however, that the distinction is now becoming blurred with a mixing of the elements and inevitably, rank seems to impact upon the effective operation of the system. Many observers now advocate the removal of the precious metal terms as it implies order of rank or importance, preferring strategic, tactical and operational instead. Indeed, the configuration of GSB within the police service is further manipulated depending on the nature of the incident being managed. For example, incidents relating to firearms, public disorder and major incident management all have variations in the application of GSB. To avoid confusion, GSB as it is applied to the management of major incidents or civil emergencies will only be dealt with in this book.

5.2.1 Command and control

An important point to remember is that the police must operate a command and control that not only delivers effective co-ordination for all responding agencies but that it can also manage its own resources too. The command and control training therefore for police managers is quite comprehensive and the whole police command and control process has been reviewed to make it less ambiguous and more consistent across the UK which is reflected in the most recent edition of the ACPO Emergency Procedures Guidance 2008.

For most organizations the process of supporting the police through the GSB method of incident management is quite straightforward in that they react to requests from the police to attend and participate within one to the management levels be it at Gold, Silver or Bronze level. In the event of a spontaneous major incident as defined within the CCA, the application and use of GSB is quite straightforward and easily understood. It is obvious from the outset that all management levels will be required because of the nature and magnitude of the event. Take for example the Lockerbie aircraft crash. It would be obvious that this catastrophic event needed a full management structure in place immediately. Therefore, all the management levels kick in immediately. But what about something less obvious and at what point would GSB kick in and up to what level?

It is worth making clear at this point that we are considering the spontaneous (sudden impact) events, the unexpected and unplanned. Planning for and managing forthcoming events in many respects is easier, as the consequences and events are largely predictable, notwithstanding that an unexpected event may occur. Therefore, the management structure can be designated and facilities put in place in advance. The challenge is in being confronted with a major incident with no notice and implementing arrangements and obtaining resources to manage it. The spontaneous event is characterized by starting with the operational response and building as the issues unfold. The event may jump to a full GSB response immediately (as in the case of Lockerbie) but in other cases may begin as a routine or normal incident.

The difficulty arises in operating the GSB system spontaneously when it develops from a 'normal' incident as it escalates and recognition grows of the need for appropriate management levels. These could be described as 'slow burn' or 'rising tide' incidents, a gradual escalation of an incident that falls between a full GSB response and a 'normal' response, see Figure 5.1. This is where effective coordination can fail. This is primarily an issue for the police, but understanding the process and the triggers that initiate the necessary management levels is important for any EPO from any background as it is this process that has such an impact and influence on the response overall. It is this period of uncertainty that can stall an effective and timely response.

Figure 5.1 Gradual Escalation of an Incident

5 Co-ordinating the Emergency Response

To explain this process it would be useful to look at this from the police perspective and how incident management should build and develop from a simple incident into a major incident and the thought processes that will inform the decision of the police to invoke the various levels on management. The implementation of these management levels can affect everyone with an emergency response responsibility. The key here is not to view GSB as a standalone off the shelf procedure that will solve all the complexity of major incident management. It must be fully integrated into daily activity and fully understood by all those with an emergency response role, in particular those in managerial or command roles.

To begin, consider how a problem is managed in everyday life and how decisions are made. When presented with a situation that requires a solution we initially think 'what is it I need to do to resolve this?' We weigh up our options, consider alternatives, we look at the implications of taking that course of action. Having decided what needs to be done by assessing all the options we then consider how we will achieve what we have decided to do. What methods are available to us, which are the best economically and practically? Having decided our preferred method, we then implement that by actually doing what needs to be done to resolve the situation.

In effect—we have been thinking strategically: what needs to be done? We have been thinking tactically: how I am going to achieve this? And finally we have been thinking operationally: doing it. Our decision making has comprised three components but we hardly think of it in those terms because it is so natural and intuitive. We have simply described the process of Gold, Silver, and Bronze.

So it can be seen that in normal circumstances the three components can easily be accommodated because the tasks faced are generally simple and not complex. In fact, in the majority of situations strategic and tactical thinking will be a small part of the overall activity, as we know what needs to be done and how we are going to do it. The bulk of the resolution is operational—doing it. It is hardly given a second thought.

But consider a situation in which the issues are more complicated and involve many people; impact upon many resources or the environment; have media implications or major financial implications—not quite so simple now! In this situation it may be necessary to separate out the components to be able to manage the situation effectively. It is simply too much to be dealt with by one person. The key to successful integration and usage of GSB is recognizing the need and the point at which to separate and invoke the levels of management as the situation directs. The implementation of GSB should be seamless and a logical progression based upon the needs of the situation. Management levels are dependent on complexity not the nature of the incident. Recalling the explanation of what is a 'major incident', it can be seen that a helicopter crash is a very unusual event but in many respects could be managed as a 'routine' incident, but how many times would a full GSB management structure be imposed for such an unusual event?

Task 5.1

Make a list of incidents that you would class as major incidents and unusual incidents. What is the distinction?

It is the consequences of the incident that matter not necessarily the cause. Incidents should be managed and decisions made at the lowest appropriate level, known as *subsidiarity*, in fact the CCA endorses this view in the guidance document *Emergency Response and Recovery (2005)* by saying 'co-ordination at the highest necessary level only'. In other words, the response and management levels must be proportionate to the incident. It must be remembered that GSB does not predetermine rank or status but acts as a descriptor of function where the Bronze or operational level is not seen as inferior, low status or low rank. It simply says 'I am operating and managing this incident at Bronze level—dealing with any Gold or Silver issues as they arise'. 'The Bronze or operational response will usually deal with most incidents or events'.[1]

Commanders

In these situations there seems to be a desire for some police officers to notionally appoint themselves as Silver or Gold Commanders, although they are detached or isolated from the incident and in many cases it is not required. Phrases like, 'I am the Gold Commander, if you want me I am at home' have no place in management. There can be no notional Commanders. Commanders need to be in their appropriate command positions at all times. It must also be remembered that unnecessary command or management structures will complicate, confuse and blur accountability.

Commanders are mentioned a great deal and in particular within command and control, but what does command mean in the context of co-ordination? Command is a term more often seen in organizations such as the police, fire, ambulance, and military services but it simply means 'management'. A Commander is a manager. The Fire and Rescue Service for example have removed all 'ranks' and replaced them with roles and managers, eg Crew Manager, Station Manager . Command is about people, and refers to people, those who manage, command, facilitate, or make decisions on behalf of their organization.

Control

Control on the other hand is about places or facilities to enable effective command or management to be administered. The Control Centres can be any location from where an organization will 'control' the incident (recall Chapter 3—Management Section). For the police it is usually police stations or other permanent locations usually operated by the police and they are there to facilitate and manage

---

[1] Civil Contingencies Act 2004. Emergency Response and Recovery, p 22.

co-ordination of both their own resources and that of response organizations. Specially constructed and adapted vehicles are termed 'command vehicles' but can be confused as 'Controls'. Command vehicles are just that—they are used by individual organizations to command their own resources. In the last chapter, reference was made to the Incident Control Post or ICP. It is arguable if a site based ICP can fulfil a multi-agency co-ordination role at operational level. Controls need to have support administration, space, seating, heating and communication for several organizations to use for multi-agency purposes. It is difficult to envisage a vehicle with that capacity. Therefore, many police forces have now designated fixed site Silver Controls at specific locations within their areas. In this way they are ready to open at short notice.

Controls support and service the needs of Commanders and Commanders should not become involved in their administration. They must be free agents to position themselves at the most appropriate location to manage the incident. The decision to open a police control centre will be made by the relevant police Commander in liaison with other agencies; this decision normally begins at the incident site where an ICP has been designated. Remember this may only be a vehicle with basic accommodation.

5.3 The Police Incident Officer (PIO)

In the previous chapter mention was made of the 'Incident Officer'. The term Police Incident Officer (PIO) is common throughout the police service and requires explanation within the context of GSB. The PIO represents the means by which co-ordination is achieved; in particular where it is not immediately obvious what management structure will be needed. The PIO becomes the focus and point of reference for all agencies responding at and around a scene of an incident. This applies to small scale incidents right up to major incidents. The PIO must be conspicuous, proactive and dynamic at the scene to provide that point of contact for responding agencies and ensure that co-ordination is begun at the earliest stage. It is the PIO who will make those first assessments and decisions in building an effective command and control structure.

The beginning of any incident will be attended by a police incident officer. They could be of any rank and if the incident remains low level and non complex that PIO will remain in place and conclude that incident without the need to escalate or invoke additional management levels, like GSB or seek more senior support.

On arrival at an incident the first police officer will make an assessment as we have already seen. From that point in time that officer is the PIO and will be assessing and reporting information and will begin liaison with any other agencies that are in attendance.

Co-ordination begins at that point. It is the responsibility of the police.

The PIO will continue assessing, making judgements, and liaising with other Incident Officers from the other services. It is from this process that a management

Figure 5.2 The Incident Officer

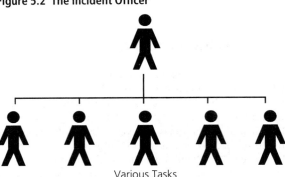

Various Tasks

Simple Low Level Incident

structure will emerge. That officer should make themselves readily identifiable as soon as possible, by wearing a PIO jacket or tabard. This may sound a little pedantic but without this identification other services will not know who they should be speaking to and co-ordination breaks down. The PIO can change from person to person as more senior or experienced officers arrive on scene but this must be logged. The PIO will begin to invoke the necessary level of management. Initially, the PIO will be dealing with all aspects of the incident at GSB combined. However, there may come a point, which could be immediate, that the PIO declares that there is a need for a Silver level of Command and Co-ordination.

The issues that would affect that decision could include:

1. If a Major Incident is declared.
2. If multi-agency co-ordination is required.
3. If there is a need for significant additional resources.

5.3.1 **Police Silver Commander**

Having made that decision to invoke the next management level, the PIO will assume the role of Police Silver Commander and begin to designate and delegate tasks to others who now occupy the Bronze management level through one or more Bronze Commanders. In terms of a fixed incident scene, the police Silver Commander should remain with the scene and in liaison with other services.

The police Silver Commander will summon resources to the scene, which may include the support of a command vehicle to assist them in scene management and communication. This vehicle could well become the ICP or indeed another emergency service vehicle may be used. The police Silver Commander may also call for the establishment of a multi-agency Silver control to support them and facilitate multi-agency co-ordination.

So where will the police Silver Commander go if they open a Silver control?

5 Co-ordinating the Emergency Response

The Silver Commander should remain where the incident scene is fixed. If the scene is widespread (eg flooding or a moving toxic cloud) it may be more appropriate for them to move to another location or into police Silver control. To manage the Silver control, a Silver control co-ordinator will be appointed by the Silver Commander or another senior officer to administer and manage the control. The Commander should be free to command. When the Silver control is operating it will require support and attendance from other services. These will be liaison officers from those organizations and not designated Commanders who will be too involved in managing the incident scene.

To recap, at this stage there is a Silver Commander and bronze Commanders in place. Co-ordination is active through on-scene liaison meetings with Bronze and Silver Commanders at the ICP, supported by a multi-agency Silver control, managed by a police Silver co-ordinator.

As the event develops and circumstances change, the police Silver Commander may accept direction from senior officers or make a judgement and recommendation that a Gold level of management is required.

Again, this decision is informed by liaison with other agencies and senior officers recognizing a need to separate out the Gold elements. Issues that would be considered in informing that decision may include:

1. Multi-agency Silver control being opened?
2. It is a Major Incident?
3. The incident is large scale and highly complex?
4. There are multiple sites?
5. Are there multiple Silver Commanders (see later)?
6. Co-ordination of a tactical response is required. That is the introduction of additional Silver Commanders to deal with specialist issues such as the identification of the dead or the investigation.
7. Regional or national impact?

8. Significant policy decisions to be made?
9. Potential major expenditure?
10. Necessary to agree a policy framework with other agencies?
11. High profile media reaction?

A full command structure is illustrated in Figure 5.4.

5.4 **Activating Management Levels**

The activation and implementation of the correct management structure is determined by need. It is managed at the lowest appropriate level. In a spontaneous, unplanned incident the management structure will grow, sometimes almost instantaneously. At other times it will grow very slowly as the facts emerge, perhaps as result of a 'slow burn' or 'rising tide' event. The incident management structure will plateau at some point within the incident response. The diagram Figure 5.3 below illustrates this by comparing different types of incident and the management development. Some incidents are rapid on-set and some are slow, breaching the management thresholds if necessary.

Task 5.2

Consider sudden impact or rising tide incidents and make a list of five scenarios for each.

What is it about each incident that would define it as such?

It will be noticed that some incidents remain in the Bronze region and co-ordinated by the Police Incident Officer without recourse to implementation of a formal GSB management structure. On the other hand some incidents will rapidly reach beyond Gold requiring regional co-ordination. In the example it is terrorist-related but could be a nuclear event.

5 Co-ordinating the Emergency Response

Figure 5.3 Response Curve

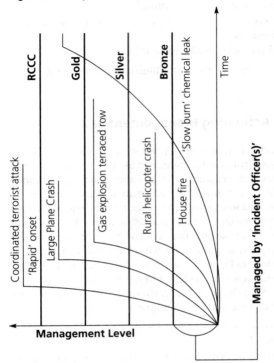

5.5 **Strategic Co-ordination Centre**

When Gold Control—or the Strategic Co-ordination Centre (SCC) as it is correctly known—is opened, the Police Gold Commander will chair multi-agency Strategic Co-ordinating Group (SCG) meetings. The SCG will agree policy and strategy and will delegate that for implementation by Silver Commanders. All management staff in police control centres should be identifiable by tabards displaying their role within the centre. This simple requirement is important for those attending the SCC, who may be unfamiliar with the key staff running the centre.

The SCC is a strategic 'co-ordination' centre. Note the word co-ordination is emphasized. Each participating agency will have its own 'strategy' which may have been agreed within their own organization but the role of the SCG is to co-ordinate those strategies by agreeing to accept, modify or re-configure them, if necessary, in the light of the collective aims and objectives to achieve the most effective response. The SCG will address the 'what we have to do' questions. That decision making process can legitimately contain elements of tactical functioning in offering advice on 'how we achieve what we have to do'. But there must be a clear separation. Typically, an SCC will appear serene and slow moving, with deliberation and due consideration. Whereas, a Silver Control will appear to be dynamic, fast moving but controlled.

An important issue to remember is that control centres facilitate two crucial activities within the management process. Firstly, it is a decision making forum and secondly it is an information processing facility. The two must not become confused. Commanders and senior managers must not become embroiled in administration and in practical information processing. To do so would distract the Commander or senior manager from decision making. To that end a Gold Commander will normally nominate a Gold Control Co-ordinator to take responsibility for information processing, analysis, briefing and communication. This will ensure that Commanders and senior managers are free agents able to concentrate on key decisions.

5.5.1 **Multiple Silvers?**

In as much as there can be several police Bronze Commanders or operational functions operating together to achieve a common objective there may be multiple police Silver Commanders. This is not a concept universally accepted. Some management structures prefer instead to have one Silver Commander supported by Bronze Commanders managing all other functions.

However, some of the functions now required in major incident management extend beyond operational capability in terms of resourcing, so a Silver Commander level is justified. For example:

1. Senior Investigating Officer (SIO)
2. Senior Identification Manager (SIM).

Indeed, in a widespread event with multiple sites, a separate Silver Commander for each site may be essential. For example, separate townships, separate terrorist incident sites, or flooding sites. This is where a Gold Commander is essential to co-ordinate their efforts and make decisions relating to the allocation of resources. These would be police command meetings which would not involve other agencies per se.

5.5.2 **Two essential SCC sub-groups**

A recently introduced feature of the SCC, brought about by the Buncefield Oil depot fire in Hertfordshire in 2005, was the introduction of the Scientific and Technical Advice Cell (STAC) to ensure timely co-ordinated scientific and technical advice during the response to an emergency.

Figure 5.4 Police Basic Full Command Structure

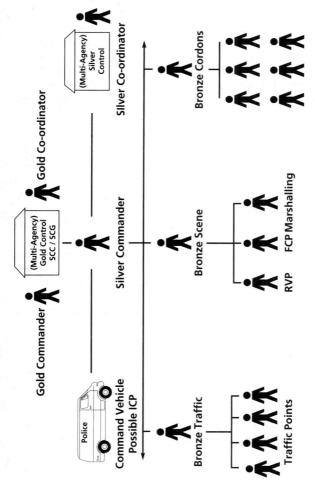

5 Co-ordinating the Emergency Response

The Scientific and Technical Advice Cell (STAC)

The STAC should be formed as a standing sub-group to offer advice to the Strategic Co-ordinating Group (SCG) when required. The SCG will also need to identify a designated STAC lead and who would co-ordinate the work of the STAC when activated. The STAC should bring together technical experts from those agencies involved in the response and who may provide scientific and technical advice to the Gold Commander on issues such as the impact on the health of the population, public safety, environmental protection, and sampling and monitoring of any contaminants. The purpose of the cell would be to ensure that, as far as possible, scientific or technical debate was contained within the cell so that the SCG (and others involved in the response) receive the best possible advice based on the available information in a timely, co-ordinated and understandable way. To that end there is no 'ideal' STAC. Each STAC will be configured to address the hazards presented. Given that a number of agencies will be involved in the response, the STAC lead and the SCG should identify the core membership of the STAC, as well as any other membership that may be required on an ad-hoc basis. To ensure the effective working of the cell, membership and attendance should be strictly controlled by the cell lead.

Task 5.3

Can you list ten situations where a STAC would be useful?

The term 'return to normality' is sometimes used to describe recovery, which is never the case. The impact and consequences of any significant incident will result in change at some level. During the emergency response phase to any incident it is important to consider the longer term recovery issues. These issues could involve impact on a business, the environment and health or welfare of a community. Decisions made during the emergency response could create longer term problems during the recovery phase if not thoroughly thought through. It is therefore crucial for all stakeholders to be at the heart of that decision making process to have influence on how both the emergency phase and recovery phase are managed.

Recovery Working Group (RWG)

To that end, the SCG under the lead of the police will usually call for and create a Recovery Working Group or RWG. This group is normally chaired by the local authority in whose area the incident takes place. It operates at the same time as the SCG and STAC and will consider the implications of dynamic decisions on future issues and advise the SCG accordingly.

The RWG will also provide that continuity link when the emergency phase has passed and the lead is formally handed over to the local authority to manage by the SCG/Police Commander. The RWG will become the focal point to activate all the resources and support that can be obtained locally, nationally and internationally to mitigate the effects of the incident. Appropriate grants, funding and aid will be sought using central government support.

Recovery management is as much of a challenge as responding to the emergency itself. For example, in flooding situations the recovery phase represents a larger scale operation than the response phase and will take years. The impact on communities is devastating. The decontamination alone will disrupt communities, the environment and business. Strategies will need to be carefully integrated and co-ordinated to ensure the most effective and rapid means of bringing relief to those affected by the incident.

5.6 **Regional and National Co-ordination**

The CCA introduced additional layers of resilience management to ensure better communication and co-ordination at both Regional and National level. This facility was introduced by the establishment of Regional Resilience Teams working from Regional Government Offices.

Task 5.4

Consider the role and function of the regional tier of co-ordination through the RRF/RRT and the RCCC. Refer to the CCA guidance. Can you think of five situations in which their co-ordination would be needed?

5.6.1 **Role of Government Offices**

The Government Offices (GOs) provide a link to central government during a non-terrorist emergency and may be the first place that government departments turn to for situation reports on non-terrorist incidents. The GOs are likely, therefore, to have a role to play in most emergencies that could generate ministerial interest or national/regional press coverage.

The underpinning principle in major incident management in the UK is that it is dealt with locally under the auspices of a Chief Officer of police who has overall responsibility. GOs will only become involved if they can contribute and support the response. Gathering information to brief the centre may be a key role for them. However, the greater the significance of the incident, and the press and ministerial interest, the more the GOs will be able to provide support and assistance. They should be made aware of significant incidents in a liaison capacity. Therefore local plans should have a Task or action to alert the GO/RRT (see below) of any significant incidents.

5.6.2 **Regional Resilience Teams (RRT)**

A Regional Resilience Team (RRT) has been established in each of the GOs to co-ordinate the response of the whole government office. These small teams are the first point of contact in GO areas for any resilience issues.

The GOs may need to be represented at Strategic Co-ordination Centres (SCCs) to ensure links to regional and central government are maintained so a member of the RRT may undertake this role.

5.6.3 Regional Civil Contingencies Committee (RCCC)

With the introduction of the Civil Contingencies Act 2004, the concept of a Regional Civil Contingencies Committee (RCCC) was introduced to provide a regional level of co-ordination to incidents where the local level experienced difficulty in managing the incident(s) or where the incident crossed over local boundaries and a degree of regional co-ordination was required.

An RCCC, made up of agency representatives of emergency services, local authorities, the government office and others as applicable from across the region will be charged with improving the co-ordination of the response to an emergency across a region with a particular, but not exclusive, focus on consequence management and the recovery phase after an incident. The RCCC response to an incident is another option available to central government and local responders to be used where it can add value.

Checklist—The role of the RCCC

This is likely to vary depending on the nature of the incident, however it is likely to include:

1. collating and maintaining a strategic picture of the evolving situation within the region, with particular, but not exclusive, focus on consequence management and recovery issues
2. assessing whether there are any issues that cannot be resolved at local level
3. facilitating mutual aid arrangements within the region and, where necessary, between regions to resolve such issues

---

4. ensuring an effective flow of communication between local, regional and national levels, including the co-ordination of reports to the national level on the response and recovery effort

5. raising, to a national level, any issues that cannot be resolved at local and regional level

6. ensuring the national input to response and recovery is co-ordinated with the local and regional efforts

7. guiding the deployment of scarce resources across the region by identifying regional priorities

8. providing, where appropriate, a regional spokesperson.

One important issue must be made clear and that is the relationship between the Chief Officers of Police and the regional co-ordination function. The emergency response is driven locally under the general co-ordination of the police with the delegated authority of the Chief Constable who holds responsibility for policing in each police force area. This raises the question of who is in charge of a regional emergency. The answer is that the individual Chief Police Officers retain responsibility and authority in their jurisdiction but liaise closely with each other using the Regional Civil Contingencies Committee (RCCC) to act as a co-ordinating instrument. The RCCC holds no additional authority or direction over Chief Police Officers. Sometimes the term 'Platinum' is used to describe this regional contribution. Clearly this is misleading as it infers authority or direction.

The RCCC will not interfere with local command and control arrangements, unless specifically empowered to do so by Emergency Regulations giving emergency powers. The role of the RCCC is to add value to the response, usually where there is more than one SCG operating and there is a need to co-ordinate.

Therefore the Act created a structure intended and designed to mobilize the combined resources of the nation in support of the local response to any scale of event.

KEY POINT

Emergency powers

The Civil Contingencies Act 2004 updated the Emergency Powers Act 1920. Only in extreme circumstances will emergency powers be invoked by the Government. It involves the making of temporary legislation to apply across the UK or to any of the English regions or devolved administrations under the control of a Regional Nominated Co-ordinator, or in the case of devolved administrations an Emergency Co-ordinator.

5.7 **Lead Government Departments**

In terms of co-ordination beyond the regional level, there may be cases where the nature and size of event requires central government support. It must be emphasized that this function is not intended to take away the main focus of the response which will always remain local, but it is rather to add support and assistance in delivering the most effective means of managing the incident.

The Government has created a list of Lead Government Departments (LGD) to oversee this co-ordination function depending on the nature of the emergency. By default the Civil Contingencies Secretariat will facilitate the activation of the appropriate LGD or indeed take the lead themselves in certain cases. The list containing the main LGDs is shown in Figure 5.5.

The process of invoking central government support and/or co-ordination will normally route through the Regional Government office's Regional Resilience Teams (RRT). Upon opening of an SCC/SCG the appropriate RRT should be notified, not least because they sit within the local LRF. They in turn will notify central government via the Civil Contingencies Secretariat (CCS), who will in turn assess the need to facilitate the activation of the appropriate LGD or

---

5 Co-ordinating the Emergency Response

Figure 5.5 Lead Government Departments

Emergency	England	Wales
Any—will then be passed onto relevant LGD.	Initial and immediate lead is the Cabinet Office Civil Contingencies Secretariat (CCS)	The HR (Facilities and Emergencies) Division of the Welsh Assembly Government (WAG)
Flooding	Department for Environment, Food and Rural Affairs (Defra)	Dept. for Environment, Planning and Countryside (DEPC) of WAG
Radiation (Civil)	Department for Business, Enterprise and Regulatory Reform (BERR)	BERR in consultation with (DEPC)
Radiation (Terrorist)	Home Office	Home Office
Radiation (Military)	Ministry of Defence (MOD)	MOD and supported by HR (Facilities and Emergencies) Division of WAG
Radiation (Civil Transport)	Department for Transport (DfT)	DfT and supported by HR (Facilities and Emergencies) Division of WAG
Hazardous Materials (non-terrorist)	CCS would lead and determine the most appropriate LGD	HR (Facilities and Emergencies) Division of WAG
Offshore Installations	Health and Safety Executive in the Department for Work and Pensions (DWP)	As England
Search and Rescue (Civil)	Department for Transport Maritime and Coastguard Agency	As England
Search and Rescue (Military)	MOD	As England

Figure 5.5 Lead Government Departments (cont.)

Emergency	England	Wales
Storms / Weather	DfT–Transport BERR–Power Supply Flooding–Defra Building–Department for Communities and Local Government (DCLG)	Department for Economic Development and Transport (DEDT) of the WAG–Transport BERR–Power Supply DEPC of WAG–Flooding DEPC of WAG–Building
Transport Accidents	At sea–DfT (MCA) On land–DfT	At sea–DfT (MCA) On land––DEDT
Dam Failure	Defra	DEPC
Animal Disease	Defra	DEPC supported by Defra
Food Contamination	Food Standards Agency (FSA)	FSA in Wales
Infectious Disease	Department of Health (DoH) supported by Health Protection Agency (HPA)	Office of Chief Medical Officer (CMO) supported by Public Health Laboratories Service

---

Task 5.5

For the following incidents which would be the LGD and the local co-ordination lead?

1. Outbreak of smallpox
2. Civil nuclear accident
3. Falling satellite
4. Reservoir breach
5. US Military aircraft crash

Task 5.6

Can you think how existing legislation may be changed in an emergency?

For example, long distance drivers' hours may be relaxed to allow more food to be transported.

5 Co-ordinating the Emergency Response

Figure 5.6 National Co-ordination

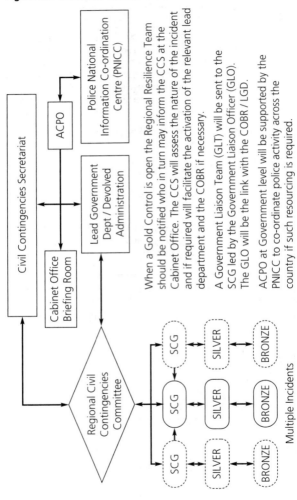

When a Gold Control is open the Regional Resilience Team should be notified who in turn may inform the CCS at the Cabinet Office. The CCS will assess the nature of the incident and if required will facilitate the activation of the relevant lead department and the COBR if necessary.

A Government Liaison Team (GLT) will be sent to the SCG led by the Government Liaison Officer (GLO). The GLO will be the link with the COBR / LGD.

ACPO at Government level will be supported by the PNICC to co-ordinate police activity across the country if such resourcing is required.

equivalent devolved administration facility or indeed lead the co-ordination themselves.

In some cases of national emergency or indeed where a number of LGDs are operating, the government may convene their crisis management facility known as COBR or Cabinet Office Briefing Room. That committee will be chaired by the Prime Minister, Home Secretary, or a senior government minister.

Within that group will sit key stakeholders and LGD representatives. ACPO will usually be present representing the police service and have at their disposal the Police National Information Co-ordination Centre or PNICC to assist in co-ordinating information and resources of the police nationally.

If the government become involved in co-ordinating centrally they will also become responsible for the national communications strategy. This communications strategy will be co-ordinated with the local responders via the SCG and MBC. The National Co-ordination Centre (NCC) will be activated to drive national media communication. The Home Office may also take the lead in managing a government Media Centre to deal with terrorist type incidents or a LGD for non terrorist incidents. The NCC will co-ordinate media appearances of ministers.

Another function of the Cabinet Office is the lead with regard to warning and informing the public where local arrangements would prove insufficient or in effective. The diagram shown at Figure 5.6 illustrates the framework of national emergency management.

5.8 **Managing within the SCC/SCG— Recording and Sharing Information**

The Control Centre(s) at all levels and across all response organizations will be pivotal in managing emergency response. To that end, capturing and recording information and processing that information is the fuel that drives the response engine. There will have to be a system in place to record, assess and disseminate that information. All control centres will need a system to record messages. That can be a simple paper message form or a sophisticated computer-based system. But remember that no matter how good the IT system is, a paper backup is essential.

This area cannot be overstated. All decision making must be recorded together with telephone messages and indeed any verbal exchanges that are relevant. Documentation will be scrutinized at any follow-up inquiry and everything is subject to disclosure, which means all documents and computer records may be seized and used in evidence in some circumstances—assume it will be. Remember—"Preserve and Protect" all documentation. A clearly defined audit trail must exist.

Paper flow and logging systems adopted within control centres must be tested and understood by all staff designated to perform roles within the room, which may also include advising other multi-agency staff.

The ability of agencies within a control centre to communicate, exchange, share and record critical information is vital for the successful management of an incident. CCs must have in place a robust system to ensure effective information exchange is achieved between all participants. The system must be:

1. reliable
2. secure from external hacking
3. capable of identifying the inputter
4. easy to use
5. capable of reproduction into hard copy
6. tamper-proof.

The system can be electronic but must have a back up in cases of IT failure.

A simple example of a paper message form is shown in Figure 5.7, together with instructions how to use it shown at Figure 5.8 and a paper flow chart shown at Figure 5.9, which again can be adapted to suit individual needs. Ideally, it should be produced in pads and on self-carbonating paper. The suggested colours are white, blue, and yellow which is the scheme used in the example.

These forms can make the basis for a messaging system in any Control Centre. They can be used as the primary means of processing information or as the back-up should an electronic system already be in place.

5.8.1 **What should be recorded?**

What is committed to a messaging system for sharing is a matter of professional judgement for the individual and will be aided by appropriate training and familiarization sessions. But it is better to encourage participants to input information than not to. It must always be remembered that in the context of an inquiry 'if it is not written down it never happened'. It must also be remembered that many inquiries are years after the event.

External agencies using electronic information sharing systems must ensure that they are secure as far as reasonably possible and data protection issues are addressed. For example, personal information relating to the deceased and injured must be managed in compliance with regulations. In addition these systems must not undermine the role of the police in terms of investigation, acting on behalf of the coroner or where circumstances direct the use of police family liaison officers (FLOs) and social service crisis support teams, who will be working closely with families affected by the incident. If attending a police control centre, message management systems will be in place for everyone to use. Although the police cannot force anyone to support or commit to such a system of recording messages or information, it must be remembered that it will not be the police who are stood up in court or public inquiry if someone failed to record vital information—it will be them!

5 Co-ordinating the Emergency Response

> **Task 5.7**
>
> List five reasons why recording information within a control centre is good practice.

> **Task 5.8**
>
> Using the format and information above, can you think of a format and prepare a system that would better suit your organization?

5.8.2 Crisis meetings

Meetings will be specifically convened to address certain areas of management. This can be from combined multi-agency meetings at low level to deal with operational, tactical and some strategic issues, to separate meetings set up to deal with strategic issues only such as at the Strategic Co-ordinating Group and using tactical and operational meetings to implement the direction from Gold.

Every control centre will conduct meetings of key responders within the organization and/or outside the organization to agree response options, be it strategic, tactical or operational. Effectively chairing these meetings is vital to a successful outcome. At whatever level these meetings take place, the same principles apply and that can be Strategic or Tactical Co-ordinating Group meetings or operational meetings. It should be borne in mind that crisis meetings differ from the type of meeting that most people will be familiar with in day-to-day business. These 'normal' meetings tend to be consensus management meetings as opposed to crisis management meetings. That said, it does not mean that a crisis meeting goes forward without consensus but the crisis meeting requires firm structure and discipline. After all, the issues on the table will require quick decisions, often under stressful conditions with clearly defined aims and objectives within a group who may have never met before. So how is such a meeting started?

Figure 5.7 Message Form

INFORMATION/ ACTION / MESSAGE FORM

Information Source (Tick)

NUMBER

☐ Phone in	From: Time (24 hour) and Date
☐ Fax	Organization:
	Contact No
☐ e-mail	
☐ Verbal	To: Senior Management (Tick) ☐
☐ Self	Others:

INFORMATION / ACTION / MESSAGE - Use Ball Pen

(Use continuation sheet if necessary)

Recipient Response

Time (24 hour) Date received   Received By.......................................

☐ Acknowledge only (Tick)

ACTION TAKEN

RESULT OF ACTION - IF APPROPRIATE

Return this yellow copy to the Information Manager

Completed ....Information Manager

5 Co-ordinating the Emergency Response

Figure 5.8 Information Management System

- INCOMING telephone or fax messages to the Emergency Control Centre for an action and / or passing information must be recorded on an INFORMATION FORM for central logging.

- OUTGOING messages for central logging must be recorded on an INFORMATION FORM.

- INTERNAL communication need only be recorded on the INFORMATION FORM if the information is required OR necessary for central logging.

- The message must be completed accurately and contain sufficient detail to inform the recipient exactly what is required, or what information is being passed on. One action or piece of information - one form, please.

- Complete the three copies; BLUE, YELLOW and WHITE, they are self-carbonated.

- All three copies will be taken to the INFORMATION MANAGER. The Information Manager will check that the form is fully and correctly completed. A unique number will then be issued by the Information Manager from a simple matrix of numbers.

- The BLUE form will be immediately returned initialled and endorsed by the Information Manager, to the originating organization or person. The BLUE form will be retained by the organization themselves which will act as a receipt.

- The YELLOW form, duly endorsed, by both the originating organization or person and Information Manager, will be passed to the relevant recipient where there is a need to know the information contained in the information or to take appropriate action. This will be carried out by a clerk / runner.

- The Information Manager will pass the white copy to the senior management loggist for recording on the master log, who will then hold it in a General Pending tray.

  NOTE: If one message requires attention by more than one recipient, sufficient YELLOW photocopies will be made by the clerk / runner (YELLOW paper should be available).

- The recipient willl endorse and acknowledge the YELLOW copy and indicate what action has been taken. This will be entered as an 'ACTION' and initialled. The YELLOW copy must be returned to the Information Manager without unnecessary delay.

Figure 5.8 Information Management System (*cont.*)

- The Information Manager will examine the YELLOW copy to ensure it has been actioned and pass it to the senior management loggist who will record any new information from it onto the master log.

- The senior management loggist will then attach the YELLOW copy to the white copy from the general pending tray and place both forms in a file dedicated to the originating organization.

The chair at the first meeting will introduce themselves and explain the purpose of the meeting. A draft set of terms of reference (TOR) will be agreed which will set out the aim of the group and the key objectives. This will set the framework and parameters for the meetings and the TOR should be given to all those taking part. The chair must also be clear about the management of the meetings, timing, how they will be run—basically the rules. Discipline needs to be maintained to ensure the meetings are on time and remain focused at all times.

An interesting feature of multi-agency meetings is the coming together of different organizational cultures. This can have a significant effect, sometimes adversely, on decision making and is often overlooked in particular by those who are not aware of this potential obstacle. Such interaction can result in conflict and tension as competing priorities and different agendas come together for co-ordination. Each organization attending a meeting will bring with them a set of values and expectations of how 'business' will be done and if the meetings are police led or in police facilities for example it can be a daunting prospect for those not used to it. Blue light organizations tend to be more accustomed to crisis management and perhaps project a style that can be perceived as mildly intimidating and can prevent some of those present from being as participative as they would like to be. The result is a decision making process that can be stifled and inhibited. Group dynamics can play an important part in effective decision making and being aware of the potential pitfalls can offset or mitigate the effects.

5 Co-ordinating the Emergency Response

Figure 5.9 Message Flow Chart

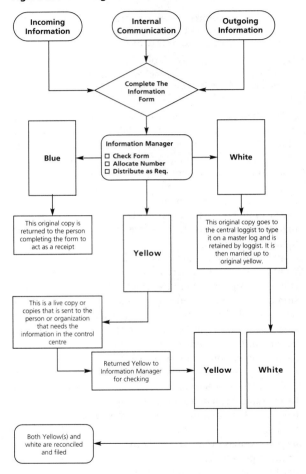

Professor Irving Janis has written extensively on a phenomenon known as 'Groupthink'.

> Groupthink is a type of thought exhibited by group members who try to minimize conflict and reach consensus without critically testing, analysing, and evaluating ideas. During groupthink, members of the group avoid promoting viewpoints outside the comfort zone of consensus thinking. A variety of motives for this exist such as a desire to avoid being seen as foolish, or a desire to avoid embarrassing or angering other members of the group. Groupthink may cause groups to make hasty, irrational decisions, where individual doubts are set aside, for fear of upsetting the group's balance.[2]

In other words, some groups, in order to preserve a sense of unity and conformity within the group will sacrifice their objectivity and criticism, often unconsciously.

This syndrome can relate to any group with common values, similar ethos and status. It predominantly relates to highly cohesive groups with a strong identity and bond, in particular where there is a disciplined and well ordered hierarchy, where the tendency is to default to conformity. To that group should be added the police but they should not be singled out, but simply acknowledge that it is they who occupy the chair when it comes to co-ordination. It must also be added at this point that group cohesion will not inevitably lead to groupthink but it is a necessary condition and one to be aware of and watch out for. According to Janis[3] there are symptoms to look for:

1. Illusions of invulnerability creating excessive optimism and encouraging risk taking.
2. Rationalizing warnings that might challenge the group's assumption.

---

[2] I Janis (1996) 'The Risk Dilemma' in H Kunreuther and P Slovic (eds) *Challenges in Risk Assessment and Risk Management* (London: Sage).
[3] Ibid.

3. Unquestioned belief in the morality of the group, causing members to ignore the consequences of their actions.
4. Stereotyping those who are opposed to the group as weak or stupid.
5. Direct pressure to conform placed on any member who questions the group, couched in terms of 'disloyalty'.
6. Self-censorship of ideas that deviate from the apparent group consensus.
7. Illusions of unanimity among group members, silence is viewed as agreement.
8. Mindguards—self-appointed members who shield the group from dissenting information.

Task 5.9

Take a few minutes to consider the above. How many times have you witnessed one or more of these conditions?

Janis[4] went on to suggest a number of ways to avoid group-think. It is not suggested all should be implemented but consideration of a combination may avoid the development of groupthink.

1. Leaders should assign each member the role of 'critical evaluator'. This allows each member to freely air objections and doubts. *This should be explicit at the beginning of the meeting.*
2. Senior managers should not express an opinion when assigning a task to a group. *Doing this at the beginning can adversely influence the task.*
3. The organization should set up several independent groups, working on the same problem. *Doing this can break up cohesion and obtain independent views on the same issues.*
4. All effective alternatives should be examined. *No issue should be disregarded if raised.*

---

[4] Ibid, pp 209–215.

---

5. Each member should discuss the group's ideas with trusted people outside the group. *Taking issues back into the organization to seek advice and opinion.*
6. The group should invite outside experts into meetings. Group members should be allowed to discuss with and question the outside experts. *If possible experts who can add value through knowledge should be used to evaluate the group's assumptions.*
7. At least one group member should be assigned the role of Devil's advocate. This should be a different person for each meeting. *This is an important one and probably the one we see most often. How many times have we derided or become impatient with a fellow member because they seem to have opinions or ideas that we perceive as simply outrageous? Every healthy group needs one!*

Recent commentators have claimed that Janis's theory has been underestimated. Be aware and account for it!

Another tactic to avoid groupthink would be to loosen tightly cohesive groupings by promoting regular and structured multi-agency interaction. This is best achieved by joint training and exercising where organizations can begin to understand and appreciate the views of others. In that way the symptoms as described by Janis will diminish and become defuse as relationships develop between organizations and agencies. Organizations, within the emergency planning community who continue to ignore or even acknowledge the importance of multi-agency working will become susceptible and vulnerable to groupthink as they become more isolated. All organizations must feel confident and comfortable to be able to express their views and opinions that may not always concur with the group consensus in a multi-agency context.

5.8.3 **Running meetings**

In terms of running meetings always ensure that they are 'minuted' and if possible tape recorded. A common error with such meetings is that they are too long. Regular, short, focused meetings of no more than 30 minutes every two hours are ideal. The chair will need to address the following:

1. Ask everyone present to give a short summary of issues currently affecting them, or requiring urgent action, including any other agencies if they are present, including the police.
2. Establish common objectives. Address any conflicts and co-ordinate effort. Identify any actions—be explicit and identify where the action lies. Write it down on a board.
3. What are the medium and longer term issues that can reasonably be foreseen? Try to anticipate—what provisions have to be made to address those issues. Resourcing is a key issue—management resilience.
4. Ensure that media considerations are addressed and agree a media strategy—remember that the police will co-ordinate the media but you have a say how the media will be managed, eg how press releases, interviews, and conferences will be approached. Be explicit as to the parameters as to your media requirements without compromising the police objectives. Push for an early press release.

5.8.4 Resourcing police controls (agencies)

When the police open control centres there is an expectation that other agencies can fully support them. That also includes an obligation upon the police who may be required to position a liaison officer in other control centres operated by other organizations and agencies. This is part of the overall co-ordination and liaison arrangements. The first planning consideration is, 'can that commitment be resourced?' Have personnel been identified in the planning process? If operating a single Silver Control and Gold Control (SCC) agencies, may have to provide two representatives 24/7 as a minimum—a significant undertaking.

The police will as a matter of priority set up a logistical cell in an SCC to manage staff and resourcing.

For agencies attending police control centres it can be a daunting prospect and that can sometimes be overlooked by the centre staff. Police staff must try to ensure that agencies attending are afforded full support. That will include providing them with appropriate parking, efficient and courteous reception arrangements. To have agency colleagues without parking, in particular when carrying equipment, or being kept waiting is unacceptable.

Agency colleagues require efficient reception and briefing procedures upon arrival and afforded comfortable surrounding within which to work. This also applies to any liaison officer or manager attending any control centre, be it police or any other organization.

5.8.5 **Criminal liability**

Another important issue in particular for non emergency response personnel, for example company representatives attending control centres, is an ever increasing concern relating to their potential criminal liability and therefore their ability to participate. Although this may sound strange, in many circumstances where there are fatalities, a company representative connected to the incident in a police control centre may feel or perceive themselves to be treated a little like a suspect or feeling not as inclusive within the management process as they would expect. This can result from situations where the company representative is excluded from certain meetings or conversations seem a little 'guarded' with them. Why is this? In the early stages of an incident there may be potential issues related to criminal culpability, which will focus on the companies involved, for example a transport or industrial processes. It could be argued that such companies may compromise the inquiry and/or incriminate themselves in any future proceedings. This has to be expected but can be managed.

First, let's deal with the issue of potentially compromising any inquiry. The priority in all cases is to save life and prevent further distress and injury to those involved. If using the knowledge and experience of a company representative to alleviate or reduce that, there is little reason to exclude them at all, indeed it would be difficult to defend.

In addition, compromise will only result from issues relating to the cause of the incident resulting in the fatality, injury or other consequence, so avoiding comments or opinions on that subject should avoid any compromise. Addressing the consequences is the key and if the company representative feels at any time that they are being excluded they should challenge this and seek a clear explanation for that behaviour and make a note of what was said and by whom. On the other hand can a company representative incriminate themselves?

The answer is potentially yes. It is possible that a company may be criminally culpable and anything said 'can be taken down and used in evidence' to coin a phrase. But again if that is the case, the company still has a responsibility to offer assistance to reduce the impact on those involved and indeed to be seen to be assisting. This could be ultimately critical to the company survival after the incident notwithstanding they may face criminal charges. Again, the key here is to avoid becoming involved in answering incriminating or compromising questions. They should focus on the here and now and managing consequences and avoid references to what caused the incident or any procedure leading to the incident. There are no failsafe rules as to what can or cannot be said but a little foresight and commonsense should be applied. There are specialist advisors and trainers who can assist in training company personnel on these issues.

Task 5.10

Reflect on some of the issues that may face an industry representative attending a police control and write down what they are.

5.9 **Co-ordination—Putting it All Together**

Understanding emergency management co-ordination is vital to every EPO from whatever background. It is the basis upon which all response is configured and therefore plans are prepared to integrate fully into that system.

Finally, to conclude this chapter and to illustrate the initial co-ordination processes, an example scenario has been chosen to illustrate how a management structure will emerge from a routine incident.

A police officer is out on routine patrol on a 'normal' day going about their duties dealing with incidents, making decisions and resolving situations. Remember the simple decision making example earlier, dealing with the three components, GSB and finding the solutions within the scope of our experience and knowledge.

The officer is called to a small car fire on a garage forecourt and the fire and rescue service is already present and there are no injuries reported. The officer, has spoken to the Fire Incident Officer (Crew Manager) and there appears to be no complicating factors, quite routine. The officer decides what needs to be done and that is to protect the public by keeping them away and manage nearby traffic congestion whilst the fire service deals with the matter. The police officer knows how to do that and is able to do it alone. The police officer is the police Incident Officer and effectively operating at strategic, tactical and operational management levels. Remember, that GSB is not rank but role orientated. They can do this because the situation is simple and 'manageable'.

Suddenly the owner of the car returns to the garage clearly upset that his car is on fire and informs the police officer that there are three oxyacetylene cylinders in the boot of the car. On hearing this information the Fire Incident Officer (Crew Manager) orders a 400 metre cordon around the car and the immediate evacuation of all those in and around the garage. The police officer immediately recognizes the need for more resources to carry this out and the need to pass this information to the media because of the potential traffic congestion this will cause, the potential damage should the cylinders explode and to warn the public to keep away.

The officer calls for support and immediately directs arriving colleagues to a safe Rendezvous Point (see Scene Management and Figure 4.5) and assigns various tasks to fellow officers to assist in evacuation and traffic management. The police officer retains regular communication with the Fire Incident Officer (Crew Manager) at an agreed Forward Control Point and they decide there is a need for an ambulance on standby in case of injuries. The ambulance service is told to send their ambulance to a Marshalling Area which has been agreed by the police officer and Fire Incident Officer. The police officer knows what to do and how to do it and is co-ordinating the incident effectively but it becomes apparent that they are unable to actually carry out all the operational tasks.

The officer decides that it is necessary to become solely 'tactical' to focus upon how the situation needs to be managed. The officer is also satisfied that the strategic elements are within their scope and understanding, which senior colleagues are now aware and agree. The officer now declares and assumes Silver Commander and delegates operational tasks to other officers via a Bronze Commander. For example Bronze cordons (400m), Bronze traffic management and Bronze evacuation. In this situation the Silver Command function is discharged from the scene, as it is the most effective location to co-ordinate the scene. The officer uses the police patrol vehicle as the initial Incident Control Post (ICP) at a safe location away from the garage.

There is no strategic level of management at this time. The current Silver Commander is joined and replaced by a more senior officer who formally takes command. The previous Silver Commander remains as the new Silver Commander's staff officer. The Silver Commander is dealing with any strategic elements at this time. The situation is now consolidated and effective cordoning and traffic management in place. The officer has directed that a Silver Control Room is opened at the police station to assist in tasking and management. The Silver Commander asks for a Silver Co-ordinator to be designated to manage the Silver Control and that all relevant agencies are made aware of Silver Control being open and requesting agency liaison officers to attend there as soon as possible.

As the driver of the car is spoken to by the police it becomes apparent that the driver can offer no reasonable explanation as to why the cylinders were in the boot. Further enquires reveal that the driver is suspected of association with known terrorist groups and the car may be in the process of being made ready for use in a terrorist act. At this point the implications of this development would direct the Silver Commander to consider the need for a Strategic level of management or command. To assist them in making that decision they may take the view that this case has:

1. exceptional circumstances;
2. large-scale implications;
3. regional, national and possibly international impact;
4. significant policy decisions to be made;
5. potential major expenditure; and
6. a necessity for agreeing a multi-agency policy framework.

The Silver Commander in liaison with senior officers agree to move quickly to a Gold Commander level of management in the light of this information and open a multi-agency Gold Control and Media Briefing Centre to assist and deal with the strategic elements of the incident. A Gold Commander is appointed to manage the strategic level. Full incident management is now ongoing and developing via the Silver Control and Gold Control, which is opening.

The incident now has the full management structure in place which was implemented as required, as the situation escalated. There would have been no need to go straight to full GSB on the initial incident. This example highlights how a normal incident can be managed using GSB and invoking the separate management levels as needed. Although this is a simple example, it is intended to illustrate how GSB can be a very flexible management tool and how seamless it should and can be. The processes demonstrate how GSB can be fully integrated into daily activity and should be proportional to the situation.

5.10 **Summary**

This is a very important chapter as it explains the full co-ordination structure. You should now understand how the police instigate co-ordination by using the Gold, Silver and Bronze management system. You should also now appreciate how the regional and national structures support the local response. The importance of information sharing, recording information and managing crisis meetings has been described in detail together with how control centres are managed and operated.

5.11 **Conclusion**

We have seen how the police are responsible for co-ordination. If that co-ordination is not effective the whole response can be compromised. The starting point for effective co-ordination begins, or should begin early and will set the pace or rhythm for the whole response.

Training and exercising will ensure those skills are acquired and retained by those responsible for emergency response. In the remaining chapters we will look at how we can achieve an exercise programme that will deliver those skills.

Chapter 6

Exercise Design

Overview

In this chapter we will cover:

- General principles
- The basic scenario
- Aims and objectives
- Exercise types
- The Seminar Exercise
- The Desk Top Exercise
- The Control Post Exercise
- The Live Exercise
- Communication Exercise
- Modular exercising
- Simulation exercising
- Visualization
- Making the right choice
- General costs and cost recovery

6.1 Introduction

Having the knowledge to choose the right exercise is so important for the overall success of the exercise and achieving the aim and objectives. Making the right choice will ensure that the plans are properly evaluated and as a result it is hoped that lessons are learned and fed back into the planning processes, so setting up a continuous cycle of improvement.

Exercising is a key part of the emergency planning cycle (Figure 6.1). The exercise will reveal any shortcomings in

Figure 6.1 Emergency Planning Cycle

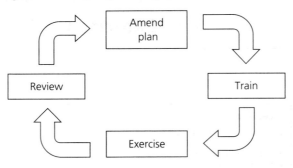

the plan which will lead to a review, which in turn will lead to amending the plan and then training staff in the revised arrangements. We then evaluate the plan again and the process continues. As we mentioned in an earlier chapter the plan should be a living, dynamic piece of work, constantly evolving and improving. Choosing the wrong exercise can compromise that planning cycle and in fact can devalue the exercise, resulting in people who are involved becoming reluctant to take part in future exercises. The right exercise will maximize the learning potential and also produce an exercise that is interesting, enjoyable and cost-effective.

6.2 General Principles

An exercise should not in itself detract from the agreed aim and objectives by being unnecessarily complicated. If the participants spend most of their time trying to understand, or interpret the 'rules' of the exercise, or are absorbed by the technological 'play station' wizardry they are not concentrating on the objectives and it is a bad exercise. The exercise elements should be 'invisible', in other words the exercise should only facilitate the activity and not become the activity itself.

The golden rule is to keep it as simple as possible to achieve the exercise objectives.

An exercise should be a true and honest evaluation, a snapshot on the day. It is of no use to over plan an exercise to such an extent that it is devalued by rehearsing the players, leaking exercise information or briefing players on the scenario. It then can become a choreographed play. This may be a temptation when the exercise is required for validation reasons, for regulators for example, but it is counterproductive and the rehearsed elements will be watched for and spotted by a good exercise assessor.

Exercising is not a training event in itself. An exercise is intended to evaluate training, processes and procedures. It should not be used to test participants or be a substitute for properly structured training. An exercise will be a learning experience but training and exercising are structured very differently. Exercising can however be configured to extend training into testing individuals but that has to be made clear and assessments prepared and participants sufficiently briefed. The danger in using exercising for personnel evaluation is that a flawed plan, poorly chosen exercise or a badly constructed exercise can create real confusion and uncertainty which is no fault of the person being assessed and therefore rendering the personal evaluation suspect and unreliable. In general, training and exercising should be kept apart, the only exception being within a seminar type exercise which we will discuss later.

The first consideration in exercising is what is the requirement? This will inform the choice of scenario.

6.3 **The Basic Scenario**

Deciding to hold an exercise can be driven by a number of different factors. For example an EPO may be faced with a need to evaluate arrangements for a particular forthcoming event or operation. They may also be directed by a risk assessment such as that provided by the Community Risk Register or within the organization as part of a policy for exercising plans against a given scenario. It could also be because a similar event has recently occurred, perhaps elsewhere and there is a need to evaluate existing arrangements in case it happens again! It could be a requirement by law if one is required to exercise to satisfy a regulator or it could simply be that it falls within a testing cycle for the plans. On the other hand there could be a need to exercise a particular plan or part of a plan which is generic and a scenario has to be created to fit. For example, testing Rest Centres, the scenario can be very flexible. It could be anything from a flood to a toxic cloud. So the exercise may be scenario driven or plan driven.

But whatever the reason to hold the exercise, the scenario chosen is key to its success. There are some basic general principles to consider from the outset. When considering a scenario it is important to keep it simple and realistic. A complicated scenario will overwhelm a group and they can easily lose sight of the objectives. An unrealistic scenario will 'turn off' a group of exercise players.

Another consideration is the context of your scenario. Are the settings and people involved appropriate? Ensure that the scenario does not create alarm or concern. For example, do not choose a specific community or minority group as the perpetrator or cause of the event. Everything must be done to avoid insulting, isolating or demonizing a section of community. After all exercising should be primarily a unifying and learning experience for all, remembering that an informed and cohesive community will react better in crisis than a divided one. If the scenario involves criminal activity such as terrorism be sympathetic and considerate before choosing who will be responsible for the act! Do not reinforce stereotypes.

Also, some transport companies will be sensitive to using pictures of their trains, planes or ferries in case it gives the impression that they are not safe. Industry too can be sensitive, and for good reason, creating scenarios which in reality would not or could never happen can send the wrong message to local communities. By choosing a local chemical site to use as a subject of an exercise may alarm local residents thinking that there must be a good reason why there is an exercise, 'is it really that dangerous?' There is no difficulty with that as long as it is managed with a sound information and media strategy which can in fact reassure that community that a proactive and responsible approach is being adopted for community safety. It is so easy to overlook these points in the scenario development process but it could cause problems later on for the EPO. A little thought early on can save many difficulties and issuing apologies.

The scenario must also include some simple and obvious information. But again choose this information carefully because it can change the whole dynamic of an exercise. For example:

- Time/date—may influence resources availability, eg Bank Holiday, early morning, etc.
- Weather conditions, temperature, wind speed, visibility, and wind direction can affect the whole exercise in terms of rescue.
- Traffic conditions—can inhibit and constrain response activities.
- Those involved, eg young or elderly, foreign nationals, infirm, etc.

These simple considerations if used correctly can have a profound effect on the response elements of an exercise even before the scenario is developed.

During the scenario development consider what will add to the realism. Think about photographs, pre-prepared news inputs in audio or visual, mapping, edited film footage from real events, and computer-generated effects. But only add material if it will add real value and not distract or confuse those taking part.

We will look in more detail later about developing a scenario with a worked example.

Task 6.1

Can you think of at least five examples where the inappropriate choice of an exercise scenario could cause you difficulties?

6.4 Aims and Objectives

Whatever the reason for exercising, once that decision is made there will need to be a careful examination and consideration of the aim and objectives. The aim and objectives will develop the scenario. In making the right choice of exercise format there is a need to decide exactly what it is that has to be achieved. Examine the plan being evaluated or look at the basic scenario being considered and identify exactly what it is that needs to be evaluated. That will be the 'aim'. There will only be one aim. The aim should be quite broad, almost strategic in terms of its scope.

Some examples of aim might be:

1. To test the existing companies' major incident procedures (this could be a COMAH or REPPIR site—see later).
2. To test the media handling arrangements following a major incident.
3. To test the emergency plan for an aircraft emergency at any town airport.
4. To test the emergency arrangements for a terrorist chemical attack in a town centre.

The aim describes your overall goal. This will be underpinned by a series of 'objectives'. The objectives can in fact be viewed as tactical in scope as the aim is strategic. The objectives will break the aim down into activities which together will achieve your aim. In simple terms it will look like Figure 6.2. This is a simple single organizational type exercise or a component part in support of a multi-agency exercise.

Figure 6.2 Aim and Objectives

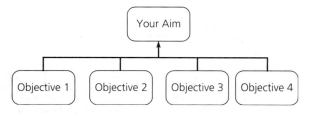

Task 6.2

Category 1 Responders have a duty under the CCA to exercise. What is the duty on Category 2 Responders?

Where several organizations or departments are involved, a single overall aim should be agreed. This gives the exercise focus and a unity. Each organization will then consider its individual aim which should complement the overall aim and be supported by a series of their own objectives. The objectives will drive the exercise and must be compatible with the objectives of the other participants. This is important because it would be no use in an organization choosing an objective if that is unachievable because another agency or department will not support that objective. The process will start with a 'proposed' aim suggested by the lead organization that is running the exercise and each support organization or department will look to examine that proposed aim and set their own objectives to meet that aim. This is done by consensus and possibly by some compromise but the benefits of compromise far outweigh the negatives aspects when there is an opportunity to interact across other organizations or departments. Figure 6.3 shows how the process works with the ultimate end result being an agreed overall 'Aim' underpinned with a series of compatible objectives.

Figure 6.3 Multi-Agency Aim and Objectives

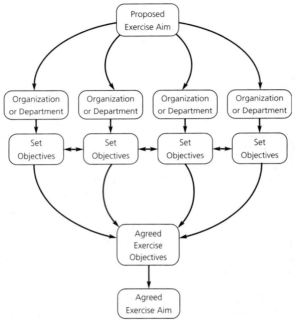

Task 6.3

Think of an emergency or crisis scenario you would like to test from your current or previous work place environment—for example a fire, a major IT failure or building collapse caused by a gas leak.

Set the Aim and support the aim by listing at least five objectives.

Taking the aim in example 3 above, the agreed final multi-agency aim is 'To test emergency plan for an aircraft emergency at any town airport'.

The agreed multi-agency objectives for each participating organization will be different but will all complement each other and dovetail. The Fire and Rescue Service objectives might be:

1. To assess the initial activation, notifications, mobilization and co-ordination of the emergency response.
2. To examine the liaison interface with all the blue light services at the airport.
3. To test the adequacy of the Emergency Control Centre (ECC) at the airport.
4. To test the effectiveness of the crisis management team within a multi-agency context for the airport.
5. To manage a co-ordinated media response in liaison with the police.
6. To assess the liaison arrangements and joint working practices with the airport Fire Service.
7. To test the upgraded breathing apparatus.

Many of the above Fire and Rescue Service objectives could not be achieved without other services agreeing to complement them with their own objectives, in particular where there is a multi-agency element. Co-ordinating all the objectives for a large multi-agency exercise, to make them fit, is a task for an exercise planning team which can be achieved through discussion with all those taking part. It is not difficult but is a case of negotiating and shaping the objectives until a coherent set emerge that can be agreed and signed off.

Ideally the aim and objectives should dictate and drive the type of exercise that takes place. After all they are the agreed priority objectives designed to fully evaluate the plan. However, there is a practical relationship between the aim and objectives and the type of exercise that can in fact be realized. There may be constraints on time, resources or finances so the ultimate decision will rest with the planning team as to what type of exercise can be realistically achieved, which we will now explore.

6.5 Exercise Types

Having agreed the aim and objectives what exercise choices are there?

Exercise types generally fall into four categories.

KEY POINT

Exercise types

- The seminar exercise
- The table or desk top exercise
- The control post exercise
- The live exercise

6.5.1 The seminar exercise

A seminar exercise is essentially a meeting in two parts. The first part will be used to introduce a new or revised plan and the second part will be to test understanding and knowledge. The emphasis will be on problem identification and solutions rather than decision making. It will also be primarily designed to focus on one aspect of the plan which will have been identified and agreed by the exercise planner(s). This exercise deliberately introduces a structured training element which will include a personal evaluation method. For example, at the end of the seminar a multiple choice question paper or quiz, taken individually or in teams, based upon the plan can be introduced.

Although the plan will have undergone quality assurance in the writing stage this exercise can also highlight any issues within the plan that may need revision, prior to re-circulation and can indeed form part of the QA process.

This type of exercise can accommodate large numbers of people, is low cost and requires a small amount of planning. It can be completed in half a day. It can be either an internal event for key players within the organization or can involve external support agencies. If the latter is chosen it is useful to use them as a panel of experts to contribute by giving a short overview of their role and assisting with questions from the group during the exercise.

This type of exercise can be managed and facilitated by one person.

Task 6.3

Exercising and training should be considered as two separate activities. Compare and contrast the potential learning outcomes and objectives from both activities to reinforce that distinction for yourself.

6.5.2 The table or desk top exercise

This is probably the most common exercise type and for very good reasons. It is cost-effective, involves decision making and good interaction between players. It is a safe learning environment but can create realistic pressure and scenarios. The usual format involves syndicate groups made up of 8–10 people of up to 8 syndicates. The groups can be made up of multi-disciplinary, multi-agency or single issue group who focus on only one aspect of the plan, for example a senior management or strategic group.

This format can cover a large amount of topics based upon a given scenario. The scenario is developed in stages by paper feeds requiring each syndicate to address a series of problems, perhaps 3–4. Depending on the format of the exercise, all syndicates will address the same problems or will address a specific aspect. Choosing the syndicate make-up is important for achieving the aims and objectives.

Multi-discipline table

The most common type is the 'multi-discipline' table. This is made up of people from different agencies or departments at similar management level. They behave as a unit and are effectively self-contained dealing with all the issues as a team. It is almost as though each syndicate is competing with the others. This is not such a bad thing as it creates a team spirit and a factor that many facilitators make use of to drive the exercise. This format is good because it exposes the group to a wide range of issues from the practical operational issues to strategic thinking. It also gives each player good insight into the roles, including limitations of the others within the group and is a superb networking opportunity. This is also a useful format to consider the impact of 'Groupthink'. How does each group arrive at consensus and how does group dynamics affect decision making. This is an interesting issue for the facilitator.

Single agency

Another format is 'single agency'. For example each table could be all company, police, fire, local authority etc. This format would require physical interaction between tables by 'forcing' players to seek advice and information from the other tables. Although this sounds useful, in practice single agency tables can become isolated and reluctant to interact unless the facilitator ensures this happens. The onus is on the facilitator to make this work.

Management level

Another format is 'management level'. In this format it is multi-agency or cross department but the tables are divided up into management levels. One or more tables will address operational issues, another tactical and another strategic. Again it sounds quite useful to focus on decision making and developing skills at that appropriate level. Interaction between tables is essential for this to work. There has to be a continuous dialogue between tables to keep the exercise running smoothly. The facilitators and presenters play a key role in managing this type of exercise.

There are other formats and variations on the main three. The one chosen should deliver the best fit for the aim and objectives.

Each syndicate will be required to give feedback followed by general facilitated discussion. Added realism can be added by film, audio, mapping and photographs. Many such exercises are punctuated by short presentations from 'experts' in particular aspects of the emergency response, for example the Police, Fire and Rescue Service, business continuity manager etc. These exercises usually have a panel of experts to offer advice and support and each syndicate is facilitated to ensure the group remains focused and all players have an opportunity to take part.

Task 6.4

Although most table top or desk top exercises are actually carried out at tables and desks, can you think of an environment where the principles of table top would work without tables?

At least one day should be allowed for these exercises.

6.5.3 **The control post exercise**

This type of exercise primarily is focused on communication, decision making and information sharing, all critical aspects of any plan. It also tests the adequacy of the facilities used to manage the incident. The 'control post' refers to the locations or control centres where incident management actually takes place. In effect, it is a live exercise but without any operational activity. There is nothing to see on the ground. All the activity is confined to control centres. Each control centre becomes 'live' upon the declaration of an event. Players can be introduced in real time to test response times or pre-positioned at the start time. The exercise is driven from an exercise control room and managed and monitored by an exercise team including umpires located at each control centre working to a separate communications network. Although the exercise is initiated by the given scenario because there is no real activity on the ground, the exercise is 'driven' from exercise control by a script of 'exercise drivers or inputs' and fed into the control centres at pre-determined times or at the request of the umpires. The exercise drivers are simply telephone messages, fax or e-mail messages from pretend players creating problems or questions that require a response.

These can range from questions from the media, local politicians, and members of the public to government ministers. There are also controlled players which we will discuss later who role play and drive the exercise forward. The exercise can become very real to the players and heated!

These exercises will usually be full day exercises.

6.5.4 **The live exercise**

Live exercises are clearly the most accurate and realistic method of testing any emergency arrangements and probably the easiest to understand in that it is the operational activity that is tested. In some cases live exercises are the only viable option to test emergency arrangements, for example, evacuation procedures, media management, casualty handling, decontamination procedures, scene management, body recovery etc. They can be configured to exercise a small part of a plan right up to a full scale major live play exercise involving a whole organization and hundreds of players. They can also be combined to form part of a control post or a table top exercise. The combined control post and operational live play represents the most ambitious exercise as it completely replicates the real emergency but in many ways is more complex to manage. The reason for this is that not only do real events have to be managed but sitting above that is an exercise management layer which would not exist in reality, which in turn has to be managed.

Clearly, live exercises by their very nature are costly in terms of the use of resources and the consequential impact on day-to-day business by extracting those resources for an exercise. They can also be hazardous and create potential public concern, all of which has to be managed. With that in mind it is important to have a high degree of confidence that the players are trained and prepared. But that does not mean rehearsing as we have already discussed. If players are not prepared then consideration of a table top may be more appropriate. Running a full live exercise with ill prepared staff can be a risky undertaking in terms of wasted time and resources. Planning too has to be comprehensive and requires several months to plan. But the potential learning from a live play exercise is enormous and in those terms can be value for money provided the planning and execution of the exercise is effective with a comprehensive debrief process to extract that learning which is fed back into the planning process.

The key to a successful exercise is ensuring that the exercise itself does not become the goal. The exercise should enable the activities to proceed without becoming an obstacle. Exercise management operates in the background. Ambiguity and confusion as to what is real or notional play will frustrate players and in all exercises all the players need to be fully briefed as to the exercise format and rules.

6.5.5 **Communication/alert/call-out exercise**

Allied to and often preceding a control post or live exercise is a communications, alert or call out exercise. Trying to combine both in a realistic test can be too problematic. If the alerts fail or response fails or is delayed, the control post or live exercise can be seriously compromised and a lot of effort and money wasted.

This kind of exercise simply evaluates and tests the alert communications. That is, are you telling the right people? Are they in turn telling the right people? Are they on the right telephone numbers? Have you got the right contact details? Can they turn out? Communications networks tend to work in cascade. For example, your operator tells four key people or organizations and each one of those tells a further three and they in turn tell another half dozen. It is easy to see that if one number is wrong or not accurate, the effect can be significant. A large proportion of the emergency response can be compromised if contact details are incorrect.

An advantage of this exercise is that one can confirm that the real emergency numbers do work and during the exercise one can substitute some of the real numbers to reduce pressure on day-to-day activities and reduce the potential for false alarms. 'Controlled players' can also be introduced to make and field these calls so the usual telephone/communications operator or control room staff are not tied up thus preventing day-to-day activity continuing.

False alarms

False alarms during exercises can have serious consequences. It is not unheard of for hospitals to be put on emergency alert or the media to run a story as though it was real. This reinforces the need to prefix all exercise communications with the exercise name and make it clear it is an exercise and not real. Therefore in any live exercise or control post exercise, proper and adequate measures must be taken to avoid false alarms. This is an issue often watched for by umpires, who will intervene to stop this. Creating concern and potential panic in the community is probably the worst case scenario coming from an exercise. Again, proper measures, notification, and advertising must be considered. The media element of the exercise planning team should address this.

No notice tests

Having said that, there are occasions when one wants a very realistic test of communications, alerts, and call outs.

A 'No-notice' test will give the most accurate picture of how effective the communications links are. If calling people out with no notice they will be unprepared and will give a spontaneous and honest response on their ability to turn out. But when contacting people on call out lists they should not be told initially it is a test. If they know it is a test they will be inclined to be over optimistic and confirm that they can respond. If they think it is for real it may come as a surprise how many people are unable to turn out. But obviously they should be told at some point that a test is being run, preferably after they have been asked the question!

KEY POINT

No notice exercises

No notice exercises quickly highlight any wrong or inaccurate numbers held in the plan.

A compromise to a no notice test is to give notice that it will be within a certain period, perhaps a day or within a week commencing. Giving notice of a communications, alert or call out exercise clearly reduces potential false alarms but it also creates an artificial result. If a person is notified of a communications test they will prepare for it by making sure that they or someone else is on that phone at the right time and prepared to say the right things—so this is not really an accurate test, which can lead to a false sense of security!

Task 6.5

List three reasons why it is desirable to separate call out and notifications testing from a live or control post exercise.

6.5.6 **Modular exercising**

Increasingly, organizations are choosing to exercise their larger plans in a modular fashion. It simply means assessing the exercise requirements and deciding which aspects of the plan are best suited to various forms of exercising (as described above) and 'bolting' them together. For example, a communications exercise and a control post exercise or a live exercise up to a point and then remaining aspects by table top. The advantage is that they can:

- be spread over time;
- be smaller in scale;
- be more focused on target groups; and
- be more cost-effective.

6.6 **Simulation**

Computer-simulated/driven exercises are a highly specialized method of exercising and for many software developers are a potentially very lucrative enterprise which seem to be gaining in popularity. Clearly they are out of reach for most organizations to own outright due to the hardware and software needed to operate the system. They have to be bought in or participants have to attend a specialist centre, which is not always convenient. It is also questionable what added value such systems add to basic exercise formats. Essentially they are there to add realism but even the most sophisticated simulations can easily become a 'computer game' and detract from the actual exercise objectives as the players becomes engrossed in the entertainment value of the simulation.

To carry out effective and meaningful exercises computer simulations are not needed and in many cases not even desirable. But that has to be balanced against visualization.

6.7 **Visualization**

Task 6.6

Having considered both simulation and visualization in exercising can you articulate the differences between the two in a way that creates a clear distinction?

Visualization reinforces a message. People more easily assimilate information presented in graphic form or pictures or indeed in solid objects. The use of mapping, scene photographs, site plans, models and simulated media audio and visual inputs during an exercise are of great benefit and value to create an atmosphere of realism. The difference between this and computer generated simulation is that there is a point at which the simulation becomes the focus of interest whereas the exercise and its aims and objectives must remain paramount.

6.8 **Making a Choice**

Returning to our earlier example—let's remind ourselves of the five objectives for our airport exercise which have now been jointly agreed by the planning team.

1. To assess the initial activation, notifications, mobilization and co-ordination of the emergency response.
2. To examine the liaison interface with the blue light services and the airport.
3. To test the adequacy of the Emergency Control Centre at the airport.
4. To test the effectiveness of the crisis management team within a multi-agency context for the airport.
5. To manage a co-ordinated media response in liaison with the police.

This is not a new or revised plan. And it has a number of objectives so a seminar exercise would not be appropriate. The intention is to choose the simplest format or combination of formats to achieve our objectives in the most economical way. Now we will consider each exercise objective in turn to see what exercise format best suits.

Objective 1

This objective can be broken down into two parts: activation and notifications followed by mobilization and co-ordination. Activation and notification elements would be best tested by a communications exercise. This could be done as a separate exercise in advance. Mobilization and co-ordination could be achieved by a live test or table top or control post. The easiest option is table top. Each syndicate could be asked the question, 'what are the initial mobilization and co-ordination arrangements in the plan?' By discussion and then explaining this, any anomalies and ambiguities will be exposed.

Objective 2

This could also be achieved by a live test or table top or control post. But again the easiest option is table top. With multi-agency support these areas can be examined and explored in great detail, supported by a panel of experts.

Objective 3

This would require a control post exercise to actually test the facility. However a small scale control post exercise would achieve this objective using the scenario and inputs and creating a modular exercise.

Objective 4

This could be achieved by a live test or table top or control post. Again the easiest option would be by table top. Having all the participants in one room discussing their respective roles and responsibilities will scrutinize that interface.

Objective 5

This could be achieved by a live test or table top. But with a multi-agency group this could be achieved at a table top exercise, especially if supported by a group of invited professional media.

Conclusion

The difficulty with this exercise is dealing with objectives 1 and 3. A modular approach is required to meet all of these objectives or indeed the planning team may revisit the objectives and reject them if necessary if resources and time will not allow an extended modular approach. But assuming there is a requirement to meet all objectives, in this case the best option would be to carry out a table top for objectives 1) part, 2), 4) and 5); 3) would require a control post exercise and the remaining part of 1) would be a communications exercise.

The exercise programme would look like this:

- **Module 1**—Communications exercise. Objective 1) Activation and Notification. Carried out in advance of the main exercise and used as part of the introduction to inform the table top exercise.
- **Module 2**—Table top exercise. Objective 1) Mobilization and co-ordination and the remaining objectives of 2), 4) and 5).
- **Module 3**—Small scale control post exercise. Objective 3) carried out after the table top and using the information in table top injects to create driver inputs.

6 Exercise Design

This example, although quite complicated, is only intended to illustrate the process of configuring exercise formats to meet aims and objectives. It also introduces the idea of modular exercising. The terminology used will be explained in more detail in the next chapter.

Checklist—Things to remember when choosing an exercise format.

Seminar

- Good for introducing new and revised plans
- Low cost
- Focuses on problem solving
- Single presenter
- Minimal planning
- Can accommodate large numbers
- Structured for training
- Mainly for internal use
- Achievable in half a day

Table top

- Can test a wide range of parts within a plan
- Cost-effective
- Excellent interaction potential
- Explores decision making
- Can be realistic
- Good for multi agency or multi disciplinary
- Significant planning required
- Requires facilitation and presenter
- Requires a full day

Control Post

- Will test the critical communications, decision and information sharing
- Will test control facilities
- Very realistic experience for participants
- Extensive long term planning required
- Planning team necessary
- Requires exercise control/management
- Separate communications network required
- Debrief required
- Will impact upon 'normal' business
- Will incur significant costs
- May invoke cost recovery from blue light services

Live

- The ultimate test of operational systems and procedures
- Can be configured to test small or large parts of a plan
- Can be combined with table top and control post
- Extensive long term planning required
- Will impact upon 'normal' business
- Requires health and safety management
- Can be very costly to run
- Requires an exercise management team
- Extensive debriefing required
- Can promote confidence in your organization amongst communities
- May invoke cost recovery from blue light services

Apart from the training element in the seminar exercise, exercises are *not* examinations. Players should have access to all plans and anything they would have access to normally from day to day. It is not a test of memory for the players.

Whichever exercise format is chosen, with a systematic approach a successful exercise is easily achievable.

6.9 **General Costs**

Exercising will incur costs either directly or indirectly. We will discuss 'cost recovery' next, but there will have to be consideration for paying for professional speakers, venues, catering, props, writing materials, visual and audio aids etc.

Cost can be kept to a minimum as many of these costs can be met from internal resources and sharing amongst agencies. It is essential though that costs are identified early and factored in and most importantly to identify who will pay. Consider funding and sharing costs, in particular through the Local Resilience Forum. It is hard to envisage a significant exercise not including some support or input from the LRF.

6.10 **Cost Recovery**

Two pieces of legislation created the right for blue light organizations to recover costs incurred in taking part in exercises to test plans created under that legislation. They are the Control of Major Accident Hazards Regulations 1999 (COMAH) and the Radiation Preparedness and Public Information Regulations 2001 (REPPIR). The introduction of the legislation created some difficulty for the emergency services in that there was no nationally agreed pricing structure or methodology to apply those 'charges'. 'Charges' are placed in apostrophes because it is cost recovery, not charging for services. It is explained as cost neutral as the money recovered goes back into emergency service operational budgets. This lack of agreed methodology resulted in vast anomalies across the UK. Some emergency services cost recovered and others did not. Some 'charged' tens of thousands of pounds and others very little or not at all. In addition, the 'broker' tasked with negotiating and managing cost recovery was the local authority but many local authorities did not take on this role.

Some attempts have been made to resolve the disparity but there still remain significant differences in approaches to cost recovery. Indeed, some Local Resilience Forums have extended the cost recovery principle to all commercial organizations.

Task 6.7

Research the two pieces of legislation mentioned in the text concerning cost recovery and create a flow chart to illustrate the process.

The rationale for this is based upon equity and even-handedness. If an organization is in business to make a profit and is required to exercise for either regulatory reasons or just good management, why should the tax payer subsidize that through the emergency services? Indeed, some organizations who pay cost recovery actively promote their contributions as putting back into emergency service budgets money that can go to support core activities such as tackling crime or reducing fires, a commendable attitude. On the other hand, businesses support the community in other ways and through taxes and after all it gives the emergency services valuable opportunities to practice. Whatever the view, cost recovery is a fact that has to be factored in and budgeted for if it applies.

If an organization is subject to cost recovery or is an emergency service considering how to apply it, how does any organization know that they are paying for or are asking too much? How does any organization know if the emergency services are unwittingly specifying too many staff and passing the cost on? Perhaps a bit cynical but it reflects opinion. It is difficult to know what should be paid or asked for unless a specialist consultant is engaged to review and assess the invoice. By consulting with peers, similar organizations in other areas or consulting the local authority should assist

in making these decisions. After all it is the local authority who should be co-ordinating the application of the
COMAH and REPPIR regulations on cost recovery.

KEY POINT

Cost issues

Important issues to consider are how and by what rationale
organizations levy the costs. How transparent is the process?
How well is it broken down and itemized?

Training benefit is a key term that can be used in this
process. If being 'charged' cost recovery, an organization
should be presented with how training benefit is calculated.
Training benefit is the positive learning experience that the
emergency services will gain from taking part in an exercise. Some services will apportion a percentage to this based
upon a player's previous experience and training. This is
in recognition that opportunities will arise where certain
aspects of a particular exercise role may hold training benefits for some participants and the exercise will be a useful
vehicle to develop that participant, without hindering the
exercise. Clearly there are roles that the emergency services
carry out every day, and doing it again in an exercise will
not advance their skills or training one bit. In particular,
where the emergency services are repeatedly asked to take
part in many exercises per year. But there is acknowledge-
ment that some emergency staff will benefit from the experience and that should be accounted for. An example of a
sample exercise benefit matrix is illustrated in Figure 6.4.

For each player a general assessment is carried out based
upon previous experience and relevant training. In this
case four areas are evaluated; each area will carry a 25%
allowance against training benefit. For example if a player
ticks three criteria, that will attract a 75% allowance, which
results in a 25% discount, ie 100%–75% = 25%. This is not
a definitive or officially endorsed process but represents a

Figure 6.4 Exercise Benefit Matrix

Role/Name	Key Skill Area	Previous Experience			%
Rank/Grade for costing purposes.	Each area carries equal weighting making up 100% benefit for no relevant competencies.	YES (tick)	NO (tick)	Full Costs	Office Use Only
Gold Commander Name........... Rank	1. Performed Gold Commander for major Incident 2. Chaired Multi-agency strategic meetings. 3. Participated in civil nuclear exercise. 4. Attended nuclear incident management training/seminars.				
Staff Officer to Gold Commander Name........... Rank	1. Performed Staff Officer to Gold Commander. 2. Participated in any other Gold Control function. 3. Participated in civil nuclear exercise. 4. Attended nuclear incident management training.				
Senior Gold Co-ordinator Name........... Rank	1. Performed the role of Senior Gold Co-ordinator. 2. Participated in any other Gold Control function. 3. Participated in civil nuclear exercise. 4. Attended nuclear incident management training.				

model to consider as a rationale or methodology to add some objectivity to the training benefit evaluation process. Without some rational process the figure can become purely subjective and difficult to audit.

There is no doubt that the emergency services will endeavour to achieve a balanced approach to ensure an efficient and effective exercise response, delivered by skilled and knowledgeable personnel. This is particularly important for the overall success of any exercise, for the police in particular, who play such a key role in the overall co-ordination, communication, and management of all emergency situations. An efficient emergency service will from the outset of any planned exercise be open, transparent, and flexible in the selection of key personnel and the likely costs that that may incur.

6.11 **Summary**

- You will be aware of the need to use exercising as a management tool.
- You be able to recognize and formulate aims and objectives.
- You will be able to choose and mix and match exercise types to create the ideal exercise.
- You will understand and factor in cost recovery.

6.12 **Conclusion**

Exercising is a vital management tool in today's business environment and that initial analysis as to the form and type of exercise is crucial. Choosing the right exercise will deliver cost-effective and beneficial rewards for any organization and lead to a planning cycle which is built on continuous improvement and development.

Understanding cost recovery is, again, a relatively new concept still bedding-in across both private and public sector. It is a significant issue for many and in particular the smaller organization, so choosing the right exercise directly affects the costs incurred.

Having considered what exercise types are available we will now look at how the exercise is managed.

Chapter 7

Exercise Management

Overview
In this chapter you will learn: • Who is who in exercise management?   • Using the input script   • Staffing schedules   • Controlled play and free play exercises   • Exercise control   • Communications networks   • Timelines   • Compressing time   • Preparing an Exercise Order   • Preparing a player's information pack   • Preparing the debrief schedule

7.1 Who's Who in Exercise Management?

Now that the exercise aim, objectives and type are understood it is now time to consider how the exercise will be managed. This falls into two parts. Firstly, this chapter will concentrate on the key personnel that will be involved in planning the exercise and taking part; and secondly the exercise structure and how that is developed to deliver the aim and objectives.

7.1.1 Exercise Director

Planning the exercise itself will be described in more detail in the next chapter but for clarity it should be understood that the Exercise Director should be agreed and confirmed at the first exercise planning meeting. Unless otherwise agreed, whoever initiates the exercise will provide the chairperson at the planning meetings. When all participating organizations or departments are assembled, at the first planning meeting, a core planning team will be agreed. These may involve other agencies too. There will be a need to agree who will be the overall Exercise Director. The Director will have overall responsibility for the exercise and can terminate and significantly alter the exercise as required. This is a key appointment and a role that requires training, qualification and experience; this is endorsed by the CCA. Although the Exercise Director need not chair the planning meetings, which is often a task delegated to an exercise manager, the director must be closely involved with the exercise throughout the planning process and consulted when necessary.

In addition to the director the following is a list of those who may be operating within an exercise:

Checklist—individuals who may operate within an exercise

- Director
- Manager(s)
- Players
- Controlled Players
- Umpires
- Assessors
- Observers
- Facilitators
- Assistants
- Inputters

We will take a closer look at each of them in turn.

7.1.2 **Exercise Managers**

Exercise Managers are usually drawn from the planning team and will manage discrete aspects of the exercise, for example:

- Exercise Control, Gold Control Centre (SCC), Silver Control Centre, etc.
- Observers' chaperone (for high level/VIP observers)
- Exercise facilitator or presenter for table tops
- Individual organizational activity of a single agency, eg the company, police service, fire service etc.

They will be designated as directing staff, working at all times to the Exercise Director, acting as liaison between the umpires and assessors. Where numbers of exercise management staff may be limited they can also have a role as exercise umpires and assessors.

7.1.3 **Exercise Players**

As the name suggests, these people actually take part and have a role within the exercise. They have a role within the plan. They are not scripted in the exercise scenario at all apart from the exercise format and exercise rules. They should be briefed just before the exercise starts and have had a players' information pack outlining all necessary information.

7.1.4 **Exercise Controlled Players**

These players are introduced into the exercise with a role to play but are scripted in parts of the exercise scenario. They may be for example, casualties, suspects, witnesses, members of the public or exercise inputters. They may also become and role play senior managers and commanders to direct players in free play exercises (see below). For example, you can introduce a controlled player to act as a Gold Commander to take all Gold decisions without having a full Gold Control. They can be assisted by a handful of organizations instead of scores of real players—as long as that facility or aspect is not being tested.

7.1.5 **Exercise Umpires**

Exercise umpires are the eyes and ears of exercise management. For that reason they must be easily identified by wearing a suitable tabard. They will communicate directly with exercise managers and the director through exercise control, if there is one, or face to face. Their job is to operate in the background watching and listening to exercise play to ensure the exercise is on track. They can be approached by players to clear up any ambiguity and they can confirm that a request has been actioned or completed. 'Notional' play is a matter for the umpire to manage. Certain requests for example will have to be dealt with as notional because to carry out the request or action would be unrealistic and may involve the activation of resources or facilities that are not taking part. The notional elements within the exercise will be agreed and worked through in the planning stage. Umpires can also communicate with players to clarify level of understanding and rationale for actions if acting as assessors but will usually confine their comments to players in response to questions about exercise play or to intervene to change exercise play at the request of exercise control or for safety reasons.

Notional exercise play

What do we mean by notional in this scenario? As an example assume that the planning team have recently tested the Control Post aspects, perhaps in a modular fashion as we have already looked at and are now concentrating on the operational and tactical elements. However, there will still be a need for a Communications Centre, Gold Control, and MBC to ensure the exercise runs. This is achieved by having controlled players acting as Communications Centre, Gold Commander, and MBC Manager. They will each have an assistant to make notes and take phone calls. They can be positioned in Exercise Control. The notional Communications Centre will manage the initial operational response until the Silver control centre goes live. In reality, the day-to-day Communications Centre(s) will manage the incident until the management structure is in place. The notional Gold Commander and MBC Manager will each field and reply to questions or requests put to them by other live centres, principally by Silver Control. The Gold Control can consist of controlled players from other organizations and/or departments each acting as their Gold or MBC advisor. In this way it is possible to achieve a Gold and MBC element with a handful of controlled players and not scores of people as would be the case in running a full Control or MBC.

7.1.6 Exercise Assessors

The Exercise Assessor's role can be combined with the umpire role but on complex or large scale exercises separate and independent assessors may be brought in. This is a matter for the planning team and the exercise director. Exercise assessors are sometimes used to ensure a more objective assessment of the exercise is carried out and that the exercise had not been 'rehearsed' or 'choreographed' to obtain a good result for the benefit of regulators! Exercise umpires, if assessing their own organization in a multi-agency environment may be inclined to be a little too subjective. In any event both the umpires and assessors will have a crucial role to play in the debrief process. Assessors must be easily identifiable. Assessors can communicate with players to clarify level of understanding and rationale for actions.

7.1.7 Exercise Observers

Exercise Observers must have a legitimate role to play in an exercise. They should not be simply there for a 'day out' and a free lunch. Observers must add value to the exercise by providing feedback in written questionnaires prepared by the planning team or to achieve some aim. For example, inviting senior managers may change opinions positively on the usefulness of exercising and free up resources for future exercises.

Inviting the real media may provide useful publicity and subsequently reassurance to the public. Inviting local politicians again may engineer support and confidence. Observers must be closely chaperoned and not left to wander. They should be separated into small groups and managed. Restricting observers to specific areas is useful to prevent their interference with the exercise. This can be achieved by having designated observers' observation areas. They must also have a thorough briefing to ensure that they fully understand the exercise as their ability to ask questions may be restricted. Observers must not communicate with players as it can be too distracting and may confuse the players and influence the exercise play. Observers must also be easily identifiable and wearing badges. It is not unheard of that rogue observers can access exercise sites!

7.1.8 Facilitators

Facilitators are usually drawn from the planning team and act as umpires in a table top exercise format. If not drawn from the planning team they will require a comprehensive briefing as to their role as an action from the planning meeting. Not only will they require a good knowledge of the plan being evaluated but a good understanding of the exercise and objectives in order to 'steer' discussions and exercise play in the right direction. They are there to guide and assist only. They should not be drawn into being a group leader or answering questions directly.

KEY POINT

Tip for facilitators

A useful tip for facilitators in table top exercises is to hold any additional ancillary documents and plans, which are mentioned in the provided plans, in a briefcase. If they are asked for by the players the facilitator can produce them, but only if asked for!

7.1.9 Exercise Assistants

Quite simply they are not playing in the exercise but are nominated to a task to ensure the smooth running of the exercise. These tasks can be:

- player liaison in the holding area/room (see later)
- distribution of refreshments
- general transport for observers
- observer chaperone assistant
- telecommunication support
- IT support
- security.

7.1.10 Exercise Driver Inputters

Driver inputters are controlled players in exercise control. They will be seated at a desk with a telephone and the driving script within which, in chronological order, will be the inputs prepared by each participating organization to introduce information into exercise play. It is useful to have each organization designated a colour as the single script will be used by all. This will allow other inputters to be aware what is going on around them and going into the exercise at any given time. The inputter will usually be from the organization with general responsibility for that type of input. For example, company inputs from a company manager, health related may be by the ambulance service, Health Protection Agency or Primary Care Trust, public safety interest issues from the police etc. In that way they will have enough knowledge to sound credible and be able to ask and respond to pertinent questions, if required. A sample driving script extract can be seen in Figure 8.2. This relates to a chemical tanker spill producing a toxic plume. The exercise code word is 'Mayflower'.

7.2 **Using the Input Script**

Please note that each inputter has a phone number. The inputter must give this number to the receiver of the call and the inputter must be asked to be called back. It is useful for each inputter to have a note pad to record what was said on each call so they can respond to call backs as accurately as possible. Clearly they are pretending to be several people. This becomes more important as the inputs mount up. It is also useful to chase up calls that have not been returned. This increases pressure for the players as it would in real life. This is actually quite a fun exercise as the inputters can role play vulnerable, angry or concerned people. They should also note the nature of the calls and where they are going. Some issues will not be strategic and go to the SCC and others will be strategic and go to Silver. Umpires will watch for this to assess if the information is managed and routed to the right location for an answer. This is so important as the question and response must be managed at the most appropriate level, ie it is no good at the Strategic Co-ordination Centre dealing with purely operational issues and vice versa. The inputs must be configured to reflect the type of question and at what level it is aimed. Within the driving script the input question or statement can be marked with an (S), (T) or (O) to indicate if the general nature of the question is aimed at strategic, tactical or operational level. Will Gold pass a tactical message down or does Bronze pass a strategic message up?

7.3 **Staffing Schedules**

Common to all exercises will be a requirement to set out an exercise staff and player schedule. On a larger exercise this could involve up to a hundred people so a means of identifying roles, locations and function will be essential. Where costs are involved it is an audit of the hours worked and the rate applied. It will include everyone involved, for example the exercise players and everyone on the exercise management team. A simple spreadsheet will accommodate this and will include information such as that listed in the checklist below:

Checklist—a typical staffing schedule

1. Exercise Site.
2. Position—where they will be positioned during the exercise.
3. Function—Player, Controlled Player, Management, Support etc.
4. Role—their task. For example, communications operator.
5. Hours—engaged in role. Time from to time to including total hours.
6. Hourly rate—include this column but leave blank unless you are submitting it for cost recovery purposes. Then include total cost.
7. Training benefit analysis—a percentage reduction for cost recovery purposes.

Only include columns 5, 6, and 7 where you are actively pursuing cost recovery.

A typical schedule would look like Figure 7.1. This example is a schedule for a major control post exercise. Although it is centred on police facilities, the format is applicable across any organization. It is a useful document to keep track of any personnel changes or amendments.

Figure 7.1 Staffing Schedules

1. Exercise Site	2. Position	3. Function	4. Role	5. Hours	6. Rate £	7. Training benefit %
Police HQ	Communications Room	Duty Officer	CP			
		Communications Officer	P			
	Entrance Door	Security	A			
	SCC & MBC	General Staffing – IT Support	A			
		Transport Services	A			
Silver Control	Main Police Station	Silver Commander	P			
		Silver Co ordinator	P			
		Silver Staff Officer	P			
		Communications Operator	P			
Bronze Control	Local Police Station	Bronze Commander Tasking	P			
		Logistics	P			
		Communications	P			
FCP		Liaison Officer	CP			

Key: P = Player CP = Controlled Player A = Assistant DS = Directing Staff

Figure 7.1 Staffing Schedules (*cont.*)

1. Exercise Site	2. Position	3. Function	4. Role	5. Hours	6. Rate £	7. Training benefit %
Exercise Control	Conference Suite	Exercise Director	DS			N/A
		Police Exercise Manager	DS			N/A
		Exercise inputs	CP			
		Exercise inputs	CP			
		Exercise logistics	A			
Exercise Umpires	SCC	Umpire	DS			N/A
	Communications Centre	Umpire	DS			N/A
	Main Police Station Silver	Umpire	DS			N/A
	Main Police Station Silver	Umpire	DS			N/A
	Local PS Bronze	Umpire	DS			N/A
	MBC	Umpire	DS			N/A
Exercise Ass'ors						
SCC	All Areas	Assessor	DS			N/A
MBC	All Areas	Assessor	DS			N/A
Company Site	ECC	Police Liaison Officer	CP			

Figure 7.1 Staffing Schedules (*cont.*)

1. Exercise Site	2. Position	3. Function	4. Role	5. Hours	6. Rate £	7. Training benefit %
SCC	Police Gold Command Room	Gold Command	P			
		Staff Officer	P			
		Senior Gold Co-ordinator	P			
		Gold Support Officer	P			
		Communications	P			
		Loggist	P			
		Clerical	P			
	Police - Gold Media Room	Media Officer	CP			
	Multi-Agency Room	Room Manager	P			
		Information Manager	P			
		Call Taker/ Liaison Officer	P			
		Clerk/Runner	P			
		Clerk/Runner	P			
	Reception/ Booking in	Reception / Help Desk	P			
	Reception/ Booking in	Reception / Help Desk	P			

Figure 7.1 Staffing Schedules (*cont.*)

1. Exercise Site	2. Position	3. Function	4. Role	5. Hours	6. Rate £	7. Training benefit %
MBC	Conference Centre	Media Gold Command	P			
		Media Manager	P			
		MCC Manager	P			
		Press Officer	P			
		Press Officer	P			
		Clerical	P			
		Clerical	P			
	MCC	Media Officer	CP			
	Multi-Agency Room	Room Manager	p			
		Information Manager	P			
		Call Taker/ Liaison Officer	P			
		Clerk/Runner	P			
		Clerk/Runner	P			
	Reception/ Booking in	Reception / Help Desk	p			
	Reception/ Booking in	Reception / Help Desk	P			

The schedule can be used to list all those who would be taking part in the exercise. It is a convenient way of keeping track of those involved and noting any changes.

7.4 Controlled Play and Free Play Exercises

Controlled play exercises are based upon a strictly managed script with set times for events to occur. Controlled play exercises effectively guarantee that all the objectives will at least be addressed. However, controlled play exercises tend to restrict the freedom of players and some spontaneity is lost in running with ideas and testing the flexibility of the plan. Can the plan deal with the unexpected events if it is so heavily scripted and controlled?

Free play exercises in which the basic scenario is given to players and their actions determine future events are very exciting and stimulating for players. The main disadvantage with this type of exercise is that it requires very careful umpiring because the umpires will be constantly managing the play by having to answer queries from players as to what is and is not to be taken as play. Never underestimate how involved players can get in an exercise—it can become their reality! For example, is the request from a player notional or real? They may ask 'Do we assume the hospital has been notified or do we have to do that?' To keep the exercise on track, this type of exercise will also require many more controlled players who will also need to have to hand a vast array of background information to answer any queries from players. For example, 'can I get sufficient Red Cross volunteers here within two hours?' In a free play exercise, consideration should be given to having a supplementary exercise control group, a 'dynamic think tank' of experts set apart who can answer any questions from the players via the umpires.

Probably the most serious flaw with free play exercises is losing control of it and actually missing parts of the plan that really need to be tested or evaluated.

7.5 **Exercise Control**

Exercise Control is the engine room that drives an exercise and for a control post and live exercises probably presents the most challenging aspect of exercise preparation and management. It is located separately from any exercise site. It is at exercise control that the exercise will be managed, monitored and driven. The exercise director will sit in exercise control together with the exercise manager(s). Exercise control will also house the exercise driver inputters, the people who will input the messages by telephone, fax, or e-mail for each service or department from a prepared and timed script. Exercise Control will operate on a separate communications network to the exercise itself (see below). Exercise control can be viewed as a management and communications layer that sits above the exercise. The umpires act as the field operatives for exercise control who have regular and direct communication with exercise control at all times. They are the eyes and ears of exercise control. Figure 7.2 illustrates a typical exercise control.

7.6 **Exercise Communications Network Overlay**

Figure 7.3 illustrates the exercise communications layer which is put in place to manage the exercise through exercise control and out to the umpires acting at each of the live sites. The dotted lines indicate exercise communication only.

Task 7.1

There are two communications networks in a control post and live exercise. Explain why that is necessary.

Figure 7.2 Exercise Control

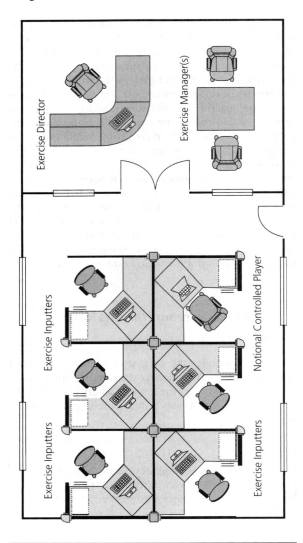

Figure 7.3 Exercise Communications Overlay

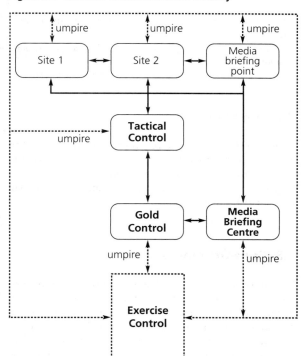

In this example there are two active operational sites 1 and 2, a forward media briefing point, a Silver Control Centre, a Gold Control (SCC) and a centralized Media Briefing Centre.

The exercise communications network operates independently of the actual communications links, if in fact they are being tested in the exercise. It is therefore important that all the telephone and radio call signs are held in exercise control so that the exercise managers can contact the exercise umpires at all times.

Task 7.2

Identify a location suitable for an exercise control in your workplace.

Draw a sketch and position the key players within that room.

7.7 **Time Line**

A time line (Figure 7.4) is a very useful way to 'visualize' an exercise particularly where multiple sites are involved and how activities relate and interact. Laid against each other it is easy to see what is happening where and when. We will look again at timelines in planning the exercise.

7.8 **Compressing Time**

Compressing time is a very effective way of moving an exercise on, particularly for table top exercises. In real time it would take many hours to set up certain facilities, access certain resources or for things to actually happen, so compressing time is the only realistic way to achieve this. This is where a detailed time line will clarify the timings. The time factor is also very important to introduce pressure and drive decision making. Careful use of time can enhance an exercise greatly. Introducing exercise inputs as 'T' time of incident and then 'T' + 1, 'T' + 6 etc. can bring into play identified exercise objectives which in real time could not be achieved: eg emergency mortuary management issues which in reality would take 12–24 hours to set up. This can be discussed with an exercise input given as, eg, T + 12.

Figure 7.4 Exercise Time Line

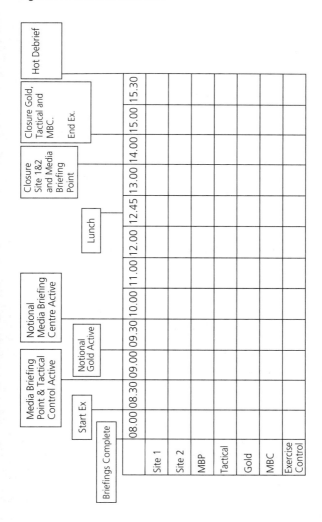

> **Task 7.3**
>
> Consider a scenario over an extended period and create a time line using 'T' at points at which significant events could take place.

7.9 Exercise Order or Programme

This document describes the entire exercise and will develop as the planning process proceeds. It is the definitive exercise programme outlining the management structure and is used by the Exercise Director, Exercise Manager(s), planning team, facilitators, umpires, assessors and observers. It is usually made up as follows:

Cover

- Exercise name/time/date/venue/logos.

Foreword

Senior manager signatory including:

- General reason for exercise.
- Support and importance of exercising.
- Encouraging those to get involved.
- Enjoy the day.

Timetable for the day

- For seminar and table top exercises include times of sessions and breaks during the day or course of the seminar.
- For control post or live exercises include the start time and estimated finish time only.

Introduction

- Specific reason for exercise.
- The planning team—who are they?
- CV for exercise management staff and presenters.

This is a good section to highlight the profile of those taking responsibility for these important roles and adds to the credibility of the exercise.

Aim and objectives

- Include all those submitted to the planning team by all participating organizations and departments.

Exercise management

- Format—type of exercise.
- Managers—their role.
- Umpires—their role.
- Assessors—their role.
- How the exercise will be run—briefings.
- Vocabulary—code words.

  - Exercise…Startex. Begin exercise.
  - Exercise …Hold. Suspend exercise.
  - Exercise…Resume. Resume exercise after hold.
  - Exercise…Abort. Emergency termination.
  - Exercise…Endex. End exercise.

Task 7.4

The exercise vocabulary is not fixed. Can you think of a vocabulary that could be applied to a live exercise scenario? Think of all the activity that will occur and try to think of code words to publish with an Exercise Order.

Communications

- This is probably the most important section. Without good and effective communication during control post and live exercises, the exercise will fail.
- Dedicated radio channels for the exercise play and exercise control should be separate. All telephone numbers in use in the exercise should be in a directory as part of the players' briefing pack. All telephone numbers both land line and mobile/radio call signs should be displayed upon a board in exercise control.
- All exercise communication should be prefixed with the exercise name to prevent any confusion if the message reaches the 'real' world.
- All non-participating communication centres and switchboards should be advised in advance of any exercise to avoid any false alarms.

Exercise inputs

- For table top exercises the questions that will be asked of the syndicates and suggested model answers to assist the facilitators, presenters and observers.
- For control post and live exercises do not include the driver inputs but a simple section to describe the process only.

Debrief process

- All exercises should be debriefed. Clearly, the more complex the exercise the more thorough the debrief.

Glossary

- It is useful to have a comprehensive glossary of terms. Although there is generally a common language for

exercising there are some anomalies across organizations and industries.
- Many observers will not understand many of the terms used.

7.10 **Players' Information Pack**

A player information pack can be as simple as a briefing sheet sent by e-mail. It can also be more comprehensive including identification tabard, identification badge, directions to venues etc. Every player must receive a minimum of information which is outlined in the checklist below.

> **Checklist—Minimum amount of information for each player**
>
> - Exercise name
> - Date
> - Exercise duration
> - Report time/Briefing time
> - Reporting to who
> - Start time
> - Dress—particularly if outdoors!
> - Location
> - Their precise job description—be explicit that it is or is not a personal test
> - Exercise rules
> - Refreshment arrangements
> - Use of mobile phone information
> - What to do if sick
> - A debrief form
> - Health and safety information
> - Glossary of terms

> **Task 7.5**
>
> Looking at the list of details above, list in order of priority the most and the least important to the player.

7.11 **Debrief Schedule**

The debrief is the most important link between exercising and realizing positive change in working practices in emergency planning. Recording information for debriefing purposes must have structure and clarity otherwise the debrief will become unfocused and ambiguous. It may also result in lessons being missed or an organization avoiding responsibility for implementing change. Throughout the exercise process, all participants should be working to address specific areas of the plan and designated objectives which should be grouped together into a 'Debrief Schedule' under 'activity areas' see Figure 7.5. Therefore, during the planning process a debrief schedule document should be produced which reflects the 'activity areas' under which the debrief will be focused. These are general areas of activity and based around the objectives, for example:

- Information exchange
- Team working
- Alert notifications
- Set up Control Centre
- Interpretation of information
- Communication
- Information sharing
- Decision making
- Media management
- Etc.

Looking at the agreed aim and objectives, decide how they can be categorized into 'activity areas' as shown above for example. The activity areas have to be created to suit the

Figure 7.5 Debrief Schedule

Activity Area	Sub-Issue	Areas for improvement	Positive comments	Organization commenting
Activation	• Alert • Decision to activate • Etc	There was confusion as to the interpretation of the incoming alert information	Once the correct information was received a very quick management decision was made.	Police / Fire / Ambulance
Notification	• Telephone • Call out • Etc	The telephone contacts were out of date. The call out list was also out of date.		Police
Set up of facilities	• Reception • Briefing • Etc			
Information sharing	• Message systems • Etc			
Decision making	• Meetings • Etc			

exercise. The activity areas will be subdivided into sub-issues. For example, if one of the objectives is the 'set up of the emergency facility' (an activity area) consider (as sub-issues) what was the parking like? What was reception like? Were attendees properly briefed on arrival?

The debrief team (set up as a sister group to the planning team) will divide up the feedback or evaluation forms from the exercise into the activity areas and assign sub-issues. This will keep the debrief focused and give it structure. It will also make allocating and identifying actions a lot easier. An example of a partially completed debrief schedule is shown in Figure 7.5.

You can see from the short extract above that a picture of common areas for concern or best practice will soon emerge as the debrief team begin to populate the schedule following the exercise and transfer the information from the evaluation data. There will be more about that in Chapter 10. This debrief schedule will then create the action tracking table document which we will look at later.

The debrief flow chart shown in Figure 7.6 gives an overview of the debrief process from initial aim to action tracking.

7.12 **Summary**

You now understand the role of key personnel used in an exercise and how the exercise structure is shaped to manage an exercise. The concept of exercise inputs and the role of umpires has been explained together with preparing for the debrief. The manipulation of time has been explained and the use of timelines to clarify the progress of the exercise. Finally, the preparation of the exercise 'instruction' or order has been covered with the provision of a player's information pack to assist everyone to get the most from the exercise.

Figure 7.6 Debrief Flow Chart

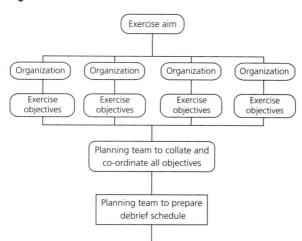

7.13 **Conclusion**

Perceived sometimes as a complicated topic, exercise management is straightforward if approached in a methodical and systematic fashion. Developing an understanding of the roles and how they interact is vital for a successful exercise. Following the basic principles outlined above will produce an exercise that will test and evaluate plans to the full and create a learning environment that is not only very informative but fun too!

Chapter 8

Planning and Organizing the Exercise

Overview

In this chapter you will cover:

- Basic exercise preparation
- Planning meetings
- Developing the scenario—Exercise Mayflower
- Driver inputs
- Preparing resource boards
- Seminar exercise checklist
- Table top checklist
- Control post exercise checklist
- Live exercise checklist

8.1 Introduction

Having gained an understanding of the exercise management process and the key people that are involved, the detailed planning process can begin. In this chapter we will be consolidating the knowledge gained so far and looking in more depth at the practicalities of planning an exercise. A worked example will be used to bring together the processes in a logical manner. The easiest approach to planning the exercise is by considering what each of the four formats already described will require. But there are some basic planning preparations to consider for any type of exercise.

8.1.1 Basic Preparation

There are some common preparations and considerations for all exercises—see the checklist below for information.

Checklist—Common preparations/considerations for exercises

- Senior management support—The EPO should inform the highest ranking manager of their intentions. Obtain their endorsement and a commitment to participate, even if it is just to open the exercise.
- Notify people early—The EPO should identify all those who should be invited to the first planning meeting, both internal and external. Do not underestimate the time needed to secure their attendance. Several months' notice will be needed to get it into diaries and to ensure their absence during the exercise can be covered. Once they agree to take part make sure the emphasis is on them to find a replacement should they have to back out. It does no harm to use the senior management endorsement as a means of reinforcing the request.
- Involve the LRF—If other agencies are involved ensure that the relevant planning group is notified. This will usually mean the Local Resilience Forum (LRF) secretary, this is crucial to obtain the support of any external agencies.
- Book early—Book the necessary rooms and facilities well in advance including any catering that may be needed.
- Financial support—Secure any finance that may be required or at least inform those who manage finance within the organization or approach the LRF. Find out if the LRF supports cost recovery in which case the blue light services and local authority may charge a fee to take part.
- Reserves—Ensure there are stand-ins or reserves for key exercise presenters, facilitators, and managers.
- Start drafting key documents—Begin to consider a draft 'Exercise Order' and 'Players' information' pack.

- Contingencies—Plan for and include contingencies for a situation that the exercise, as planned, is adversely affected. There may be a need to consider postponing it, downsizing or changing a venue quickly. It could be affected by real events such as sickness, bad weather or a real crisis. The consequential costs incurred in abandoning an exercise could be very significant. The more resource intensive the more detailed the contingencies need to be. If cost recovery is involved, ensure that the issue of cancellation is discussed and documented. Accept that the emergency services will always participate on condition that there are no real events that require operational response. Some organizations try to deploy staff on overtime to prevent such cancellations taking place, in particular where there is a major training benefit for them.

8.2 Planning Meetings

8.2.1 Beginning the planning stage

As alluded to in the previous chapter, a lead individual will take overall charge of exercise administration. The lead individual will be a person from the organization who is effectively 'sponsoring' the exercise (ie the organization who has initiated the exercise)—this is not the Exercise Director. The Exercise Director task usually, but not always, falls to a person from that initiating organization. The responsibility for exercise administration and overall manager is usually that of the EPO, contingency planning or business continuity manager from within that initiating organization (who will also invariably be an exercise manager too).

Begin to consider who will make up the planning team. All those who have a part within the plan must be invited initially. The core planning team will eventually become smaller but not to invite a key stakeholder could create tension and arguably with some justification. At this stage it is quite arbitrary but err on the side of inviting too many to the first planning meeting and then agree a core planning team.

8.2.2 The Core Planning Team

The lead person will be responsible for:

- ensuring an Exercise Director is appointed;
- scheduling the exercise planning meetings;
- preparing the agendas;
- monitoring planning actions;
- collating aim and objectives;
- collating driver inputs and arranging the script preparation;
- co-ordinating the preparation and production of the Exercise Order; and
- co-ordinating the preparation and production of the Players' Pack.

The initial invitation to attend the planning meeting should be in good time and wide ranging. At the first planning meeting the core planning team will be selected and agreed. In that way key stakeholders within the plan will have a say who attends the meetings or by what means they can be kept informed if they choose not to attend, perhaps being copied into e-mails and circulation. In this way they can contribute at any time.

Depending on the scale and complexity of the exercise, the planning team may meet many times and will certainly have a key role to play in the exercise.

One of the first tasks of the planning meeting will be to begin the initial exercise planning processes. The example that follows illustrates how that can be achieved in six steps.

8.3 Developing the Scenario—Exercise Mayflower

We have already looked at the basic issues to consider in deciding on a scenario and how aims and objectives are constructed. More specifically how does it work in practice?

This simple practical example will illustrate the whole process—called exercise 'Mayflower'. The process can be summed up in the illustration shown in Figure 8.1.

It is a six-stage process that will result in the production of precise and relevant exercise drivers and inputs to address all of the exercise objectives.

This process is relevant for table-top, control post or live exercises.

Figure 8.1 Scenario Development Stages

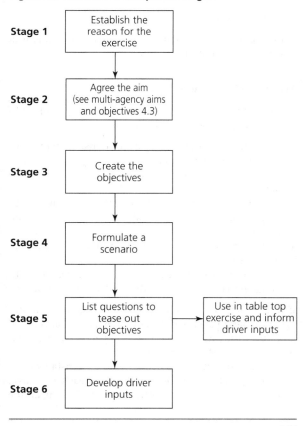

8 Planning and Organizing the Exercise

To set the scene—Bridgestone is a small rural village within which sits the ACME chemical company.

Stage 1—What is the reason for this exercise?

This exercise has been chosen because there is a concern to local residents of Bridgestone Village and the emergency services, and other emergency responders including the company, wish to evaluate their emergency arrangements.

Stage 2—Aim

'To test emergency response arrangement for a chemical tanker incident in Bridgestone Village'.

Stage 3—Objectives

These are the combined objectives of all those involved in planning and are required to meet the aim.

1. To evaluate the ACME company response to an incident involving one of their tankers.
2. To examine the emergency response and joint working of the emergency services.
3. To consider the implications of a widespread impact of a toxic chemical spill and possible deposition on agricultural land.
4. To examine the warning and informing arrangements to protect the public.
5. To examine the management issues in dealing with evacuation over an extended period for local residents.

If it is decided to use a table-top format consider multi-agency tables made up of the police, fire, ambulance, local authority, the ACME chemical Company, Environment Agency and the Health Protection Agency.

Take each objective and decide what circumstances will explore that objective. Do the same for each objective. At this stage it may seem a little disjointed bolting all the circumstances together. What will happen eventually is that a situation or scenario will begin to emerge that will build into a coherent and realistic situation which address-es each objective.

- To meet objective 1 we need a tanker crash involving ACME.
- To meet objective 2 we need a major incident involving all blue lights.
- To meet objective 3 we need spreading toxic plume.
- To meet objective 4 we need large numbers of people that need to be warned and kept informed.
- To meet objective 5 we need large numbers of people dis-placed from their homes.

Stage 4—Scenario

Drawing everything so far together, we could consider the following scenario:

'It is 0930 hours on 21 March 2008, Bank Holiday Friday. The weather is fine and the road is dry. The wind is a light north westerly. The ACME chemical company tanker is intending to make a delivery to their chemical plant locat-ed in the High Street, Bridgestone Village. The tanker veers for no obvious reason as it approaches the gate and collides with a bus and car. The bus is carrying 35 pensioners on a day trip and the car contains two people.
Note: A map provided would show that the chemical incident is located in a small village of about 20 shops and near a large school and housing estate. The wind direction indicates that the toxic plume will blow over the estate.

Three elderly people remain trapped, as are the drivers of the tanker, bus and car. The car passenger has escaped and called the emergency services.

People in the vicinity are choking and having difficulty breathing. Local residents have been warning of the poten-tial of such an incident for years and the press are already ringing the police.

This is the basic scenario and introduction. Now consider what paper feeds or inputs will drive this exercise or how this will affect any driving inputs for a Control Post or Live exercise.

Stage 5—Questions

To tease out the issues/objectives, consider asking the following questions of the syndicates:

1. Having been made aware of this incident what would your organization's initial response be?
2. What Command and Control arrangements would be put in place?
3. How would the casualties be managed in the initial stages?
4. How would local people be made aware of the incident and advised how to protect themselves?
5. What impact would this toxic substance have on surrounding farmland and livestock?
6. How would an evacuation be effected or would it be necessary?
7. How would the media be managed?
8. What kind of investigation may follow such an incident?

There may be more questions that could be added to address specific local issues but we have moved from aim to objective to scenario to questions—it is a logical sequence. Even if it is a not a table top exercise, still prepare the questions. They will clarify the outcomes of the exercise and they will be invaluable in preparing driver inputs for a Control Post or Live exercise. Therefore the final stage would be to develop the driver inputs if the intention is to run a Control Post or Live exercise.

Stage 6—Driver inputs

Figure 8.2 illustrates an extract from a driver script from the above incident. Preparing the script is a major task for the

Figure 8.2 Input Driver Script

	Input by	Input Time	From	To	Where	Text – Prefix each message with the words 'Exercise Mayflower'
1	Fire	08.54	Mrs Green 3 High St. 020 45345	Fire	Police Tactical Control	My husband is a fire-fighter and I understand he has collapsed at an incident in Bridgestone Village. What can you tell me?
2	Ambulance	08.47	Dr Patel Surgery 12 Low St. 020 45341	HPA	Police Strategic Control	I have a couple of patients who are complaining of chest tightness. Can this be as a result of the chemical spill?
3	Police	09.00	Mr Graham Global Products Ind. Estate 020 34467	Police Liaison	Company Emergency Control Centre	We are next door to the ACME site can you advise if we should evacuate our building?
4	Company	09.05	Mr Brown 7 Small St. 020 45346	Company ACME	Company Emergency Control Centre	I can see a yellow plume of gas coming from the ACME factory. Is it safe to go out?
5	Company	09.10	Mrs Evans 33 Garden Street 020 34567	Company ACME	Police Strategic Control Centre	My husband was working in the ACME factory this morning. My friend tells me he has been injured is that true?
6	Police	09.15	Daily Mercury 020 34567	Police	Police Strategic Control Centre	Can you tell me the time of the next press briefing?
7	Local Authority	09.20	Red Cross 020 12346	Local Authority	Police Strategic Control Centre	Are you evacuating and if so where is the rest centre?
8	Fire	09.30	Mr Simmons FBU 020 45345	Fire	Police Strategic Control Centre	I understand this site is highly toxic. Can I be reassured that our members are fully protected?

planning team as it is a follow on process from agreeing the aim and objectives. Each organization or department will submit their inputs to the planning team having agreed the overall objectives and the master script will be compiled from those submissions. It is worth keeping these scripts after the exercise as they can, with some modification, be used again and again.

These driver inputs will be used by Controlled Players from Exercise Control. Careful and detailed briefing will be required to assist and prepare the Inputters. The ability to manage several conversation and enquiries, as several different people and remain in character is daunting but can be very rewarding and fun.

Task 8.1

Continue the list of inputs and create another 15.

8.4 **Preparing Resource Boards**

Whichever exercise is chosen, be it live, control post, or table top, a key factor in the developing scenario will be resourcing. This is an aspect often overlooked. Exercises seem to have infinite resources and unlimited staff working continuous hours without days off but as everyone knows, the reality is that depending on the time of day resources can vary enormously. For each exercise a decision will have to be made as to the level of resourcing to allow. There is of course an option to run with unlimited resourcing: if for example, there is a need to concentrate exclusively on one aspect of the plan where resourcing is not an issue. However this will create a false dynamic within the exercise leading to a false sense of security; those taking part will assume and rely upon unlimited resources, which in reality is never the case.

Using 'actual' resource numbers can be a very sobering experience for senior managers when they see how fast they are swallowed up and additional resourcing is required urgently. Creating inputs that explore how additional resourcing can be obtained, from where, from whom and how long will it take will focus the mind of many managers. If using resource boards, which are essentially staffing and resource schedules introduce them at the beginning of the exercise to each of the organizations taking part. Resource schedules can be arranged in the planning stage for each organization. They can be displayed on dry wipe boards in a live exercise, control post, or table top exercises. They can also be handed to facilitators or umpires in paper form to manage on behalf of the players.

To get a feel for the level of resourcing available for any given exercise at a particular time and date, approach the HR department or those who prepare the duties or staffing levels. Then consider the available hardware such as vehicles and specialist support equipment. A list can then be prepared as to what level of resourcing could reasonably be expected.

Task 8.2

If possible—for any given time, day, and date (your choice)—ascertain what level of resourcing/staffing is available within your organization and what specialist skills and knowledge they have. It is important for planning purposes to have this information. Who holds such information? Can you get access to it out of hours as the emergency planning officer?

We will now consider the planning issues related to the four main types of exercise. The following lists could be used to prepare agendas for the meetings and/or prepare information to players.

8.5 **Seminar Exercise**

The date and start time of this exercise will be known. Send out invitations to all those taking part at least two weeks in advance, with the following information:

1. Time, date, and location of exercise.
2. Dress code (if any—possibly uniform or non-uniform).
3. Catering arrangements.
4. Advise participants of the limited use of mobile phones.
5. The timetable for the day (they will know when mobiles can be used).
6. Set out the aim of the exercise.
7. Inform participants that there will be a test at the end of the exercise.
8. Inform them that they are responsible for finding a replacement if necessary.
9. Prepare the questions for the test paper based upon your aim and emergency plan content.
10. Inform the participants which plan is being used (this will give an opportunity to pre-read if they wish—some will!)
11. Prepare how you intend to present the plan. The plan format suggested earlier lends itself to a systematic presentation. In other words, take each section in order using the contents page as a guide.

A word on dress code—an exercise is a professional activity attended by experts and senior managers who will give their time and support and will expect a degree of 'professionalism' from participants, particularly where the uniformed services are involved. If participants turn up in T-shirts, shorts, dirty training shoes etc. it reflects poorly not only on the participant but the organization they represent—try saying smart but casual and don't be frightened to say no trainers or football shirts.

Include separate invitations to those external agencies that will make up the 'expert' panel.

Task 8.3

Can you suggest reasons why using a test paper or quiz will be a useful activity in a seminar exercise?

8.6 Table Top Checklist

It will be necessary to allow at least 3–4 months' planning time for a table top exercise. The time between meetings allows for actions to be completed in good time. It is important that actions are actively followed. Setting out a provisional schedule of planning meetings will be useful even if it is amended as the process proceeds. The following schedule is suggested as a minimum, more planning meetings may be necessary depending on the completion of actions:

First Planning Meeting

- Invite representatives of all participating organizations and internal departments who have a role within the plan. Obtain their contact details and circulate on the day to everyone present or before the end of the meeting if possible.
- Confirm who the lead organization or department is for the exercise.
- Confirm who the lead person is.
- Discuss a date for the exercise.
- Outline a scenario—discuss.
- Discuss the exercise 'aim'.
- Ask for 'objectives' to be forwarded to the exercise lead prior to the next meeting.
- Agree an exercise name.
- Agree the core planning team.
- Discuss a policy on exercise observers—see Observers.
- Discuss Exercise Director, Exercise Facilitator(s). Two main facilitators/presenters and one facilitator per table.

8 Planning and Organizing the Exercise

- Discuss policy on Exercise Assessor(s).
- Agree table top format.
- Discuss venue—will you need microphones?
- Discuss media involvement to promote and report the exercise.
- Discuss exercise logistics—badges and administration.
- Discuss any costs and agree where those costs lie.
- Agree/confirm the schedule of planning meetings.
- Create an action tracking list and whose action it is.

Second Planning Meeting (two–three weeks later)

- Confirm exercise aim.
- Update exercise objectives.
- Decide on Resources Boards.
- Confirm the scenario.
- Agree/confirm the presenters and facilitators.
- Agree venue.
- Agree the table top format—syndicate make-up/presentations by guest speakers/expert panel.
- Draft the exercise inputs.
- Agree what additional material is required, eg photos, maps, audio/visual inputs.
- Discuss exercise inputs and agree 'model' answers.
- Present draft 'Exercise Order'.
- Check action list for outstanding actions and add new ones as required.

Third Planning Meeting (two–three weeks later)

- Assemble all exercise management team for briefing. Including main facilitators, syndicate facilitators and presenters (if available). Also include the facility manager to confirm catering and reception arrangements.

- Visit/check venue/seating and audio/visual.
- Agree exercise inputs and agree 'model' answers.
- Agree Exercise Order and players' briefing pack.
- Prepare the debrief document schedule or headings based upon the objectives.
- Run through any additional material—flip charts, photos, maps etc.
- Agree what plans will be made available to the players.
- Schedule the first debrief meeting.

8.7 **Control Post Exercise Checklist**

Allow 6–9 months' planning time for this exercise. Setting out a provisional schedule of planning meetings will be useful even if it is amended as the process proceeds. The points below will assist in preparing a planning meeting agenda.

The following schedule/actions are suggested as a minimum:

First Planning Meeting

- Invite representatives of all participating organizations and internal departments who have a role within the plan. Obtain their contact details and circulate that day to everyone present or during the meeting if possible.
- Invite all those who have an exercise support role such as catering staff, telecommunications, facilities managers, HR managers etc. for each of the locations being used.
- Confirm who the lead organization is for the exercise.
- Confirm who the lead person is.
- Discuss a date for the exercise.
- Outline a scenario.
- Agree the exercise 'aim'.

- Ask for 'objectives' to be forwarded prior to the next meeting.
- Discuss media objectives both real and exercise.
- Agree an exercise name.
- Agree the core planning team.
- Discuss a policy on exercise observers—see Observers.
- Agree Exercise Director.
- Discuss policy on Exercise Assessor(s).
- Discuss which sites/control centres will be active.
- Discuss where the site will be for exercise control.
- Agree exercise logistics—badges and administration.
- Discuss any costs and agree where those costs lie.
- Discuss any Cost Recovery issues and agree how this will be administered.
- Agree/confirm the schedule of planning meetings.
- Arrange to have the exercise videoed and/or photographs taken.
- Create an action tracking list and whose action it is.

Second Planning Meeting (4–6 weeks later)

- Confirm exercise aim.
- Update exercise objectives.
- Decide on Resource Boards.
- Confirm the scenario.
- Confirm Exercise Director.
- Agree/confirm exercise managers and umpires.
- Agree site for exercise control.
- Agree exercise communications.
- Draft/collate the exercise inputs.
- Agree what additional material is required, eg photos, maps, audio/visual inputs.
- Present draft 'Exercise Document' (or Exercise Order).
- Check action list for outstanding actions and add new ones.

Third Planning Meeting (4–6 weeks later)

- Update scenario if required.
- Confirm exercise objectives.
- Confirm exercise inputs.
- Confirm active/live sites.
- Present updated Exercise Order.
- Update on observers and their management.
- Confirm umpires and exercise managers (and assessors if operating).
- Confirm communications network for both exercise and exercise management.
- Collate all relevant telephone numbers for both exercise play and exercise management.
- Prepare the debrief schedule and activity areas based upon the objectives.
- Agree Exercise Order and players' briefing pack.
- Agree how players will be introduced into exercise— pre-positioned, called in as required by umpires or in real time.
- Confirm media arrangements and any Media Briefing Centre (MBC).

Fourth Planning Meeting (4–6 weeks later)

- Assemble all exercise management team for briefing based upon Exercise Order. Include Director, exercise managers, umpires and assessors.
- Visit and check live venue(s) inc MBC.
- Visit and check Exercise Control.
- Sign off Exercise Order and players' briefing pack for printing.
- Run through additional material.
- Agree what plans will be made available to players.
- Check communications directory.

- Fix dates to brief driver inputters.
- Schedule the first debrief meeting.

Fifth Planning Meeting (4–6 weeks later or just before the exercise)

- Brief senior exercise players.
- Brief any controlled players.
- Brief exercise support staff and assistants.
- Final briefing of Exercise Management Team.
- Revisit all control centres—final inspection.

Task 8.4

Can you suggest why taking video and photographing an exercise can be beneficial?

8.8 **Live Exercise Checklist**

Live exercising is the most realistic form of exercising. Some aspects of emergency response can only be accurately tested or evaluated by live exercising. Depending upon the nature of the exercise, it can be quite modest in scale and can exercise only a small part of the overall plan. In fact it can form a module of a larger exercise including components from table top and control post.

The primary issue for concern in planning for a live exercise is the safety of all those involved. Where there is a site or multiple sites, including the use of props such as buildings, trains, vehicles, shipping or aircraft, extensive risk assessment is needed. Close observation of all activity sites is vital as are clearly understood rules of disengagement should a real incident occur. Dedicated health and safety officers must be deployed at all times to supervise activities.

For a major live play exercise allow 6–12 months' planning time. The points below will assist in preparing a planning meeting agenda.

The following schedule/actions are suggested:

First Planning Meeting

- Invite representatives of all participating organizations and internal departments who have a role within the plan. Obtain their contact details and circulate them that day to everyone present or during the meeting if possible.
- Invite all those who have an exercise support role such as catering staff, telecommunications, facilities managers, HR managers, potential site owners etc.
- Agree the exercise 'aim'.
- Ask for 'objectives' to be forwarded prior to the next meeting.
- Confirm who the lead organization is for the exercise.
- Confirm who the lead person will be.
- Discuss any Cost Recovery issues and agree how this will be administered.
- Discuss and confirm the need to live exercise. Combined exercising options?
- Discuss the proposed location of the exercise site or sites.
- Discuss the use of notional live sites—where controlled players are used. See next chapter.
- Discuss which sites/control centres will be active.
- Discuss where the site will be for exercise control.
- Discuss the use of Resource Boards (real or notional resources).
- Consider time of year and likely weather conditions.
- Consider what additional props may be needed, eg dummy casualties, wreckage, artificial smoke etc.
- Consider a public awareness strategy to prevent concern and panic.

- Agree a media policy to observe and report the exercise. How are you going to promote the exercise?
- Discuss media objectives both real and exercise.
- Discuss a date for the exercise.
- Outline a scenario.
- Agree an exercise name.
- Agree the core planning team.
- Discuss a policy on exercise observers—see Observers.
- Agree Exercise Director, exercise umpires.
- Discuss a policy on Exercise Assessor(s).
- Agree exercise logistics—badges and administration.
- Will you need on-site toilets?
- Discuss any costs and agree where those costs lie.
- Agree/confirm the schedule of planning meetings.
- Try to arrange for the exercise to be videoed and/or photographs taken.
- Create an action tracking list and whose action it is.

Second Planning Meeting (4–6 weeks later)

- Confirm Exercise Director.
- Confirm the scenario.
- Confirm exercise aim.
- Update exercise objectives.
- Decide on Resource Boards.
- Consider any proposed site and arrange for site visits.
- Discuss a contingency in case the weather is not suitable for the exercise—what else can you do?
- Discuss additional props needed for the exercise.
- Agree what additional material is required, eg photos, maps, audio/visual inputs.
- Agree site for exercise control.
- Agree/confirm exercise managers and umpires.
- Draft/collate the exercise inputs.
- Present draft 'Exercise Order' (or exercise programme).
- Check action list for outstanding actions and add new ones.

Third Planning meeting (4–6 weeks later)

- Update scenario if required.
- Confirm exercise objectives.
- Confirm exercise inputs.
- Confirm active/live sites.
- Confirm site locations.
- Confirm all props are available and booked/sourced.
- Present updated Exercise Order.
- Update on observers and their management.
- Confirm umpires and exercise managers (and assessors, if operating).
- Confirm communications network for both exercise and exercise management.
- Collate all relevant telephone phone numbers for both exercise play and exercise management.
- Prepare the debrief schedule and activity areas based upon the objectives.
- Agree Exercise Order and players' briefing pack.
- Agree how players will be introduced into exercise—pre-positioned, called in as required by umpires or in real time.
- Confirm media arrangements and any Media Briefing Centre (MBC).

Fourth/Fifth Planning Meeting (4–6 weeks later)

Please note that a fifth meeting may be needed to be able to visit all sites depending on their distribution.

- Assemble all exercise management team for briefing based upon Exercise Order. Include Director, exercise manager, umpires, assessors.
- Visit and check live control centre(s) including MBC.
- Visit and check Exercise Control.
- Visit exercise site(s).

8 Planning and Organizing the Exercise

- Sign off 'Exercise Order' and players' briefing pack for printing.
- Run through additional material.
- Agree what plans will be made available to players.
- Check communications directory.
- Fix dates to brief driver inputters.
- Confirm exercise evaluation forms.
- Agree the debrief team.
- Schedule the first debrief meeting.

Sixth Planning Meeting (4–6 weeks later or just before the exercise)

- Brief senior exercise players.
- Brief any controlled players.
- Brief exercise support staff and assistants.
- Final briefing of Exercise Management Team.
- Distribute all exercise documents.
- Revisit all sites—final inspection.

Task 8.5

During live exercises a public information strategy is important. Can you suggest why that is?

8.9 Summary

- You will now be aware of the basic preparation to be taken for exercise planning meetings.
- You now understand the key issues that need to be addressed in planning for a meeting for any type of exercise.
- You will be able to prepare a comprehensive agenda for a planning meeting.

8.10 **Conclusion**

This chapter has concentrated on preparing checklists to assist in creating a logical planning process to the exercise. Preparing agendas is an important part of the meeting process. It will keep the planning process and discussion on track and, together with completing actions associated with those meetings, the overall planning should be problem free. Approached in a systematic way, preparing for an exercise is a straightforward activity.

The next chapter will consider how to actually run the exercise on the day including the final preparations and ensuring it all goes smoothly.

Chapter 9

How to Run the Exercise

> **Overview**
>
> In this chapter, you will cover the following:
>
> - Running and managing a Seminar Exercise
> - Running and managing a Table Top Exercise
> - Running and managing a Control Post Exercise
> - Running and managing a Live Exercise

9.1 **Introduction**

Having now looked at the main types of exercises, the key participants, scenario development and planning the exercise, we can turn to actually running the exercise on the day. We will look at this from the perspective of the exercise manager and/or main presenter, who may have also chaired or jointly chaired the planning meetings. We will assume that it is the EPO.

9.2 **The Seminar Exercise**

The day before or earlier that day, the EPO will arrive at the venue, which will have been pre-booked in advance, and checked that refreshments have been ordered. The room layout will be in the form of group tables of between 8–10 people. It is a good idea if the groups are mixed up into senior and junior staff with a mix of expertise to assist in sharing information.

9 How to Run the Exercise

The room is laid out in 'cabaret style', as illustrated in Figure 9.1. This is ideal for interaction and forming teams. The IT should be checked, for example the PowerPoint projector and that the presentation is working correctly. Ensure that the multiple choice questions (about 30 questions) and answers are prepared and there are sufficient copies for all. A hardcopy plan should be placed on each table with notepaper and pens. Label each table A, B, C etc.

Figure 9.1 Exercise Room Layout

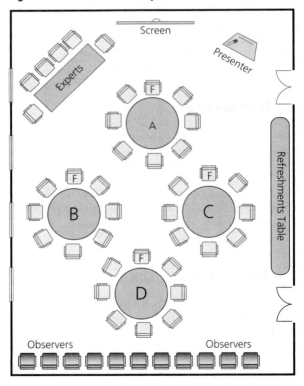

The exercise programme may look something like the example below:

Example—Seminar exercise programme
Instructions for the EPO:

09.30: Reception
Set up a reception desk and issue badges. Try to make the first name prominent. A seating plan should be displayed prepared by you earlier. Again, ensure you have a good mix of experience and skills. Registration is important to record those who have attended and for health and safety reasons should an evacuation be required. Try to get e-mail addresses at registration. Coffee/tea should be provided.

09.45: Opening
A senior manager should do this if possible. You should have approached and secured their attendance during the planning process. It is a good idea to prepare a draft of what you would like them to say!

09.50: Introduction
At this point, you thank the opening remarks and everyone for attending. You will then introduce yourself with a little background. You should then ask everyone to introduce themselves to each other on their tables, not to the whole seminar. Allow about 5–10 minutes for this.
Cover health and safety and domestic arrangements. Explain the format for the day and explain the purpose of the test or quiz at the end of the seminar.

10.00: Presentation of the Plan
Your presentation will begin by showing the hard copy plan to the group and the importance of the session. Work through the plan sequentially in section order referring to the main headings and drawing out the most important areas. Constantly ask for thoughts and their observations. Make sure you address all the areas that will appear in the test later.

If you have assembled an 'expert' panel frequently refer to them for comment.

11.00: Coffee

11.15: Resume—as above

12.30: Finish/Lunch

13.30: Quiz

Offer a quick resume of the critical areas of the plan. Explain the purpose of the quiz. The emphasis is on it being fun. Refer to it as a quiz and each table can form a team. This will promote discussion. Offer a token prize for the winning team.

14.30: Finish the quiz and collect the question papers. Break for coffee.

14.45: Answers to the quiz

Resume and go through the paper giving the correct answers. Do not be too hasty to move on if there is a query on any question. Take this opportunity to clarify, leave no doubt. In fact, there may be occasions where some very useful and valid suggestions are made to amend the plan. Take these points on board and thank them for their comments. This engenders ownership. If you have an 'expert' panel ask for final comments from them.

15.30: Conclusion

Conclude the session. Announce the winning team. Ask for any final comments. Hand out a simple feedback sheet and ask them to complete. Ensure that you encourage them to make contact with you if they have any further questions—give them your details.

16.00: Finish exercise

Task 9.1

Create an evaluation sheet that is suitable for this type of exercise

9.3 **Table Top Exercise**

In this example we will have syndicates as 'units' of equal knowledge and expertise.

It is a good idea to visit the venue the day before and check out the audio and visuals. Contact any presenters to confirm their attendance. It is also a good idea to have some back-up audio visual (AV) in case of failures. Also, make sure the catering is scheduled and reception arrangements are in place. Check that badges are ready and the tables have the necessary documents, such as plans, maps, photos, notepaper and pens, with A1 flip charts. Label each table A, B, C, D, E etc. as in Figure 9.1. The table layout is the same for the seminar exercise. If the venue is a hotel or conference centre meet the facilities manager and discuss final points.

In this exercise it is assumed that the EPO has managed to enlist four presenters to give four 15 minute inputs on subjects relevant to the plan.

The exercise programme may look like the example below:

Example—Table top exercise programme.
Instructions for the EPO:

08.00: Final Checks

Arrange to meet exercise management staff at the venue for a last minute briefing. Check out AV and that all presentations loaded on computer and displaying correctly. Check out the microphones if the venue is large. Ensure reception is ready.

09.00: Reception

A seating plan should be displayed in a prominent position. This will be prepared before the day ensuring you have the right mix of people in the syndicates to suit the format you have chosen for this exercise.

Registration is important to record those who have attended and for health and safety reasons should an evacuation be required. Try to get e-mail addresses

---

of those present by handing out an attendance list if you do not have that information at registration. Coffee/tea should be provided.

09.30: Opening

A senior manager should do this if possible. You should have approached and secured their attendance during the planning process. It is a good idea to prepare a draft of what you would like them to say!

09.35: Introduction

At this point you thank the opening remarks and everyone for attending. You will then introduce yourself with a little background and ask players to introduce themselves to their tables.

Then introduce the other principle facilitator and each facilitator on the tables. Introduce the expert panel—a short CV provided by them will assist you. Cover health and safety and domestic arrangements. Explain that the exercise is about testing systems, processes and procedures and is not an examination. Encourage all to get involved and enjoy the day.

The exercise will now be explained, for example:

- It is a syndicate based table top exercise.
- Each syndicate is made up of . . . Explain the makeup of the groups, and how they are facilitated to assist your discussion.
- 'A scenario will be outlined and you will be asked to consider a number of issues arising from the incident as described. These will be in the form of a number of written questions or paper feeds, as they are sometimes called. You will be given a set time to do this and one syndicate will be asked to give the primary feedback. Feel free to use the flip charts to outline your response. Please nominate a spokesperson to do this. We will then open the issues up for general discussion'.

'Please feel free to ask the advice of the expert panel at any time and use the plans on the tables which will deal with this incident'.

'I will now outline the current circumstances' . . . as prepared by the planning team. This will be the general situation with all attendant details leading up to the incident.
There is an example of an introduction and questions in
the chapter dealing with scenario development.
- Read the current circumstances and refer to any video,
  photos, maps already prepared for the purpose.

10.00: Hand out the questions, first input, usually 3–4
       questions and start the clock, say 30 minutes.
       Near the end of time, it is a good idea to inform
       which group will be giving feedback. Count them
       down from 10 minutes.

10.30: Ask the nominated syndicate to give feedback and
       facilitate the response ensuring that maximum
       information is extracted. Your Exercise Order should
       have prompts to assist you.
       Open it up to the whole group and ask for contribu-
       tions from the expert panel. Facilitate the following
       discussion.

10.50: Conclude feedback
       (At this point you can introduce a presenter to cover
       a relevant topic—15 minutes)

11.05: Second input. Develop the scenario.

11.35: Second feedback session

12.00: Second presenter (15 minutes)

12.15: Third input. Further develop the scenario.

12.45: Third feedback session

13.00: Conclude third feedback session

13.00: Lunch

13.45: Re-start with third presenter

14.00: Final fourth input

14.30: Fourth feedback session

15.00: Coffee

15.15: Final presenter.

15.30: Debrief/lessons learned. At this point you will refer
       to your facilitators to summarize the learning points
       from each syndicate. These will be collated and form
       the debrief report. This should be forwarded to all

> those participating and where necessary fed back
> into the plan. Leave evaluation sheets on each table
> for players to complete.
> 16.00: Conclusion and closing comments. This should be
> delivered by a senior manager.
> 16.15: Disperse

Task 9.2

Create an evaluation sheet that is suitable for this type of
exercise

9.4 Control Post Exercise

In preparing for a Control Post exercise, the live control
centres, including the media briefing centre (MBC) if being
used, should be available for use at least the day before the
exercise and subject of a visit by all the planning team,
including the director, umpires and assessors.

Formal briefings should have been held for all those planning team members and those involved in the exercise management, for example, security, catering, facilities managers
etc. Arrangements for observers will be confirmed as they
will need a briefing away from exercise activity and brought
to the venue(s). Exercise control should be visited and scrutinized to ensure the exercise driving scripts and telephone
numbers are posted.

Depending how it has been decided to introduce players, either pre-positioned at the start of the exercise or their
attendance is controlled from a 'holding' area, is a matter
for the planning team. A holding area is useful if the attending players would have had to travel long distances to the
control centre. A holding area means that they can travel
the night before and be introduced in a gradual fashion to

simulate a more realistic staged response and that enables briefing arrangements to be tested by the exercise players on their arrival. The players can be notified and brought forward to the control centre as they are needed, by an umpire contacting the holding room and requesting their attendance.

A staged response will also reduce the log jam of attendees at the control centre reception for booking them in. But if a holding area is agreed it should be visited to ensure that players, as they are directed to the holding area, have a comfortable spacious room with refreshments. In the holding room, arrangements must be in place for the players to have contact within the respective control centres as they would have in reality by either land line or mobile phone. To this end all telephone numbers must be posted in the holding room as they appear in the Exercise Order. The holding area will need to have at least two exercise assistants to deal with the reception of players and escorting them to the control centre(s).

Any controlled players will receive a separate 'edited' briefing and it is permissible to brief senior management staff taking part in the exercise on the general conduct of the exercise only, in particular the role of umpires, assessors and observers.

Ensure that all key management staff playing in the exercise in control centres in particular are wearing tabards displaying their role. This is important for those who may be attending the centre for the first time and unfamiliar with the roles.

We will assume that there are five live control centres and a media briefing centre operating:

1. Company Site Emergency Control.
2. Police Strategic Co-ordination Centre (Gold Control).
3. Police Silver Control Centre.
4. Police Bronze Control Centre.
5. Local Authority Emergency Room.
6. Multi-agency Media Briefing Centre.

9 How to Run the Exercise

Figure 9.2 illustrates the communication links between the centres and exercise control.

Exercise Control with communication links with all active centres and the players holding area. The dotted lines show the interaction between the active sites.

Figure 9.2 Control Post Exercise Module

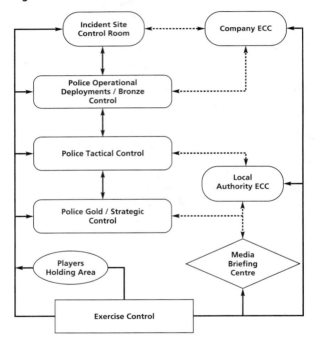

The exercise programme may look like the example below:

Example : Control Post Exercise

The instructions are for the EPO who is exercise manager in exercise control.

07.00: Arrive at exercise control. Contact each umpire/assessor in turn and confirm that they are in position at each live site.

07.30: Assemble exercise control staff and Exercise Director and brief the exercise inputters.

08.00: Contact all umpires to confirm that their senior management players have been briefed on the conduct of the exercise.

Contact 'Observer Liaison' to ensure observers are in position.

Contact player liaison assistants at the holding area(s), if one is being used.

08.30: Startex—Exercise start. Contact each umpire to declare the exercise is running at each control centre.

Ensure exercise inputs are on time.

Keep regular contact with all umpires and exercise assistants.

Deal with any questions and/or refer to the Exercise Director for decision.

The exercise will proceed and create its own momentum. As lunch time approaches ensure that agreed refreshments arrangements are implemented.

The exercise will terminate on the instructions of the Exercise Director. This can be at the request of any regulators who are assessing the exercise for regulatory purposes but the ultimate decision rests with the Director to ensure that every reasonable opportunity has been used to achieve all the objectives of the exercise.

16.30: Assuming the exercise has been terminated. A Hot Debrief (see Debriefs) will be called in a site of suitable size. It should be open to all those who wish to attend. If it is an exercise required by regulators they will lead or share the debrief with the lead organization. A hot debrief will only take very brief details of perhaps three positive points and three areas for improvement. These will be recorded for use at the formal or cold debrief. (Further information relating to debriefs will follow in the next chapter).

17.00: Hot debrief to take place. The closing remarks would normally be jointly shared but led by the Exercise Director followed by other senior managers or indeed any high profile observers.

Following the exercise there will be a considerable amount of clean up and returning control centres to normality. Feedback will have been provided from several sources and we will look in the next chapter how to approach the debrief process to ensure that every piece of useful information is used to improve structures, procedures and processes including evaluating of training.

Task 9.3

Create an evaluation sheet that is suitable for this type of exercise

---

9.5 **Live Exercise**

This exercise will probably be the most challenging logistically with several days of preparation being required.

In this example we assume that we have:

1. two live sites A & B
2. one Silver Control Centre
3. one Forward Media Briefing Point
4. one notional Gold Control
5. one notional Communications Centre
6. one notional Media Briefing Centre

Figure 9.3 illustrates the communications links connecting the exercise centres and exercise control. The dotted lines in the diagram indicate exercise communications.

Figure 9.3 Live Exercise Module Example

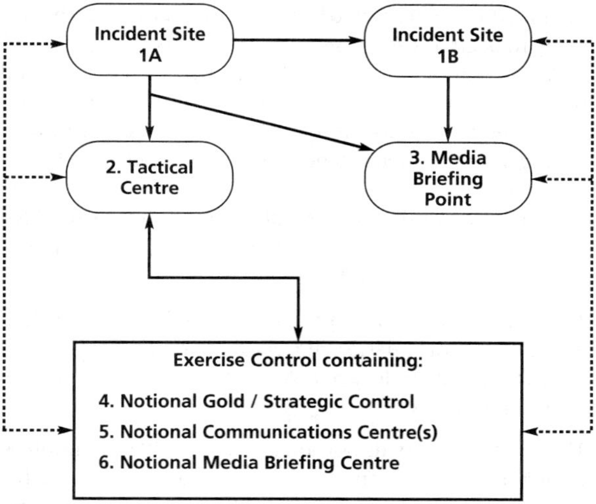

Site visits

The sites at which the exercise will take place have to be visited in the final three days and any safety measures put in place. This may take the form of cordons, lighting, directions and potentially, first aid arrangements. During the planning phase the site(s) will have been surveyed and a full health and safety risk assessment carried out. During the exercise each site will have a health and safety officer on duty ready to stop the exercise if necessary. The health and safety officer will wear high visibility clothing and will use a whistle or air horn to attract attention in the event of an incident requiring the exercise to be stopped or attract attention to an unsafe practice. Ensure that there will be places to brief players and assemble resources as holding areas prior to deployment. Consider the Marshalling Area principle as we have already seen earlier. During the final preparations a communications check is vital both for exercise purposes and exercise control.

Both the Silver Control Centre and the Forward Media Briefing Point will need to be visited to ensure everything is ready to begin the exercise.

The day before or shortly before the exercise, the full planning team, including the director, umpires, managers, controlled players, assessors and health and safety officers should visit the site(s) to become familiar with the layout and/or terrain.

On the day of the exercise all players will be assembled in the various locations and will be briefed by the umpires which will be in two parts:

1. Exercise rules, exercise programme and health and safety.
2. An update or situation report to that point for them and what their next duty or task will be—a real time briefing in other words.

This briefing is very important because it will have implications for the health and safety of all players and how the exercise will be stopped if an incident occurs which compromises safety. It will also give players the parameters within which the exercise is run. In other words, what is acceptable behaviour and practice and where to get advice and information from—eg the umpires.

It is assumed in this exercise all players are in position at 'Startex' and no real time attendance is being tested. That is not to say that all personnel are literally standing out in the open waiting to start. Initial response resources are held back in holding positions and called forward as required and directed by Exercise Control via the umpires. There is no need to have police cars, fire engines and ambulances or company vehicles screaming through the streets with 'blues & twos' or orange lights flashing, indeed it would be unnecessary, unjustifiable and perhaps unlawful.

At 'Startex' response resources will be sent to the scene by umpires as directed by Exercise Control in a controlled manner. Activity will begin at the scene as outlined in the Exercise Order. In reality, it would take a Silver Control Centre perhaps one hour to set up and begin managing the incident. Therefore, Silver Control will only be allowed to begin activity by exercise control at T + 1 hour. This is where a time line, see Figure 7.4, would be very useful to 'visualize' the stages. Exercise Control will manage the incident as the Communications Centre until Silver is live and exercise control will hand over to them.

The day programme would look like this:

Example of a Live Exercise

These are instruction for the EPO:

07.00: Exercise Control is open and contact is established with all umpires, assessors and health and safety officers. Inputters are in place to provide the agreed inputs. Confirmation is sought that all sites are ready. In particular, if the weather is suitable—do you need to implement your contingency?

07.30: Umpires will assemble their players and carry out the two-part briefing. Tea and coffee is a good idea at this time!

08.00: Startex—initial response is activated and directed to the site(s). Inputs commence as agreed in the planning stage, eg, request to open Silver.

09.00: Silver Control and Forward Media Briefing point is open and both are operating.

Inputs and live play will continue under strict supervision of the Health and Safety officers at the sites and the exercise will develop its own momentum. Be aware of players in the open being exposed to adverse weather.

Keep regular contact with all umpires and exercise assistants. Ensure catering is provided at regular intervals.

Deal with any questions and/or refer to the Exercise Director for decisions.

The exercise will terminate on the instructions of the Exercise Director. This can be at the request of any regulators who are assessing the exercise for regulatory purposes but the ultimate decision rests with the Director to ensure that every reasonable opportunity has been used to achieve all the objectives of the exercise.

15.00: Assuming the exercise has been terminated. A Hot Debrief (see Chapter 10) will be called in a site of suitable size. It should be open to all those who wish to attend. If it is an exercise required by regulators they will lead or share the debrief with the lead organization. A hot debrief will only take very brief details of perhaps three positive points and three areas for improvement. These will be recorded for use at the formal or cold debrief.

16.00: Hot debrief to take place. The closing remarks would normally be jointly shared but led by the Exercise Director followed by other senior managers or indeed any high profile observers.

The time line is a useful tool to keep track of activity. A very simple one is shown in Figure 7.4 with a basic key of green being active, red being closed and brown showing refreshments. Key 'milestones' are indicated by flags.

Following a live exercise there is considerable clean up and return to 'normality'. At this stage all the feedback will be collated in preparation for the forthcoming debriefs. The planning team will have planned a meeting to co-ordinate the collection and analysis of this information. In addition, and often overlooked following a large exercise is to ensure that letters of thanks are sent to all those who took leading roles or who made significant contribution, for example those who provided props, venues etc. In addition, a corporate message should go out for two reasons. Firstly, to thank everyone for taking part and secondly to reassure everyone that the debrief is imminent and contributions will be welcomed and fed back into the planning process.

Video and photographs should have been taken and they can be edited into a short film for debrief, training and public relations issues.

9.6 **Summary**

You have seen how each form of exercise is set up, controlled and managed.

The creation of feedback sheets has been examined and you should be aware how important it is to collate and gather that information.

The importance of graphical communications networks to add clarity to often complex arrangements has been explored.

The use of time lines to add structure has been examined.

9.7 **Conclusion**

We have looked at running four types of exercise. Although it may seem daunting on paper, the actual events are very rewarding and enjoyable. After planning for and completing the first exercises it will become very clear what needs to be done and although the examples given here only represent one format for each type of exercise there is a whole range to be achieved by mixing and matching the various types.

In the next chapter we will take a close look at debriefing. This is the culmination of the whole planning process and the one that will reap the benefits of exercising for any organization.

Chapter 10

Debriefing

Overview

In this final chapter you will cover:

- Effective debriefing
- Debrief types
- Debriefing an exercise
- What is entailed in each form of debrief
- Running the exercise debrief
- Debriefing a real event
- Completing the debrief report
- Implementing findings
- Overall action monitoring
- Spreading the word

10.1 **Introduction**

In this chapter, we will look at the process of debriefing. Although this chapter is primarily examining the exercise debrief process it will be useful to compare, and in some areas to contrast the process involved in debriefing a real event.

10.2 **Why Debrief?**

Why do we need to debrief if everything went well? A phrase still heard today. Perhaps it did, but that is unlikely. The debrief is about improvement and continuous development. What went well is just as important as what did not go so well. A good, open, honest, and progressive approach to self-analysis is a sign of a mature and healthy organization and the debrief is the demonstration of that maturity.

The right tone and atmosphere must be set from the start of a debrief process. A debrief can quickly degrade into accusations and blame for apparent failures. This must be avoided at all costs. Participants must feel free and confident to speak out and contribute spontaneously. The chair has an important role to play here.

KEY POINTS

The purpose of the debrief

- To review processes, procedures, structures, and not individuals apart from identifying potential training needs generally. It is not an opportunity to point the finger.
- To identify good practice and areas for future development.
- To promote an open and honest discussion.
- Not to compromise any ongoing investigation and acknowledge an individual's wish to decline to comment if that will compromise or incriminate them in any investigation.

This final point is important, this has been addressed earlier to some extent but the desire to have a debrief following a real incident, in particular where fatalities are involved may present difficulties for those charged with the investigation of that incident. Issues disclosed within a debrief may compromise an investigation. For that reason any decision to proceed with a debrief in such circumstances must be discussed with those carrying out that investigation, which may include the police, Crown Prosecution Service (CPS) or the Health and Safety Executive and any observations or guidelines given by them followed to the letter. However, this situation does not prevent a debrief taking place but care needs to be taken. Delaying a debrief for anything up to two years pending the outcome of a complex criminal trial would be nonsense and leave opportunities for the same thing to happen again because lessons were not learned and passed on to improve. Clearly, the need to prevent a reoccurrence is paramount.

For exercising, after months of planning and following the exercise itself there is an understandable tendency to think that the debrief and review is just a formality. In fact, the debrief and more importantly, the subsequent process that will see the implementation of lessons learned from the exercise is the most important part of the whole process.

The implementation of lessons learned must be based upon a robust, tenacious and auditable process. The planning team for the exercise or the debrief team for a real event will oversee this process and responsibility must be made clear who will carry the process through to conclusion.

In the event of a real incident, there will be some form of inquiry. It can take the form of anything from the following list to a combination of more than one of these factors:

- single agency/company internal departmental debrief and inquiry with insurers
- a multiagency debrief at which everyone's actions are examined
- a coroner's inquest
- a public inquiry
- a Health and Safety Investigation
- a police investigation.

As we have already discussed, corporate manslaughter is now a reality in modern management and managers with a directing influence on matters where lives could be lost may be held accountable for their actions. Debriefing is the first stage in realizing positive change and improvement within an organization's emergency arrangements and demonstrating a commitment to duty of care. Being able to show a robust training, exercise and review programme for plans can help negate any accusations that an organization is complacent with regard to health and safety and emergency arrangements. How an organization implements lessons learned is the key element in demonstrating that commitment. That is why debriefing is so important.

Task 10.1

Research the process and conditions to allow a public inquiry to proceed.

How do we ensure we get the most benefit from an exercise or following a real event?

10.3 **Effective Debriefing**

Debriefing is often undertaken by people who because of the very nature of their position within an organization, it is assumed they will know what to do—similar in many ways to assuming that a Chief Executive Officer (CEO) will be great in front of a TV camera ... this is not always so!

Without an effective chair, a debrief can easily become confused, disjointed and confrontational. Debriefing is not difficult but does require someone who has good communication and facilitation skills, a good and experienced chairperson for example. Detailed knowledge of the precise nature of the exercise or incident is not in itself necessary and in some cases can be a positive disadvantage. The chair should be seen as objective and independent and it is therefore useful for the debrief chairperson to be able to declare that at the debrief. Under no circumstances can a player or a person involved in a real event facilitate the debrief. With the best will in the world they will be biased in favour of their own performance and perceptions.

Choosing a debrief chair is a task for the planning team or debrief team. Whoever takes the role of debrief chair or facilitator they must have the support of the planning team or debrief team in the form of providing them with the necessary information, evaluation reports, recommendations and the final draft debrief reports to allow them to quality assure the document before it is published.

What kind of debrief format should be used? Some observations now from the outset about 'structured debriefing'—structured debriefing is a term relating to a form of debriefing popular with some organizations. It has gained popularity essentially in the absence of a real alternative methodology, such as that described in this book. It is not intended here to explain in detail structured debriefing which has some positive benefits but it does have inherent limitations. For example, the number of participants can be very limiting. This is because of the seating configuration and a requirement for participants to leave their seats to place sticky post-it notes on a board. In addition, structured debriefing only takes the debrief process to the identification of the issues and not through to action allocation and post incident implementation. The process does discourage group problem solving or decision-making. The advantages often cited for using structured debriefing are often issues that an effective facilitator or chairperson can deal with. For example, allowing those who are less assertive to take a full and active part, a good facilitator will be aware of that and address it. In essence, structured debriefing is useful for small groups with limited scope for carrying the debrief process to conclusion.

Alternatively, following the advice in this course provides a flexible framework approach to exercise and real incident debriefing. This system allows for large numbers of people to attend and to reach conclusions and implement actions. In reality the nature and scale of debriefs today often involves large numbers of people being driven by a strong imperative to issue actions to organizations to implement auditable change.

An exercise or indeed a real incident could have several debriefs. A debrief is not required for a seminar-based exercise. The objective and outcomes of a seminar exercise are different to a table top, control post, live exercise or real incident.

> **Task 10.2**
>
> Outline a number of examples where it would be undesirable to have the debrief chair as someone who took part in the exercise or incident and explore the reasons.

10.4 **Debrief Types**

There are a number of debrief formats which each have a place in the overall debrief process. They are:

- hot
- single agency
- internal
- multi-agency
- formal
- cold.

We will now consider each one and how they build into a co-ordinated debrief process.

10.5 **Debriefing an Exercise**

Getting the information—following the exercise the first task is to collect and collate all the feedback. The following activities and people will have provided most of the material:

- hot debrief (notes taken at the time)
- umpires (reports)
- assessors (reports)
- regulators (if present)
- managers (reports)
- players (through evaluation sheets)
- observers (through feedback sheets).

The format of the feedback will come in a variety of ways from evaluation sheets, written reports and observations. All that information will have to be analyzed, categorized, interpreted and set out in a form that is easily understood.

This is where the debrief schedule will help you as described earlier in Chapter 7.

10.6 **What is Entailed in Each Form of Debrief?**

10.6.1 **Hot debrief**

Hot debrief occurs immediately after the exercise (or incident) to capture key issues. It is more informal and flexible than a formal or cold debrief, as we shall see, in that a reporting debrief schedule as illustrated earlier will not be necessary. The hot debrief should be opened by and facilitated by the Exercise Director and any additional opening remarks from attending regulators or high profile observers taken. This hot debrief will be chaired by the Exercise Director and supported by any regulators.

At the hot debrief everyone involved in the exercise should have an opportunity to provide feedback. This is often extremely useful as it is fresh in the mind and usually brings out the key or 'hot' issues. Having a note taker present is essential to capture this information.

The purpose of the debrief process should be outlined and those present encouraged to offer their views. Umpires and assessors should be ready to provide at least three areas of improvement and three positive points and they should be called upon by the Director to start the feedback and evaluation at the start of the debrief. Those facilitating or chairing debriefs must try to avoid using negative language—such as bad points, criticisms or blame. Using such words can ignite a negative and defensive reaction. Use words like 'areas for improvement', 'more efficient methods', 'enhanced the procedure', 'develop the system' etc. Keeping the language positive and optimistic will encourage more constructive contributions.

At the hot debrief reinforce the need to complete the evaluation sheets provided to everyone and have them returned to a nominated person within the planning team. Use stamped addressed envelopes if necessary and have plenty of evaluation sheets available to hand out. In addition, issue an e-mail address clearly displayed for anyone to make contact with the planning or debrief team. Evaluation sheets and emails are also useful as some players may be a little reluctant to openly express their views in a hot debrief situation, particularly if it involves another member of staff—remember 'Groupthink'.

In concluding the hot debrief, outline the process of collating feedback and the production of the final report.

10.6.2 **Single agency/company/internal (formal or cold) debrief**

These are restricted to single agency or company personnel. They are carried out by organizations and companies to identify issues, which are peculiar to themselves in terms of internal processes and to co-ordinate issues to be taken forward to any multi-agency, external or cold, debrief. These debriefs are normally chaired by their own agency or company personnel who were not players in the exercise. An exercise manager for that organization or company can act as debrief chair. If however, it is an internal exercise only, an independent chair would be more appropriate from another branch or department. These internal debriefs are useful opportunities to 'iron-out' any issues before presenting to the more formal multi-agency or external debrief. Organizations may feel more comfortable discussing internal issues in a closed environment.

> **KEY POINT**
>
> In a multi-agency exercise each participating organization should hold their own internal debrief. Not to do so is a missed opportunity.

It is also important to consider using a debrief schedule as illustrated earlier, for an internal debrief too, but configure it to address the issues relevant to the company or organization based upon their objectives.

Invite everyone who took part in the exercise to the internal debrief. This is important to demonstrate appreciation for their contribution and an opportunity to personally thank everyone. It is also about building confidence in the organization in the debrief process. However, in reality there may appear to be a distinct lack of enthusiasm for this phase of the post-exercise process, but never mind. It is better to be open and inclusive than to restrict access to those who genuinely have an interest and perhaps have valuable observations to make. Again, the support of a senior manager would be of great benefit and yet again will do no harm in using their attendance to 'encourage' others to attend.

This debrief is also an ideal opportunity to nominate representatives to attend any multi-agency debriefs that are scheduled. The internal reporting and implementation of actions once identified should follow the model outlined below. See Figure 10.2.

10.6.3 **Multi-agency (formal or cold) debrief**

This is the culmination of the debrief process in which all participating organizations meet to discuss the learning outcomes of the exercise.

Multi-agency exercises, because of the sheer numbers of participants, can be very big indeed. A degree of selection and negotiating may be required to keep the numbers manageable but not at the detriment of ensuring the key people are there.

Multi-agency debriefs are usually a number of months following the exercise and it is therefore useful to recap before the debrief begins. If a video has been taken, which is essential during a live exercise, this can be shown as an introduction. A properly edited version of the exercise video is an asset for future training and briefing too.

During this debrief the debrief schedule is vital as a reference and for giving the debrief structure and direction.

10.7 **Running the Exercise Debrief**

A short meeting will be required of the debrief team/planning team to agree the format and running order for the debrief. This will be an action on the final meeting of the debrief team/planning team.

Ensure that the entire exercise planning team is available, in particular the debrief team together with the umpires and the assessors. Any debrief facilitators who dealt with single agency debriefs should also be there, in most cases they will be part of the exercise planning team anyway. The Exercise Director should also be there and representatives from all participating organizations.

The nominated chair will open the debrief and introduce the Director (if not chairing) and key personnel, usually the exercise managers, umpires and assessors. A recap of the exercise should take place as it may have been several months since the exercise. If a video has been taken this is a good opportunity to use it and refresh memories.

The debrief chair will then draw attention to the debrief schedule (see Figure 7.5) and address the first activity area. This will have been populated by the debrief team based upon all the feedback and evaluation received. General discussion will follow and an action may be identified to address the issues raised. That is then recorded by the Action Recorder (see later) on the Action Tracking document (Figure 10.2).

Participants at the debrief should be warned as to any potential restricted classification of any draft debrief report until it is finally published and even then a final classification may be assigned to it—remember the Government Protective Marking Scheme (GPMS). This could be as a result of issues which are commercially sensitive or official secrets issues.

The chair should ask all those present if, following their internal debriefs, there are issues that should be raised and declare them, almost like any other business.

The prepared debrief schedule/activity module document will be available to all those present. Two note takers will be required. One will record what was said in the form of minutes and the other will write down any actions that come out of the discussions. This person is called the '**Action Recorder**'. Actions can come thick and fast and the minute taker could be overwhelmed and possibly miss a vital word or phrase. In addition, the Action Recorder can give a summary at the end of the debrief or updates during the debrief as to what actions have been agreed. The chair would find it quite difficult to do any of this having been concentrating on the discussion.

The Action Recorder records the precise nature of the action, who it is allocated to and a proposed time scale. This action-tracking schedule will form the basis for the implementation of lessons learned from the exercise.

To recap:

Key persons present:

- Exercise Director (chair);
- all planning staff;
- umpires;
- assessors;
- regulators (if any);
- selected players—representatives;
- invited observer(s);
- minute taker; and
- action recorder.

Key documents:

- all evaluation sheets;
- logs/minutes of meetings (SCG/TCG);
- messages used (SCG/TCG);

10 Debriefing

- debrief schedule/Activity Modules (see Figure 7.5); and
- action tracking (see Figure 10.2).

Task 10.3

Can you think of ways in which the debrief chair can put participants at ease and ensure everyone has a say.

The debrief will continue using the debrief schedule as a guide and eventually all the issues relating to the objectives will be covered. At that point, the 'Action Tracking' document will contain all the actions raised and who will be responsible for leading on each.

The debrief chair will then ask the Action Recorder to read out all the actions. Participants will then be invited to comment and agree the details. If not, participants should declare any issue they have. Then the 'Action Tracking' document will be accepted.

The chair will conclude the meeting by reminding the participants how the process to move to the final report will proceed. A suggested process may look like this:

- A draft debrief report will be produced by the lead organization or department with an action summary and circulated within two (2) weeks of the debrief to all participating organizations or departments for observations. Circulation will normally be by e-mail.
- Participating organizations or departments should take no longer than one (1) week to lodge observations on the draft with the lead organization or department.
- This report will be forwarded to the Chairperson of the debrief for final approval prior to circulation.
- The report will be forwarded on behalf of the Chairperson of the debrief to the lead organization or department.
- The lead organization or department will be responsible for distribution of the report.
- Individual organizations or departments will only implement and monitor their own actions.

A typical multi-agency debrief table lay out is illustrated in Figure 10.1.

Figure 10.1 Debrief Room Layout

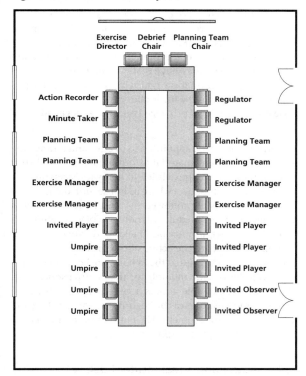

10.8 **Debriefing a Real Event**

Whereas in an exercise the information will be collected and collated as part of the exercise management process, following a real event that information will be captured and recovered by a debrief team designated by the overall incident manager and/or police commander. For inquiry and debrief purposes it is vital to recover all data from all sources as it is not only good practice but will be demanded by legislative bodies such as the HSE, coroner etc.

10 Debriefing

Issues to consider are:

- Prevent the disposal or destruction of any documents, e-mails, message forms, meeting tapes, logbooks or computer disks/drives. Print to hard copy if necessary.
- Ensure everyone is made aware of that requirement and locate those who may have that information.
- Request the information and require 'negative' returns and who gave you the information.
- Deal with any legal privilege issues—take legal advice if necessary.

A debrief team will be appointed to oversee and arrange the recovery of relevant material as outlined above and they will begin to arrange the debrief. In many respects this mirrors the exercise situation where in house 'hot' debriefs and 'internal' debriefs are followed by a multi-agency debrief although a debrief schedule will not be in place to guide the process. However, an 'Action Tracking' document should be prepared to record the actions from the debrief.

Therefore, it is suggested that a template be created to act as a reminder or aide memoir for the chairperson to use. The following example adopts a generic approach to the most common features of the beginning of an incident and its subsequent development. The template is intended to be modified and adapted to suit individual needs.

10.8.1 Managing a real incident debrief

The Chairperson, following a general introduction of the incident and the proposed conduct of the debrief, which should include a cautionary note on issues of incrimination and sub judice, would lead by providing a review or overview of the incident and using any film footage or pictures that are available. This sets the context and reminds those present of the events and allows them to re-focus on the events.

If the event led to fatalities, it may be appropriate to consider a request for a moment to reflect on those who died and their families. This is not a minute's silence but a few moments. There is no better or poignant reminder of why debriefing is so important.

In this example, it is following an incident where the police led the co-ordination, but the areas covered are as relevant to any organization in their design. Each formal real incident debrief should have a guide based upon the issues emerging from the incident and this guide should be produced by the debrief team. See the example below:

Example—Guide to a real debrief

1. General overview of incident.
   Chairperson.
2. Initial notification.
   (a) How did we all find out? Was it timely?
   (b) Did we tell who needed to know?
   (c) Were there 'information only' messages to agencies?
   (d) Did any agency stand down another?
3. Mobilization.
   (a) Were plans utilized?
   (b) Actions by agencies?
   (c) Was there specialist input or support required?
   (d) Was there a need for additional support?
4. Liaison
   (a) Basic liaison structures put in place? Did it work?
   (b) Did we start talking to each other?
   (c) Did police commander (Silver) attend the scene and liaise effectively? Was a Forward Control Point (FCP) used?
   (d) Was there adequate communication ongoing?
5. Police Co-ordination—was it:
   (a) Clear?
   (b) Proactive?
   (c) Decisive?
   (d) Inclusive?
6. Police Controls
   (a) Was formal co-ordination involved—Silver/Gold Controls Rooms?

(b) Were they supported by agencies?

(c) Were control room processes easy to use for agencies, eg messaging, actions and briefings?

7. Media/Public relations issues

(a) Media interest—local/national

(b) Media management

(c) Response agencies media co-ordination

(d) Media Briefing Centres

8. Resourcing

(a) Enough personnel?

(b) Sufficient equipment?

(c) IT back-up?

9. Welfare

(a) Personnel

(b) Health and Safety

10. Business Continuity

(a) Able to maintain core services?

(b) Impact on core business?

11. Areas for improvement—to be taken forward

(a) Each agency

(b) Actions—to whom?

(c) AOB

12. Summary

By Chair/Action Recorder taker

13. Closing

By Chair

This list is not exhaustive but is introduced to illustrate means of adding structure and progression within a debrief yet providing the flexibility that is needed. The closure of this debrief will follow in a similar way to the exercise debrief by describing the process to the final report and the implementing of actions.

Task 10.4

Outline the key differences between the conduct of an exercise debrief and a real incident debrief.

10.9 **Completing the Debrief Report**

Once the debrief is complete the 'Action Tracking' table document will be populated by the planning team. See Figure 10.2.

The debrief report will be created in draft form and may be set out like this:

Example—Debrief report

1. Foreword—A suitable foreword by the Exercise Director
2. Distribution list
3. Contents
4. Exercise overview—summary
5. Key Issues arising—top five issues
6. Action Tracking Table
7. Action tracking process

It is important to keep the document concise as a complex weighty document will be quite off-putting and less likely to be read.

10.9.1 **Implementing findings**

This is the final and most critical part of the exercise cycle and the most likely part to fail. Why will it fail? If there is no mandatory or moral imperative to implement lessons learned, for example, following an investigation, inquiry, HSE conviction, media pressure, victim or family pressure it is unlikely that there will be the appetite or drive to take action if the organization or company is not engaged or committed to learning. This is particularly true where changes or improvements involve spending money. But it can be false economy not to spend this extra money when weighed against the impact an adverse event may have on businesses or any organization. Some managers may choose to 'risk manage' by not implementing findings but such decisions can come back to haunt.

10 Debriefing

Figure 10.2 Action Tracking Document

EXERCISE .... ORGANIZATION / COMPANY ....

No.	Activity Area	No.	Sub Issues	Positive Points	Areas for Improvement	Action Point	To whom 'Owner'	Monitoring Organization	Completion / Review Date
1.		1a							
		1b							
		1c							
2.		2a							
		2b							
3.		3a							
		3b							
		3c							
→		→							

How do you manage the action tracking to conclusion? A flow chart has been created to illustrate the process. This is inclusive from the beginning of the exercise to the implementation of action. See Figure 10.3.

Figure 10.3 Action Tracking Flow Chart

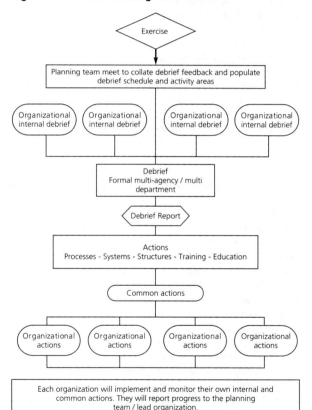

10.10 **Overall Action Monitoring**

Once the action(s) has been allocated it should be the responsibility of each organization to ensure the implementation of that action takes place. They become the owner of the action. If it transpires that this has not been done in a reasonable time, the organization may be held accountable for their failure to do so. It must be remembered that all the debrief material could be discloseable in future inquiries and failure to implement outstanding actions could be construed as potentially negligent.

Therefore, during the debrief meeting consideration should be given to a lead organization taking the role of overall '**Action Co-ordinator**'. The Action Co-ordinator may be designated by the lead organization that initiated the exercise or led by the co-ordinated response in the real incident. Being the administrator simply means that someone will monitor the action progress relating to that incident from each organization. This does not mean they have the responsibility or any authority to implement the actions but merely to monitor progress. The Action Co-ordinator may in fact report progress to the Chair or indeed to an official body such as the Local Resilience Form or sub-group.

For actions relevant to an individual organization, a named individual or post holder should be allocated this task as '**Action Administrator**' internally. If the exercise is wholly internal the Action Administrator will be solely responsible for action monitoring. The person who is responsible for the action will be the action '**Owner**'. The Administrator will contact each owner in turn by e-mail or in writing specifying the action. A completion date should be set along with review dates.

In summary, the monitoring process for a multi-agency exercise or real event will be overseen by a lead Action Co-ordinator, usually from the lead organization. Then within each participating organization, an internal Action Administrator will be appointed to follow each action with each action Owner and report back to the Action Co-ordinator.

These arrangements must be strictly adhered to, in order to:

- give the Owner responsibility and measurable accountability
- change attitudes and organizational culture as to the importance to organizational learning

If there is multi-agency action tracking, a composite action tracking document will be used by the lead organization. The document will specify where the actions lie and who is monitoring. It must be remembered that the multi-agency action tracking document held by the Action Co-ordinator is there to give a general overview of progress. Individual organizational action tracking by the Action Administrator is the original document and is evidence that actions are progressed and completed, and indeed could be cited in inquiries and investigations.

10.10.1 Spreading the word

There will be a need to disseminate any lessons learned within the organization to ensure that the improvements are fully integrated into plans. How can this be done effectively?

- Arrange a seminar exercise when the plan is revised.
- Hold short, ½ hour—1 hour, briefings for key staff.
- Post a global e-mail on the system with key points.
- Create an interesting article for an in-house magazine or a poster for rest rooms and canteens.
- Put an article in the local newspaper.
- Arrange to have a short summary taken to key management meetings by a line manager or volunteer to do a short presentation on the exercise—this is where the video will score.
- Arrange to give presentations to interest groups—this will energize management when feedback filters through to them.

Whichever method is used to implement the lessons learned it is without doubt time and effort well spent. Not fully debriefing is 'like going into a shop with your hard earned cash, carefully selecting what you want, paying for it and then leaving the shop without it'! An EPO can plan, train and exercise continually but it becomes meaningless unless lessons are implemented and the emergency planning cycle continues, increasing efficiency , developing people and the organization.

10.11 **Summary**

- You will understand the importance of debriefing.
- Appreciate the differences between an exercise debrief and a real incident debrief.
- You will understand the key elements to effective debriefing.
- You will be able to collate information from a variety of exercises.
- You will be able to organize and run a debrief.
- You will understand and be able to track and monitor actions to conclusion.

10.12 **Conclusion**

This chapter has given insights and practical advice to successfully organize and run a debrief. In addition, it is hoped that the importance of action tracking and implementation has been recognized.

Index

Index

Index

Index

Index

Index